THE NEW RELIGIOUS INTOLERANCE

THE NEW
RELIGIOUS INTOLERANCE

*Overcoming the Politics of Fear
in an Anxious Age*

Martha C. Nussbaum

THE BELKNAP PRESS OF HARVARD UNIVERSITY PRESS

Cambridge, Massachusetts, and London, England

2012

Printed in the United States of America

Library of Congress Cataloging-in-Publication Data

Nussbaum, Martha Craven, 1947–
The new religious intolerance : overcoming the politics of fear
in an anxious age / Martha C. Nussbaum.
p.   cm.
Includes bibliographical references (p.   ) and index.
ISBN 978-0-674-06590-1 (alk. paper)
1. Freedom of religion.   2. Religious tolerance.   3. Religious
discrimination.   4. Fear—Religious aspects.   I. Title.
BL640.N88   2012
201'.723–dc23   2011051712

In memory of Arnold Jacob Wolf
1924–2008

Contents

Anxiety most of all characterizes the human animal. This is perhaps the most general name for all the vices at a certain mean level of their operation. It is a kind of cupidity, a kind of fear, a kind of envy, a kind of hate. Fortunate are they who are even sufficiently aware of this problem to make the smallest efforts to check this dimming preoccupation. . . . The natural tendency of the human soul is towards the protection of the ego.

IRIS MURDOCH, *The Black Prince*, 1973

I don't know what the big deal is. It's freedom of religion, you know?
"CASSANDRA," *a stripper who works at New York Dolls*
near ground zero, on the proposed Islamic community
center next door to the strip club

PREFACE

The idea for this book began when I was asked to write a column for "The Stone," the philosophy feature of "The Opinionator," the online commentary from the *New York Times*. I wrote about the proposed *burqa* bans in Europe, with ideas that figure in Chapters 3 and 4. I was astonished by the volume, variety, and intensity of the comments I received, and fortunately I was permitted to reply in a piece as long as the original article. I'm grateful to the editors and to the seven hundred or so people who sent comments, helping me to develop some of the ideas further. At that point, the notion of writing a small book on the topic began to seem attractive. I am thankful to my longtime editor Joyce Seltzer at Harvard University Press for sharing my enthusiasm and helping me to shape the project. Chris Skene and Robert Greer provided invaluable research assistance. More recently, I'm indebted to Rosalind Dixon, Aziz Huq, Saul Levmore, Ryan Long, and Chris Skene for their generous and challenging comments on a draft of the manuscript. I presented several chapters at a Work in Progress Workshop at the University of Chicago Law School and, as always, have reason to be deeply grateful to colleagues who spent so much time reading the text beforehand and who raised such excellent and varied questions, which were crucial to the final revision: Dahwood Ahmed, Eric Biber, Jane Dailey, Lee Fennell, Bernard Harcourt, Richard Helmholz, Todd Henderson, Brian Leiter, Richard McAdams, Eduardo Penalver, Ariel Porat, Eric Posner, Mike Schill, Geoffrey Stone, Laura Weinrib, and Albert Yoon.

I dedicate this book to the late Arnold Jacob Wolf, a giant in American Reform Judaism and in my own religious life. One of the wisest people I've known, Arnold combined a passion for social justice with deep religious concern, and both of these with a genius for teaching—gruffly, maddeningly, hilariously, with a Socratic passion for argument and an un-Socratic capacity for sympathy and humor. I was very lucky that he blessed me at my adult bat mitzvah in August 2008. Sadly, he died the next December, at the age of eighty-four. Following a longstanding tradition at KAM Isaiah Israel, a Reform congregation, Arnold was a passionate advocate of interreligious understanding. He arranged joint activities with Christian and Muslim groups, as well as with local African-American churches, themselves both Christian and Muslim. (KAM, now famous for being across the street from President Obama's house, is also close to the home of Louis Farrakhan and to a large African-American mosque.) Key pieces of the liturgy were rewritten so that congregants could sing about "all the people of the world" rather than just about "the people Israel."

If you saw Arnold for the first time, you might think you were looking at one of those trolls of middle-European fairy tales, a short, round, white-bearded Rumpelstiltskin whose gruff, almost snarling voice seemed suited to a character of that cantankerous sort. But whereas Rumpelstiltskin, consumed by dislike and envy, had, I imagine, dull, guarded eyes, Arnold's sparkled, and you could see in them such variegated colors of affection, for all the people, young and old, whom he reproved, chastised, and even mocked. ("Religion is a serious business," he would say, "but this congregation is a joke.") Rabbi Eugene Borowitz, his contemporary, said at the funeral that Arnold was first and foremost a lover—and then he added, "To love Jews is no small accomplishment." You saw that accomplishment in the eyes first, because it consisted above all in real curiosity and a willingness to see the other person as the person was—and, at the same time, in a willingness to be seen, faults and all. There was no critique of Arnold that he did not make first and most trenchantly himself.

Here are two stories about Arnold that seem contradictory. In his bar and bat mitzvah classes, whenever kids would complain about something, he would say, "It's not about you." And yet, in his Torah study sessions with fellow rabbis, so one reported at his funeral, he frequently said to people, "It's always about your own life." Was he just inconsistent? I think we can put those two stories together, if we think that in a deep sense one's own life is not about oneself. Arnold believed in introspection. He did want people to let the text summon them to deeper self-knowledge and self-criticism. But in the end, any self-knowledge worth the name tells you that others are as real as you are, and that your life is not just about you, it is about accepting the fact that you share a world with others, and about taking action directed at the good of others. To self-involved teens, Arnold emphasized the focus on the other; to intellectualizing rabbis, the need for personal self-examination. But the message in the end is the same: know yourself, so that you can move outside of yourself, serve justice, and promote peace.

That, in the end, is the message I hope to convey in this book.

THE NEW RELIGIOUS INTOLERANCE

I

RELIGION:
A TIME OF ANXIETY AND SUSPICION

Once, not very long ago, Americans and Europeans prided themselves on their enlightened attitudes of religious tolera-tion and understanding. Although everyone knew that the history of the West had been characterized by intense religious animosity and violence—including such bloody episodes as the Crusades and the Wars of Religion, but including, as well, the quieter violence of colonial religious domination by Europeans in many parts of the world, domestic anti-Semitism and anti-Catholicism, and culminat-ing in the horrors of Nazism, which implicated not only Germany but also many other nations—Europe until very recently liked to think that these dark times were in the past. Religious violence was somewhere else—in societies more "primitive," less characterized by a heritage of Christian values than were the modern social democ-racies of Europe.

The United States has had a somewhat better record than the "Old World" from which its original settlers fled, many of them in search of religious liberty and equality. Outright violence in the name of religion was always a relatively rare phenomenon—endured by the allegedly "primitive" Native Americans and, more recently, by

Mormons and Jehovah's Witnesses, dissident groups that the majority perceived as strange and threatening, but not by members of mainstream religious bodies. And the United States has always been somewhat more hospitable than Europe to nonhomogeneity in dress and lifestyle, which has proven helpful to religious minorities who want to pursue their own conscientious commitments without assimilating to the culture of the majority. Still, no reasonable person could deny that religious prejudice and fear, in the form of anti-Catholicism and "nativism," anti-Semitism, and a host of other prejudices against "strange" minorities, have been a persistent blot on our society. We need only remember, for example, that not until the 1970s did "white-shoe" law firms begin to hire Jews in any significant numbers, and that only in very recent times could a majority of the Supreme Court be composed of Roman Catholics without public outrage, in order to feel humility about our own record as an allegedly tolerant and respectful culture. Still, the self-image of U.S. citizens in recent years has been that we are a welcoming and diversity-friendly society that has outgrown the prejudices of the past.

Today we have many reasons to doubt this complacent self-assessment. Our situation calls urgently for searching critical self-examination, as we try to uncover the roots of ugly fears and suspicions that currently disfigure all Western societies. At this time we badly need an approach inspired by ethical philosophy in the spirit of Socrates, an approach that combines three ingredients:

- Political principles expressing equal respect for all citizens, and an understanding of what these principles entail for today's confrontations with religious difference. (These princi-

ples already inhere in the political traditions of both Europe
and, especially, the United States.)

- Rigorous critical thinking that ferrets out and criticizes inconsistencies, particularly those that take the form of making
an exception for oneself, noting the "mote" in someone else's
eye while failing to note the large plank in one's own eye.

- A systematic cultivation of the "inner eyes," the imaginative
capacity that makes it possible for us to see how the world
looks from the point of view of a person different in religion
or ethnicity.

These ethical virtues are always helpful in a complicated world.
Why, however, are they needed with particular urgency at the present time? Let's take stock of some recent developments, focusing
first on Europe and then on the United States.

Europe: *Burqas*, Minarets, Murder

Three European nations—France, Belgium, and Italy—have now
passed laws banning the wearing of the Muslim *burqa* and *niqab*
(both of which cover the face apart from the eyes) in any public
place.[1] (In Italy, the law has only passed in the Chamber of Depu-
ties; it is now being considered by the Senate.) Despite the acknowledged fact that only a tiny minority of Muslims in these countries
actually wear these garments (in Italy, for example, one reliable estimate is 100, and even the most inflated estimate is only 3,000), these
laws—which certainly impose a heavy burden on people's conscientious exercise of religious freedom—have been treated as of the ut-

most urgency, and as addressing a public crisis of profound significance.[2]

Such developments did not go unchallenged, even by experts in women's dress. In Italy, a capital of women's fashion, no less an authority than Giorgio Armani came to the defense of the *burqa*, saying (several years before the national ban, when prohibitions were still local) that women should wear what they like. "It's a question of respect for the convictions and cultures of others," he stated. "We need to live with these ideas."[3] Still, Italians in this case ignored the voice of fashion, following concerns imagined to be even more urgent.

Meanwhile, many communities in Europe have even imposed regulations on the Muslim headscarf, which covers the hair only. In France, girls may not wear the headscarf in schools.[4] Kosovo, with its large Muslim population, has imposed a similar ban.[5] In parts of Germany, Holland, Spain, and Belgium, the headscarf may not be worn by public employees, including teachers on the job—even though nuns and priests are permitted to teach in full habit.[6] Girls in Switzerland may not wear the headscarf while playing basketball.[7] In Russia, Muslim women won the right to retain their headscarves in passport photos, but a teenage girl was recently expelled from school for wearing her headscarf, and one university in the North Caucasus has banned all headscarves.[8]

In Switzerland, after a campaign designed to appeal to fears of a Muslim takeover, a popular referendum voted by 57 percent to ban the construction of minarets associated with mosques—despite the fact that few mosques actually have minarets (only 4 in Switzerland at present, out of 150 mosques), and that in consequence the architectural issue appears to be purely symbolic.[9]

Even in small and sometimes bizarre ways, the fear of Muslims

shows its ugly head. The mayor of the Italian city of Capriate in Bergamo banned kebab shops in the city in 2009.[10] A white-supremacist
website (www.stormfront.org) has made much of this "victory," ex-
ulting triumphantly and trying to stir up disgust by describing allegedly filthy and roach-ridden conditions in those restaurants
(conditions that are pretty common the world over, but that can
still be used to inspire disgust). As the year went on, quite a few
more towns in the region of Genoa and Bergamo joined the ban. In
Lucca, a kebab shop was firebombed, and a member of parliament
from the anti-immigration Northern League called for a ban on all
foreign foods. Italy's agriculture minister, who is from that party,
defended the ban, appealing both to tradition and to concerns
about health.[11]

Northern Europe is usually imagined as a quiet zone of ideal toleration and amity, and so it is, much of the time. And yet even that
region has experienced waves of anti-Muslim sentiment. Finland, a
country I know well, has not adopted any legislative restrictions
against religious dress of any sort, and there is little political support for such a move, but discrimination in employment against
women who wear the Muslim headscarf is a common complaint.[12]
Some employers (the police and certain food stores) say openly that
they will not employ a woman wearing a headscarf.[13] Schools in
Raasepori forbade headscarves for female students but withdrew
the ban in the face of public pressure.[14] In two cases, however,
Muslim-friendly policies have themselves been dropped as a result
of public pressure. Helsinki and Espoo municipal playgrounds recently stopped serving special meals for Muslim children.[15] And the
controversial Helsinki policy of reserving certain hours for Muslim
women to use the public swimming pool at Janomaki has been can-
celed, although a new women-only slot has been created in the eve-

ning.[16] Finland displays characteristic toleration and forbearance, but tensions still exist, and the tendency of Finns to identify nonhomogeneity as foreignness is a troubling thread running through the news treatments of this issue (which typically speak of "Finns" and "Finnish culture" by *contrast* to Muslims and Islam, without inquiring how many of the Muslims in question are residents or even citizens of Finland).

In July 2011, terror struck a neighboring Northern European nation with a heavy hand. Norwegian zealot Anders Behring Breivik murdered approximately 76 people in twin attacks, bombing government buildings in Oslo and shooting young representatives of the Labour Party who had gathered on the island of Utoya for a youth camp.[17] Breivik, who has confessed to the crimes but denied fault, released, on the day of the attacks, a 1,500-page manifesto in which he outlines a theory supporting his actions, based on the idea that Europe must fight against the scourge of Islamicization.[18] He evidently has ties with a variety of anti-Islamic groups in both Europe and the United States.[19] His actions, though widely condemned, have been met with celebration by some right-wing politicians in other countries. Jacques Coutela, of France's National Front (FN), has described him as an "icon" and "the main defender of the West." He sees him as "fighting the Muslim invasion" and compares him to the French hero Charles Martel.[20] Coutela was suspended by the party, pending an investigation. Another FN member who said similar things in less graphic terms has not been suspended, however. Italian member of parliament Mario Borghezio, of the Northern League (a partner in Silvio Berlusconi's government), condemned Breivik's violence but backed his ideas, especially his "opposition to Islam and his explicit accusation that Europe has surrendered before putting up a fight against its Islamicization."[21]

The United States: Headscarves, Mosques, "Sharia Law"

The United States has not encountered mass religious violence in recent years (unless we count the Oklahoma City bombing of 1995, perpetrated by vaguely Christian members of the militia movement, whose motives were antigovernment, rather than directed at immigrants or religious minorities). Despite conditions that emphasize heterogeneity and religious pluralism, however, prejudice and occasional violence against new religious groups have never been absent from the U.S. scene. The early settlers at times exiled people whose religious views were deemed heretical (for example, Roger Williams, forced to flee from Massachusetts to Rhode Island).[22] Jews, Quakers, Baptists, and Mennonites were welcome in some colonies, but not in all.[23] In the nineteenth century, a surge of Roman Catholic immigration from Ireland and Southern Europe prompted an upsurge of virulent prejudice, as "nativism" became a popular political cause.[24] In one or another form, anti-Catholic prejudice has remained a major factor in American political life until extremely recently: during the Cold War, for example, liberal journalist Paul Blanshard, in his best-selling book *American Freedom and Catholic Power* (1947), warned Americans that Catholicism was as big a danger to American democracy as global communism. Meanwhile, smaller groups such as Mormons and Jehovah's Witnesses suffered not only prejudice but also outright violence.[25] Anti-Semitism was extremely common until the 1970s, and has still not disappeared.[26] How, then, are Americans responding to the current upsurge of religious anxiety?

The U.S. response is more varied than that in Europe, involving more religions. Jews are not exempt from suspicion—particularly if they are foreigners. Three Mexican Jews attempting to pray aboard an Alaska Airlines flight bound from Mexico City to Los Angeles

7

were required to leave the flight and questioned by the FBI.[27] After 9/11, the Sikh turban was commonly confused with Muslim dress, and Sikhs suffered at airports, and in some cases were violently attacked.[28] Sikhs continue to complain of airline searches of turbans, although the TSA has devised alternatives, such as a pat down of the turban, or even a self-pat down, after which the person's hands are screened for chemicals.[29] Recently, the U.S. army has allowed Sikh recruits to retain their turbans.[30] Sikhs have a long tradition of distinguished military service and have been passionate advocates of change. An army spokesman, George Wright, said, "It is the Army's policy to accommodate religious practices as long as the practice will not have an adverse impact on military necessity." Hinduism, too, has encountered difficulty: the first Hindu prayer offered in the U.S. Senate was disrupted by organized protesters who described themselves as "Christians and patriots." The protest, however, did not achieve its aim of stopping the Hindu prayer: the protesters were arrested in the visitors' gallery for "disruption of Congress," and their acts were condemned on the Senate floor by Majority Leader Harry Reid.[31]

Still, in the United States as in Europe, by far the largest number of troubling incidents concern Islam. No proposal to ban the *burqa* is known to me, but the headscarf has caused isolated incidents. A thirty-one-year-old Muslim woman wearing a headscarf was asked to leave a Southwest Airlines flight after a flight attendant overheard a cell phone conversation in which she allegedly said, "It's a go"—although she reports that she really said, "I've got to go," because the flight was preparing for takeoff. After patting down her headscarf and talking to her the TSA quickly recognized that a mistake had been made and did not require an inspection of her cell phone or purse, but she was not permitted to get back on the flight, because the crew was uncomfortable with her. She received two oral apologies from the airline and a voucher that she intends to give away, because she does not want to fly on Southwest again. Finally, she has received an official public apology.[32] Meanwhile, Imane Boudlal, a female Disneyland employee from Morocco, is suing Disney for the right to wear her headscarf during her job as a hostess at Disneyland's Grand Californian hotel. Her supervisors told her it was not the "Disney look," and that if she wanted to continue to wear it she would have to take a job out of sight of customers. She was then offered a compromise: a large, masculine-looking hat that she could wear over the *hijab*, which, in a photo, looks quite ridiculous. She refused the compromise.[33] Noor Abdallah, a young Muslim woman from Illinois, working for Disney in California as an intern, accepted a more plausible but still odd compromise, wearing a blue beret over her *hijab*.[34] The idea is certainly being conveyed that the sight of these women looking like themselves, namely, observant Muslim women, would be displeasing to customers. Although Abdallah is satisfied with the compromise, Boudlal continues to press her cause. Other employment-related complaints have been reported, and the number of such complaints appears to be on the rise.[35] Significantly, however, the public sphere has yet to join the fray. When a Georgia woman was denied entrance to the Douglasville municipal courthouse when she refused to remove her headscarf, the state of Georgia recommended that religious head coverings be permissible in all the state's courthouses.[36]

If the headscarf has caused problems only in isolated cases involving private employers, mosques have in at least two cases occasioned public opposition. There's nothing comparable in the United States to the Swiss minaret ban, but the zoning board of DuPage County, near Chicago, has rejected a plan to build a mosque in Willowbrook—after the same group had rejected a plan to build an Islamic education center and place of worship near Naperville and an application for an Islamic religious center in West Chicago. The county in all cases cited worries about an alleged oversaturation of religious institutions and related traffic and sewer problems, but more or less every other religion has been able to operate. Close to the Willowbrook site are a Buddhist meditation center, a Chinmaya mission, and a Macedonian Orthodox church.[37] Many Christian churches and Jewish synagogues exist in the county. So it is unfortunate to draw the "oversaturation" line at a point that fences out the region's most rapidly growing group. Associated appeals to declining property values raise the specter of bias. Another plan for an Islamic community center on 248th Avenue in Naperville was rejected by the town's planning commission in October 2011, once again with public argument focusing on oversaturation and traffic issues; but signs popped up on the property warning, "Vote No to Mosque on 248."[38]

In a related incident, a plan to build an Islamic community center in Murfreesboro, Tennessee (an expansion of a center that has existed for thirty years), led to a vociferous protest at the county commission's meeting, as hundreds of opponents packed the meeting in June 2010. Two months later, arson destroyed equipment at the construction site. The FBI was called to investigate, and other Islamic places of worship in the region increased security. Meanwhile the Justice Department defended the right of the Islamic group to build a place of worship, in response to a lawsuit brought by local landowners against the county.[39] More recently, in January 2011, an attempted bombing of the Islamic Center of America in Michigan was foiled by the police, and Roger Stockham, a sixty-three-year-old army veteran from California with a record of Islamophobia, was arrested with a large number of explosives in his possession. He was ruled incompetent to stand trial.[40]

Although in that case the perpetrator was an isolated individual, protests and threats against mosques seem to be spreading. Between May 2010 and September 2010, the American Civil Liberties Union counted thirty mosques or proposed mosques that had faced vandalism, public protest, or strong opposition based on hostility to Islam.[41]

Another issue giving rise to controversy in the United States is the potential application of "Sharia law," or Islamic law, to U.S. citizens. In Oklahoma, an amendment to the state constitution, which passed with 70 percent of the vote, provides that Oklahoma courts may draw on U.S. federal law, common law, and "if necessary the law of another state," but may not "look to the legal precepts of other nations or cultures . . . international law or Sharia law."[42] The law's primary architect, Rex Duncan, said, "This is a war for the survival of America. It's a cultural war."[43]

This ill-drafted and vague amendment (called the "Save our State" amendment) raises a host of problems—including the fact that the common law is of English origin and the sweeping indictment of international law might be construed to apply to such recognized sources of law as maritime law and treaties. But the most obvious issue is redundancy: the Establishment Clause of the First Amendment to the U.S. Constitution would already preclude enforcing in U.S. courts the legal codes of any specific religion. The law was challenged by Islamic groups on the ground that it singles out Islam for special stigmatization, and the suit was found by a federal district judge to have merit on Establishment Clause grounds; she temporarily halted the law's implementation for a further hearing, and later extended that restraining order indefinitely. She found that the law does not have a secular purpose, that its "primary purpose inhibits religion," and that it fosters excessive state entanglement with religion.[44]

The judge also noted, as have scholars, that the law would place a special burden on Muslims, since courts are permitted to enforce contracts (such as wills and marriage contracts) that incorporate language drawn from other religious traditions. As University of Chicago Law Professor Aziz Huq wrote in the *New York Times:*

> [T]he bans would deprive Muslims of equal access to the law. A butcher would no longer be able to enforce his contract for halal meat—contracts that, like deals for kosher or other faith-sanctioned foods, are regularly enforced around the country. Nor could a Muslim banker seek damages for violations of a financial instrument certified as "sharia compliant" since it pays no interest.[45]

The Oklahoma controversy gave rise to a wave of anti-Muslim sentiment across the state. It also prompted other states to draft similar measures, with an attempt to find language that avoids the constitutional problems of the Oklahoma law.[46] Perhaps most bizarre is a proposed law in Tennessee that would make following Sharia a felony, punishable by fifteen years in jail.[47] Since Sharia, like traditional Jewish law, covers a wide range of personal conduct, such as abstention from alcohol, dietary guidelines, rules for prayer, and a code of honesty in business dealings, the Tennessee law is ridiculous as written, but the very fact that it could be seriously proposed gives evidence of a high level of public ignorance and suspicion. (When such objections were mentioned to the lawmaker who drafted the bill, he replied, "I'm still researching it.")

Indeed, there is solid evidence that prejudice against Muslims is on the rise in the United States. Complaints of employment discrimination against Muslims to the Equal Employment Opportunity Commission (EEOC) have surged in recent times. Gallup, Pew, and ABC polls confirm a new upswing in anti-Muslim views.[48]

Ideas of National Identity: Homogeneity and Belonging

All these developments are deeply disturbing, and they do show that religious fear in the United States is on the rise, particularly against Muslims. Nonetheless, we find nothing in the United States that even remotely approaches the nationwide and regional bans on Islamic dress in Europe, or the nationwide Swiss minaret referendum. Can we explain this divergence? I've suggested that the United States is comfortable with heterogeneity to a greater extent than is Europe. But this difference is part of a deeper difference in ideas of national identity.

Ever since the rise of the modern nation state, European nations have understood the root of nationhood to lie first and foremost in characteristics that are difficult if not impossible for new immigrants to share. Strongly influenced by romanticism, these nations have seen blood, soil, ethnolinguistic peoplehood, and religion as necessary or at least central elements of a national identity. Thus people who have a different geographical origin, or a different holy land, or a different mother tongue, or a different appearance and way of dressing, never quite seem to belong, however long they have resided in a country.[49] One reason it was so terribly difficult for the Jews to win acceptance as equal citizens in Europe, for example—if indeed they have ever won it—was a perception that Jews were inherently different because they worshipped differently, dressed differently, used a different language in their worship, and ate different foods. To the extent that Jews assimilated, eating with others, inter-marrying, using German rather than Hebrew in their worship (as Reform Jews in Germany typically did), and dressing in "normal" style (no *kipoh,* no facial hair), they were more likely to win accep-tance—until the advent of race science and blood-based racial typ-ing, a relatively late phenomenon. Once race science took over, as-similation was no defense. Before and after that period, however, the accent has been on homogeneity and on cultural assimilation to the dominant paradigm. Difference is foreignness.[50]

It's worth mentioning that the alleged homogeneity was always to some degree fictitious, concealing differences of sect, clan, lo-cal dialect, and many other sources of internal diversity. Historians such as Eric Hobsbawm for Europe in general, Graham Robb for France, and Linda Colley for Britain have shown in detail the way in which stories of national identity are often relatively fragile and shallow constructs over longstanding divisions.[51] For Germany and Italy the same thing is even more obvious, since unity was late and even more transparently constructed. And, as historian George Mosse has indelibly shown, European unity projects frequently functioned by defining the nation against foreign or minority ele-ments that are characterized as degenerate in some way, often as the bearers of a stigmatized sexuality.[52] Thus the idea of homogeneity is both real (a majority shares a religion) and less real than it is said to be. Still, people come to believe in it and see likeness where, before, they might have seen difference.

This attitude prevails in many parts of Europe today. Finland is perhaps an extreme case, since Finns have allowed so little immigra-tion and thus have seen so few people who look different. A Finnish colleague of mine at the University of Chicago, who grew up in Finland's second-largest city, told me that she was sixteen before she met anyone who was not a Northern European Protestant. Finland exhibits in a stark and simple form characteristics that are shared to some degree by most European nations. And although Finland's ugly collaboration with the Nazis during World War II has several distinct origins, prominent among them being a hatred of Russia, anti-Semitism was widespread there, as a form of rejection of the different. Finnish nationalism is an especially clear case of the thesis that national identity is a deliberate construct, since one can trace it happening and name the people who engineered it. In the mid- to late nineteenth century, a group of intellectuals influenced by European romanticism rediscovered the Finnish language, which at that time was spoken only in rural areas (urban and educated people all spoke Swedish), and resurrected myths of national origin (for example, the *Kalevala*, based on traditional folklore but written in the nineteenth century).[53] Newly patriotic artists wrote novels of rural agrarian life, painted wonderful works of romantic expressionism depicting the national character in relation to lakes and forests, and wrote music expressing a love of Finnish nature and folklore (Sibelius being the most distinguished composer in this movement). People who had always spoken Swedish began speaking Finnish and changed their names from Swedish to Finnish names. Because language, so lately rediscovered, has been a particularly powerful vehicle of national pride, Finns often judge people alien if they cannot speak Finnish, a particularly difficult language unrelated to the Indo-European language family and related only to Hungarian and Estonian among known languages. Today, in fact, my Finnish friends tell me, an African immigrant who speaks fluent Finnish would be considered less alien by many people than a blond Protestant who speaks only English or German—although English has become overwhelmingly the language of academic life and of commerce. But there's appearance-based exclusion too, and all the different factors that make for inclusion have to be present together before a new resident's status would be secure.

Finland is a unique and extreme case of homogeneity. But all European countries face similar issues, to some degree. None has straightforwardly defined nationhood in terms of political ideals and struggles—a form of national identity familiar in many modern nations, including Australia, New Zealand, Canada, India, South Africa, and the United States, and one that eases these problems of inclusion to at least some extent. Not that the nations in this latter group lack struggles over inclusion and identity, as we'll soon see, but they start out with the door open a crack, since they allow anyone in who can join in the project of "life, liberty, and the pursuit of happiness"—or, in the case of India, of economic equality—that defines the national aspiration. Some of these nations have even mythologized immigration and difference as aspects of national identity. American schoolchildren visit Ellis Island, or the Statue of Liberty, and recite Emma Lazarus's Statue of Liberty poem about the "huddled masses yearning to breathe free." The United States has painful struggles over immigration, but the issue today revolves around *illegal* immigration, and a politics of opposition to legal immigration has never gone far here; its high-water mark was the latter half of the nineteenth century, when nativism had significant political traction. Even then, however, it remained a minority position, and today opposition to all immigration is a deeply unpopular idea. When Pat Buchanan, bearing such a message, marched in the St. Patrick's Day parade in Chicago while on his abortive presidential campaign, he was strongly criticized by the marchers, who noted that the holiday was a celebration of immigrants' contribution to the United States.[54]

India does not have many immigrants, but it does contain immense internal heterogeneity, and forming the modern nation centrally involved acknowledging all those elements (religious, ethnic, cultural, and linguistic) and forging a concept of membership that includes all on a basis of equality. This was an important effort of both Nehru and Gandhi, around which they fought a successful battle with the Hindu Right, who—explicitly tracing their picture of national identity to Europe—sought a more religion-culture-ethnicity-based conception of full civic inclusion, concluding that the Muslims could never be full-fledged citizens.[55] India's national anthem begins by listing the different regional/linguistic origins of India's people; its second stanza enumerates its diverse religious origins. All these groups, positioned equally, are said to give reverence to the moral law.

Australian self-definition, like that of the United States, is based on an understanding that most Australians are the descendants of immigrants—although recently it has become central to that identity to express remorse for the injustice done to indigenous people, and to take public pride in their distinctive culture and artistic traditions. Since many Australian immigrants were convicts, thus the "dregs" of Britain, the idea of a class-free and antihierarchical society is also very central. (For example, it is often thought un-Australian to sit in the back seat of a taxi, although in places with lots of tourists customs become confused.) Another aspect of identity that is frequently prominent is the ongoing relationship to the difficult and challenging land, something that all can share. (The novel *Voss* by Patrick White, Australia's first and still only winner of the Nobel Prize for Literature, depicts immigrants from a range of backgrounds and classes joining in a failed attempt to explore desert areas of the interior, in which national origins are dwarfed by the magnitude of the shared challenge.)

All three of these nations, then, understand membership in terms of shared goals and ideals, thus in a way that does not require homogeneity—in dress, dietary custom, religious belief, or even outward religious observance. This hardly means that people do not fear the strange and different, or associate religious minorities with danger. It does mean that there is a powerful counterweight. To focus for now only on the United States, because these ideas have to some degree been incorporated in the structure of U.S. law regarding religion, it also means that the institutional structure will be slow to swing into action in response to fear-laden sentiments, or will get a rebuff (as in the Oklahoma case) if it does. As we'll see, even the scary Afro-Cuban Santeria religion, which includes ritual animal sacrifice, got a resonant defense from our Supreme Court—and not just from its so-called liberal wing, either, but from its leading conservative, Justice Scalia, and from the moderate Justice Kennedy—when a community passed a law that targeted this religion's ritual practices while leaving other, similar practices unaddressed. Laws that stigmatize and persecute are extremely unlikely to stay around in the U.S. constitutional system.

Ideas of national identity are not forever fixed. The United States has surely gone through periods of anti-immigrant panic, during which the ideas of "nativism" (immigrants are not true Americans) redefined national identity for at least a significant proportion of the U.S. population. This can happen again, and we ought to be vigilant against the threat of a new nativism. Europe, by contrast, is perfectly capable of migrating to a more inclusive and political definition of national belonging, in which land, ethnicity, and religion would be less important than shared political ideals. So Europeans can use their concept of the nation to explain current attitudes and policies, but not to justify them. We can't tell at present whether it is more likely that the United States will increasingly resemble Europe, or that Europe will increasingly embrace (what used to be) the ideals of the United States. That future is in the hands of the people.

Despite these historical differences, then, we should be worried about the upsurge in religious fear and animosity in the United States, as well as in Europe. Fear is accelerating, and we need to try to understand it and to think how best to address it. Fear is an emotion about which, by now, we know quite a lot. Reflecting about its positive contributions and its likely pitfalls, we can return to some of our recent cases with greater understanding.

2

FEAR:
A NARCISSISTIC EMOTION

Without fear, we'd all be dead. The Greek philosopher Pyrrho, who claimed he had exorcised that disturbing emotion, led a very weird life, as legend has it. Without constant aid
from his friends, who followed him around all day, he would have
walked off cliffs and fallen into wells.[1] He wasn't much use to others, either. Once, when he saw his friend Anaxarchus fall into a
swamp, he walked on by without giving him any help—apparently
failing to comprehend the nature of his friend's predicament.[2] But
just as clearly, fear can be a source of unreliable and erratic behavior. Alarmed by an intruder who disturbed their sacred rituals, the
women of Thebes (in Euripides' chilling drama *Bacchae*) chased
down the stranger and tore him limb from limb. Their leader then
bore his head in triumph into the city—not yet aware, in the tumult
of her emotion, that she was carrying the head of her own son.

Such myths tell us that the removal of fear would produce social
disaster: obtuseness about real dangers to life and limb, failures to
protect both self and other. But at the same time, fear can produce
unreliable and unpredictable conduct, and it can be exploited by
politicians eager to whip up aggression against unpopular groups.

Fear is implicated in most bad behavior in the area of religion. History is filled with cases of fear-inspired cruel and harmful actions against members of minority religions—Jews, Roman Catholics, Mormons, Jehovah's Witnesses, to name only a few groups that have figured in recent U.S. and European history. In such cases, we can see clearly in hindsight that, although the majority's fear was about things of real importance—national security, nondomination, economic security, political stability—the connection people made between these values and an alleged threat posed by the religious minority was utterly bogus, a product of ignorance and fantasy propelled by political rhetoric. It was utterly implausible that Jews were plotting to seize control of Europe through a conspiracy of bankers. It was utterly implausible that treating Roman Catholic immigrants as equal citizens would result in the collapse of U.S. democracy. It was utterly implausible that Jehovah's Witnesses were planning to betray the United States to the Nazis (who had already put Jehovah's Witnesses in concentration camps in Germany!). And yet, all these things were widely believed, and they led to both discrimination and violence, as fantasy took center stage and became a reality that sentenced many innocent people to substandard lives and, all too often, to death.

I'll be arguing that to get a handle on our fears we need a combination of three things: sound principles involving respect for human equality; arguments that are not self-serving, targeting an alleged fault in the minority that is ubiquitous in the majority culture; and a curious and sympathetic imagination. But first we need to understand more about fear and how it works.

Let's begin with a famous example, to which we can return armed with what we learn: the myth of a Jewish world conspiracy, widely believed in late nineteenth and early twentieth-century Europe, as disseminated in two influential documents: the "Rabbi's Speech" (1872) and the *Protocols of the Elders of Zion* (c. 1902).[3] The "Speech" is actually an extract from a novel by Hermann Goedsche, called *Biarritz.* So the first extraordinary fact is that, despite the wide availability of the fictional source, large masses of people believed that the Speech was historically real, and it was even eventually invoked as a proof of the authenticity of the *Protocols.* The novel depicts a secret meeting of representatives of the thirteen tribes of Israel in the Jewish cemetery in Prague. A rabbi addressing this gathering announces that the Jews are poised to take control of the world. Using Christian civilization as a shield and operating secretly, Jews have slowly amassed huge power through their control of financial institutions and their personal wealth. Given the rising debt of European nations, they will soon be ripe for a Jewish takeover. The speech advises the Jews that they still need to do more to take over landed property, to achieve high standing in the various professions, and especially to establish themselves in the legal profession and the press—and eventually they can effect changes in financial regulation that will work to their benefit. Throughout, the rabbi keeps pointing out that the gullibility of the public is their greatest advantage: they can continue to work in secret, unsuspected, while paying lip service to Christian culture and Christian values.

The *Protocols,* first published in Russia, is a similar conspiracy fiction, a purported report of a secret meeting of an international conference of "elders of Zion" (a term made plausible by the fact that the First Zionist Congress took place around this time). Again, the basic idea is that Jews will achieve world domination through wealth and control of financial institutions, operating by "cunning and hypocrisy." In this case, Jews will prey on the dissatisfaction of workers and stir them up to socialist revolution, thus fomenting chaos in Europe that they can then use to their advantage. Once again, the text emphasizes the need for secrecy and hypocrisy, and the ease of prevailing, on account of the naïveté and guilelessness of the majority.

These texts had huge influence and are still believed in some quarters today. They show us some interesting things about how fear works. First, fear typically starts from some real problem: people had reason to be anxious about economic security, about class tensions and the possibility of revolution, about the unpredictable forces of both political and economic change that were sweeping through European societies.

Second, fear is easily displaced onto something that may have little to do with the underlying problem but that serves as a handy surrogate for it, often because the new target is already disliked. It was a lot easier to blame the Jews for political and economic problems than to search for their real causes.

Third, fear is nourished by the idea of a disguised enemy. Most good horror stories involve a clever adversary who lies low, only to reveal his true nature when it is too late for the innocent victim to seek safety. The wolf pretends to be Grandmother, and Red Riding Hood believes him—until he pounces. The deranged heroine in *Fatal Attraction* is a dead ringer for a competent, glamorous businesswoman—and only when it is too late does Michael Douglas realize that he has become enmeshed with a homicidal psychotic. And what red-blooded American woman would have a moment's anxiety about mild-mannered Norman Bates?

One of the best horror stories of all time, and one that lies very close to the *Protocols,* is the classic film *Invasion of the Body Snatchers.* This film, which fed on the atmosphere of suspicion and accusation that was prevalent during the Cold War, particularly in the

McCarthy era, ups the usual ante by imagining an entire community of look-alike clones, whose true identity is not even an object of curiosity, so harmless, so exactly like the ordinary inhabitants do they seem—until huge damage has already been done, and a few courageous people begin to come to their senses. The film cannily exploits the fact that fear thrives on the idea of hiddenness, of danger lurking beneath the façade of normalcy. The *Protocols* exploits this tendency, which is probably deep in fear's biology, to its advantage, portraying the Jews as, in effect, body snatchers who pretend to be good citizens and even quasi-Christians (paying lip service to Christian values and even intermarrying and in some cases converting)—until the reins of power are securely in their hands.

The corollary of the idea of hidden evil is the idea of superior insight: the person who sees that Jews are dangerous and evil is positioned, in this fiction, as the one who sees through the disguise before others do, the courageous one who may ultimately save the whole community, the brave scout who notices and confronts the snake lurking in the grass. The suggestion of superior insight flatters readers: they are urged to become saviors by stripping away the pretense that surrounds the evil force.

The idea of covering the face has taken on a huge symbolic significance in current debates over the role of Islam in Europe. The obsessive focus on removing the veil follows a long tradition (in fairy tales, in films, and in real life) of imagining the existence of a secret conspiracy that will pop out of hiding to kill us when its time is ripe. The tendency to fear the sudden emergence of a startling assailant is grounded in biology, and at times it has served humanity well. It can, however, be a source of irrational and inaccurate reactions.

European gentiles who believed the *Protocols* had real worries: economic unrest, political violence. People didn't really understand these forces at the time, and it is difficult to understand them even in hindsight. How simple, then, to fall into the fairy tale trap of imagining that what's feared is easily identified as a single group, already unpopular, whose differences in religion and dress had already marked them out for suspicion, and to suppose that the very respectable and respectful behavior of this group is yet one more sign confirming the workings of a hidden conspiracy. If we just tear the veil from that group, all our problems will be removed.

Fear: Biological Tendencies

Fear is a very primitive emotion. Unlike compassion, which requires perspectival thinking and is thus available only to a few species of animal, and even unlike anger, which requires causal thinking about who is to blame for causing a harm, fear really does not require very elaborate mental apparatus. All it requires is some rudimentary orientation toward survival and well-being, and an ability to become aroused by what threatens them. Not surprisingly, then, recent research has associated fear with the amygdala, a part of the brain that is shared among all vertebrates and is not associated with higher cognition. Particularly significant is Joseph LeDoux's work on emotional learning and memory.[4] By producing brain lesions in rats, LeDoux has shown that a variety of distinct parts of the brain are involved in the transmission of fright signals and the laying down of an emotional habit or memory. The amygdala, which is an almond-shaped organ at the base of the brain, plays a very central role in the process, as do the thalamus and the auditory cortex.

LeDoux carefully avoids claiming that human emotions involve similar physiological processes; they may, but this has not yet been demonstrated. Even in the case of the creatures LeDoux has studied, he is at pains to stress the complexity and variability of the physiology: the "establishment of memories is a function of the entire network, not just of one component. The amygdala is certainly crucial, but we must not lose sight of the fact that its functions exist only by virtue of the system to which it belongs."[5] If this is so for rats, it is all the more likely to be true in humans. Finally, LeDoux claims only to have uncovered some phenomena involved in fright behavior, not to have illuminated the subjective experience of the emotion of fear, in either rats or humans. LeDoux writes that he considers fear a "subjective state of awareness" involving reaction of the organism to danger, and that what he studies is therefore not that emotion: "Subjective experience of any variety is challenging turf for scientists."[6]

We do see, however, that fear is an emotion that a rat can have, in a way not utterly distinct from a human being—as is not the case with emotions such as grief or compassion. And further research shows that human fear involves deeply buried evolutionary tendencies: for example, humans appear to have a fright reaction to the shape of a snake, which is likely to have been very helpful in evolutionary prehistory. Moreover, habituated fright, LeDoux shows, changes the organism and thus proves very difficult to reverse. Once animals are conditioned by a frightening stimulus, they can be unconditioned again only by a very long process of reconditioning.

A related set of findings, closely associated with fear, pertains to the reaction of "startle," a kind of fear-laden surprise. As Jenefer Robinson argues well, startle, like fright, and closely related to it, can also be explained well by relatively primitive evolutionary mechanisms, which do not require higher cogitation, reflection, or self-consciousness.[7]

Fear and startle are valuable mechanisms, since they attune us fairly reliably to our own safety and well-being and ensure a strong aversive reaction to perceived threats and dangers. For these reasons political thinkers have often argued that fear plays a valuable role in the law: what we fear, we have reason to prevent. Thus even John Stuart Mill, who was a leading proponent of a rationalistic approach to law, argues in *Utilitarianism* that "the impulse of self-defence" is a natural tendency, either an instinct or "close to" an instinct, that rightly underlies the criminal law. It is "common to all animal nature," and it is, up to a point, a good guide to what ought to be regulated by law.[8]

Even before we delve deeper, however, we already can see that fear may not be a perfect guide. In the first place, what helped humans survive in evolutionary prehistory is not always helpful today. In some contexts it is still useful to react swiftly and aversively to the shape of a snake, but that same tendency might not be so helpful where there are no snakes but harmless things with the same shape (ribbons used in dance, for example). More important, the natural fear of the snake often gets expanded into a culturally inflected suspicion of people who are thought to be sinuous, or wily, or stealthy —traits that are often associated symbolically with minority groups. (All were associated, historically, with Jews.) We react to *perceived* danger, and that is not always the same thing as real danger. As society gets more complex, occasions for potential dissonance between appearance and reality multiply.

This problem is magnified by the tendency of the startle instinct to make us especially frightened of that which leaps out suddenly, catching us unawares. Fear and startle, as we've seen, work closely together—whether in fairy tales and horror films or in the *Protocols*, with their fantasy of a hidden enemy ready to leap forth. And in sudden times of quick perception, we may be particularly likely to be deceived, not taking time to check out what we think we are seeing.

Most important, perhaps, is an issue to which Mill immediately turns, after offering his limited justification of fear: to be a good guide for law and policy, fear must be "moralized" by "sympathy," that is, by thought about the well-being of everyone in society. Fear, argues Mill, is all about ourselves, and it "tends to make us resent indiscriminately whatever any one does that is disagreeable to us." So it is not a wholly reliable guide to decision-making in a society where we need to consider the interests of all. Mill suggests that fear, in and of itself, resists a larger view of the good: that view needs to be supplied from outside, by a different set of emotions and thoughts.

Consider this powerful description of a young soldier's fear from Erich Maria Remarque's novel *All Quiet on the Western Front:*

> Three guns thunder out just beside us. The gunflash shoots away diagonally into the mist, the artillery roars and rumbles. We shiver. . . . We feel as if something inside us, in our blood, has been switched on. . . . The moment we hear the whistle of the first shells, or when the air is torn by artillery fire, a tense expectancy suddenly gets into our veins, our hands and our eyes, a readiness, a height-ened wakefulness, a strange suppleness of the senses. All at once the body is completely ready. . . . Perhaps it is our innermost and most secret life that gives a shudder, and then prepares to defend itself.[9]

Fear is a form of heightened attentiveness—but of a self-focused, in-deed solipsistic kind. It reduces to a kind of vivid awareness of one's own body, and perhaps, at best, of a narrow circle of people and things closely connected to the body. Of course Remarque knows that it can indeed be "moralized": one of the major themes of the novel is the way in which wartime comradeship qualifies self-serving fear. But, as in Mill, the force of general sympathy is depicted as thoroughly external to fear, as a "warmth" that "tear[s] me with a jolt away from the terrible feeling of isolation that goes with the fear of death."[10] By itself, fear contracts the spirit.

Fear: Culture and Rhetoric

In social life, as Remarque reminds us, we have a lot more to fear than snakes and predatory animals. Indeed, those nonhuman sources of danger are so thoroughly under human control that what we primarily need to do for predatory animals is to protect them from us. Human societies are still threatened by many natural forces and diseases, but they are also threatened by human hostility, by war, poverty, and dangers yet more abstract than these (economic catastrophe, group discrimination, lack of political and religious liberty, social revolution).

This means that human beings have to make decisions in a world for which evolution has given them only a very rudimentary preparation. If fear is to be a helpful motivator in that world, then people will have to form a conception of their own safety and well-being, and that of their society, that is considerably more complicated than the narrow evolutionary focus on short-term bodily safety, and they will have to engage in sophisticated thinking about what threatens that well-being. None of this is instinctual. In every society, this process of extending and shaping fear is influenced by culture, politics, and rhetoric.[11] One of the best accounts of these processes is found in Aristotle's *Rhetoric,* as he gives advice to the aspiring orator about how to persuade an audience.

Fear, Aristotle says, can be defined as "a kind of pain or disturbance resulting from imagining an impending bad event that is destructive or painful."[12] Aristotle connects fear with serious damages that involve either pain or destruction: for, he says, people do not fear that they will become unjust, or slow-witted. (Notice that he lived in a world in which people usually didn't live long enough for senile dementia to be a widespread problem.) He might have added that the reason people don't fear injustice is that it never seems to be "impending" in the sense of "hanging over" us, because we think that our moral character is within our control. The reason we now fear loss of our mental faculties more than people did in Aristotle's time is that we see more clearly how little that sanity can be controlled as we age. Aristotle later makes this point explicit: people don't feel fear if they think that they control everything important and cannot be harmed.[13]

Fear, then, is connected both to a perceived lack of control and, at least centrally, to the body and our views concerning its survival and health. Aristotle adds that the bad event must also seem to be near at hand: all people know they will die someday, he continues, but they don't fear death unless it seems imminent. When we fear other people, he adds, we do so only if we think that they have both sufficient power to harm us and bad intentions so that they are plausibly seen as likely to harm us.

As Aristotle's remarks about death reveal, there's a lot of self-blinding in human life, and people tend to fantasize more control than they really have. In reality, death can come at any time (and this was more true in his time than in ours, with its much shorter life expectancy). And yet, most of the time, we just don't think about it and are carried along by a fantasy of invulnerability. People or events that puncture that fantasy are likely, then, to be particularly feared. (Aristotle's analysis thus fits with our observation about enemies who leap out from hiding.)

Interestingly, even in core cases, where fear clearly follows evolutionary prompting, it is not based squarely on the facts. If it were, we would all be carrying around a weight of fear of death that would disrupt our daily lives; blindness to the facts no doubt evolved as a valuable trait.

But Aristotle is offering advice to political speakers, for situations in which fear is not instinctual and there are numerous choices about how to view the situation. He is basically telling them that they will succeed in arousing a fear response and consequent action only if (a) they portray the impending event as highly significant for survival or bodily well-being; (b) they portray it as close at hand; and (c) they make people feel their own personal vulnerability and lack of control. If other people should be involved—and where rhetoric is concerned they usually are—the orator should focus on the power of these people and their malevolent intentions. Elsewhere he emphasizes the importance of the self-portrayal of the orator: he should make himself appear very trustworthy. Obviously this appearance will not always be used in the service of truth.

And indeed, Aristotle is not talking about truth at all: he focuses on how the situation will be *imagined* by the audience, and on the orator's power to influence those imaginings. He is certainly not aware of the biological findings we've been discussing, but he is an astute observer of human societies, and he correctly notices that there is a good deal of flexibility in how and when people become afraid, in a way that offers an opening for the orator.

But wherever there is an opening for the orator, there is room for error. Thucydides' *History of the Peloponnesian War* tells us how a demagogic orator named Cleon whipped up the democratic assembly to vote in favor of putting to death all the men of the rebellious colony of Mytilene, and enslaving the women and children. A ship was sent to carry out this grim resolution. But then a different orator, Diodotus, stepped forward and persuaded the assembly that their previous vote had been wrong. They reversed their position and sent another ship to catch the first. By sheer luck, the first ship was becalmed, and the second one was able to catch up to it. By such a narrow thread hung thousands of lives. Without deciding which resolution was correct (although Thucydides clearly favors the second), we can be sure one was wrong. Rhetoric works on the passions in the way Aristotle says, producing both appropriate and inappropriate reactions.

In the case of fear, where might error creep in? First, people need to have a well-thought-out conception of what their welfare consists in, and they do not always have that. Certainly survival and health are a part of well-being, but people make many mistakes about what is conducive to these ends. Beyond that, people often proceed on the basis of ill-considered ideas. Aristotle thinks that people who are going to be active in politics should think reflectively about what human well-being is, because often they have superficial ideas that a little deliberation would remove. He therefore spends the entirety of the *Nicomachean Ethics* working through this issue, with the explicit aim of improving political choice. Most people, he argues, overvalue money, pleasure, and honor—but through argument they can be shown that they actually do not think these things are as important as they said they were. Other things, such as friendship, virtuous activity, and political engagement, are, by contrast, often underrated in people's first "take" on what their welfare consists in. But if fear is about potential damage to one's well-being, one needs to have an accurate conception of well-being, a conception that corresponds to one's own deepest values. Most people, however, do not follow Socrates' injunction to lead "the examined life." A person who overvalues money will have too much fear of the loss of money; a person who undervalues friendship will have (initially, prior to Aristotelian reflection) too little fear of damages that may befall others. Because most people don't follow Socrates, their emotions are likely to be inconstant and at times inappropriate to the idea of welfare that they themselves hold, on reflection.

Aristotle's ideas are consistent with Mill's observation about the narrowness of fear: he agrees that most people have a conception of welfare that attaches too little importance to the well-being of others and of the community as a whole. Like Mill, Aristotle believes that people will agree on reflection that they actually endorse a broader set of ends—but without a process of argument such as he lays out in the *Nicomachean Ethics,* plus a period of time to devote oneself to ethical reflection, most people will continue to follow narrower or more selfish goals. Mill is more pessimistic yet: he holds that for people to come to care about the good of people distant from themselves a general reform of education is necessary.

Even if people have an adequate conception of their welfare, they may be quite wrong about what really threatens it. Some of these errors may be just a matter of getting the facts wrong; others may result from overestimation of some danger that is genuine, or the underestimation of other dangers. Where other people are concerned, we might have the wrong view of their intentions and plans, or of their power to affect our well-being. We may also think ourselves more vulnerable, and more helpless against the threat, than we really are. Or, by contrast, we might exaggerate our own invulnerability and thus have less fear and fewer fears than would be rational.

If we put these dangers together with the pitfalls inherent in our evolutionary equipment, we see that we may be especially misled when a putative threat is new or surprising, a sudden tear in the fabric of our invulnerability—or when we are somehow led to imagine that something that currently looks innocuous may shortly surprise us in an unpleasant way.[14]

Fear: Heuristics and Biases

Beyond pitfalls deriving from fear's evolutionary origins, recent psychological research suggests a number of specific ways in which fear may be inaccurate—or may be fomented in an inaccurate way. No doubt some of these tendencies also have evolutionary origins, although we can study them simply as widespread human tendencies. They can be used to supplement our Aristotelian analysis of fear's likely pitfalls.

One very common source of error in fear is what psychologists call "the availability heuristic": if we can readily call to mind an example of a problem that is vivid in our experience, this leads us to overestimate the importance of that problem. This heuristic is a frequent issue in thought about environmental risks.[15] If people hear a lot about a specific danger—contamination from Love Canal, for example, or increased cancer risk from the use of alar on apples, they will tend to think that danger more significant than it is and underestimate the danger of alternatives that are not vividly depicted and that remain in the background.

Another group of phenomena that has been studied in the con-

text of ethnic hostility is the "cascade": people respond to the behavior of other people by rushing to join them. Sometimes they join
because of the reputation of those people (the "reputational cascade") and sometimes they join because they think that the behavior of others gives them new information (the "informational cascade"). Economist Timur Kuran has argued that such cascades play
a large role in the context of "ethnification," the shift (often amaz-
ingly rapid) in which people come to define themselves in terms of
an ethnic or religious identity and to set themselves in opposition
to some other ethnic group.[16] Psychologist Sudhir Kakar, doing research on ethnic violence in India, has uncovered, independently,
similar phenomena.[17] Kakar's puzzle is why people who have lived
together peacefully for years (for example, Hindus and Muslims)
suddenly turn hostile, defining their identity in a way they did not
before, in terms of their religious ethnicity. His study shows that a
large role is played by respected community leaders whose reputation produces herdlike followers. A role is also played by the intro-
duction of new "information" about danger posed by Muslims, often very unreliable in reality.

We can supplement both of these accounts by thinking about the
classic work of Solomon Asch on peer pressure: people go along
with other people even in obvious errors in sensory judgment,
ashamed or afraid to have an isolated viewpoint.[18]

These tendencies are already noticed by Aristotle, since he tells
the orator that he ought to present himself as of good character
and reputation if he wants to have an effect; and of course he is supposed to inspire fear by purveying alleged information.

To these sources of possible bias in fear we can add the anxiety
most people feel about their animal bodies and the vulnerabilities
they entail. A lot of research shows that people feel disgust at hu-

man waste products and corpses, and animals or animal products relevantly like those (sticky, slimy, smelly, oozy). They also fantasize that certain groups in their society have such properties to an exaggerated degree, even when they don't—the phenomenon that I have called "projective disgust." Jews, Muslims, women, gays and lesbians, African Americans, members of the lower castes in the Hindu caste hierarchy—all have in some ways and at some times been viewed as hyper-animal and as close (somehow, through some fantasy) to the waste products people shrink from in themselves: they are smelly, they remind us of feces and blood. Disgust is very closely linked to fear: indeed it is a shrinking from contamination that is a type of fear, or at least fear's first cousin. People fear and shrink from those to whom, in some fantasy of animality, they attach these properties.

We can now connect the disgust tendency with the surprise-startle tendency. Group A fantasizes that Group B is oozy, slimy, disgusting, hyper-animal. But the members of Group B look, in fact, like the members of Group A. What could explain this dissonance? They must be hiding something. And so, the fantasy develops that underneath the innocuous exterior of these people is something hidden, foul, that could suddenly surface to revolt and overwhelm. Historian of fashion Anne Hollander has perceptively argued that such fantasies flourished when women kept their legs and hips covered by wide skirts. They were seen as a kind of mermaid: human on top, but with a secret concealed area that was unspeakably foul and might suddenly cause disgust or even death.[19] (Hence Hollander's view that the suit was an important statement of equal humanity for women.)

Related fantasies are not unknown today when people think about male homosexuality. Those men look like us: but when they get their clothes off, they mingle feces with blood in ways that are unspeakably foul and profoundly threatening to us. Pamphlet liter ature attacking same-sex acts appeals to a very primitive fear of contamination by animal products—with which gay male sex acts are somehow supposed to have a unique affinity, and which gays somehow bring to all of us (whether by desiring us, or merely gazing at us, or even by bringing foreigners, with their alien germs, to U.S. shores).[20]

Cultural historian Sander Gilman shows that similar fictions were ubiquitous when people thought about Jews. Jews were widely seen as closer to the animal than Aryans were.[21] Their noses were taken as signs of hyper-animality (partly because of a fantasized connection between the nose and the penis). But the unlikeness was imagined to be much greater once they disrobed: beneath their clothing was something disgusting and foul. Thus the idea was prevalent that the Jew's body really was different from other bodies—with cloven feet like pigs, for example, and with male menstrual periods like women.[22] To a degree this fantasy tracked anxiety about a reality—male circumcision. In that sense it really was true that Jews were different under their clothing, and that difference, a large source of anxiety for non-Jewish men, fed the fantasy of a body that was grotesque and disgusting in every way.[23] Like Jewish plots to take over Europe, the Jewish body might put on a good masquerade, but its very hiddenness offered powerful fuel to the fantasy of danger.

It's a good idea to bear in mind that people who are different often give rise to this type of pathological fantasy. If they cover their bodies, the fantasy may acquire even more power from the idea of concealment and threatened revelation. Many things are at work when people fear the Muslim *burqa*, but we should at least ponder the propensity of the human mind to imagine unutterable horror and corruption beneath many different kinds of concealing cloth.

Let's now return to the *Protocols of the Elders of Zion,* asking how our analysis of fear's deformations helps us see what made the *Protocols* so gripping, what made otherwise rational people believe an easily unmasked fiction. All of the Aristotelian sources of error are on display in spades: the author presents a group of people who are in fact quite weak and who suffer from enormous social disadvantages as overwhelmingly strong, poised for a takeover. He represents the rest of the people of Europe—who in fact have been for centuries sitting on the Jews and denying them basic equality—as, by contrast, helpless in their naïveté and gullibility. He makes this scenario plausible by some true touches—allusions to Jewish success in banking and the evident intelligence of Jews and their achievements in many sectors of society. In that sense the availability heuristic is part of his strategy: think of the Rothschilds, and you will easily believe that all Jews are rich, powerful bankers. Think of famous Jewish intellectuals, and you'll easily believe that all Jews have a preternatural cleverness and sagacity. The availability heuristic virtually guarantees a fictitious ascription of power and influence to the group: for the individual members of an oppressed subgroup who do manage to make themselves known to the majority are likely to be the most powerful and high-achieving of its members.

The conception of well-being with which the author is working is very straightforward: the security and survival of Christian Europeans. Jews are represented as threatening to that dominant group. By making the debate about a matter of such urgency, the author preempts any serious discussion of social justice for Jews, or the proper way to deal politically with religious difference.

Disgust is not directly in evidence, but the idea of hiddenness, and of a scary underside to a "normal" surface, is what the text is all about. Jews are all around you, masquerading as nice normal people. But a day will come when they will leap out of hiding and kill you.

Finally, cascades were a large part of the way the text established itself. As reputable people believed it, so too did others, and a stampede was created, which was at the same time based on the illusion of gaining new and urgently pertinent information. A cascade of this sort in this same area took place concerning the alleged guilt of the French Jew Albert Dreyfus, who was convicted of selling military secrets to the German government. In a huge reputational cascade, people first embraced his guilt on the basis of virtually no evidence—and then, cascading in the opposite direction in response to the accusations of Emile Zola and the gradual marshaling of evidence, came to embrace his innocence. These cascades and their irrationality are mordantly depicted in Proust's great novel *Remembrance of Things Past.*

Now let's turn to some current examples. First, as orientation points, I consider two cases of basically well-grounded appeals to fear. These cases show us that appeals to fear are often rational and prudent, and we can ask ourselves why, in these instances, that seems to be the right verdict. Second, I examine two cases of religion-based fear, in which the appeal to fear seems ill-grounded and irresponsible. We'll see how the insights of neuroscience, philosophical rhetoric, and cognitive psychology can be put to work to cast light on the cases, and the differences among them. In each situation we want to know how adequate the fear is to true facts and real problems, how well it steers people to take appropriate evasive action that guides them away from real dangers, or by contrast, what distortions might have crept into people's responses from heuristics that are not adequate to the real situation and from politically engineered and normatively dubious constructions.

Rational Fear: Hurricane Irene, Airport Profiling

In late August 2011, a powerful hurricane named Irene surged up the East Coast of the United States. Meteorologists kept officials and the public informed about its likely path and strength, and their information gave reason to anticipate a massive strike in the New York City area. Mayor Michael Bloomberg kept addressing the public during this period, urging caution. He repeatedly told people not to be calm, to take this storm seriously as a threat—in short, to fear for their safety. Eventually, he ordered mandatory evacuation of some low-lying areas and strongly recommended leaving others. Although he avoided the hype of the tabloids ("Mean Irene," "Monster 'cane zeroes in on NYC," "Monster! Angry Irene roars straight for U.S. and city"), he did continually urge fear: Don't swim, it's too dangerous. Check in with your relatives. Spend the night somewhere else. Get out now. Do not underestimate the danger. Although the storm, when it finally arrived, proved weaker than anticipated and did relatively little damage, people were overwhelmingly satisfied with the mayor's precautionary measures.

Here's a case where a politician whips up fear, even exploits the surprise-startle tendency by representing the danger as large, sudden, and impending—and somehow it seems right. What's right about it? First and most important, the appeal to fear was based on the latest and most accurate scientific evidence. Second, the danger was characterized in an accurate and undistorted way—as a large hurricane, not as divine punishment for same-sex marriage or any of the grotesque other things that were said at the time. Third, it was based on a conception of well-being with which nobody could argue: life and safety, both one's own and that of loved ones, should be ranked above mere habit or convenience. Fourth, Bloomberg was addressing a genuine problem: people are creatures of habit, and they are very slow to diverge from convenient routines, particularly when the sun is shining. The availability heuristic also plays a distorting role: most New Yorkers have not lived through a major hurricane, so it's easy to believe that this event will be no worse than the average rainstorm, and that the reports will prove to be a false alarm—until the storm is there and it's too late to leave. So Bloomberg was in effect disabling the distortions of the availability heuristic by making the danger available and palpable. Finally, this fear was not directed at demonizing or stigmatizing any group of people, and it did not involve fantasies of contamination. Bloomberg tried to start an informational cascade in the direction of sane and responsible behavior and succeeded, though not without the mandatory evacuations. It's very likely that people would have been lulled into complacency without the vehemence of the mayor's appeal to fear, and so that appeal to fear was instrumental to the eventual good result.

Moving closer to our primary territory: the 9/11 terrorist attacks, and other instances of terrorism connected to Islamic extremist groups, have led to a certain amount of profiling when people are selected for full-body searches in airport screenings, as well as to "no-fly" lists that bar people who are suspected terrorists. By and large such measures, if used skillfully, are reasonable. They respond to a genuine problem, and even if the number of terrorist incidents is small, their catastrophic nature makes precaution reasonable when the only downside is longer wait lines and inconvenience. In other words, the idea of well-being used in this case is one with which nobody could argue. The new full-body screeners remove the necessity for pat downs to at least some extent, and they have restored more equality in the treatment of passengers. But even now, some profiling is probably prudent and, if executed respectfully and with good information and genuine evidence, is not as such offensive.

To single out people on the basis of their religion or ethnicity is always problematic, because it risks stigmatizing a group and exacerbating tensions. For that reason, it's best for intelligence to be fine-grained rather than crude, best, for example, for security workers not to stop everyone named Ali because the name Ali is on a no-fly list, and certainly not to stop all Muslims qua Muslims, a policy as inefficient as it is stigmatizing. Errors and insults of many types are by now legion, and they are inefficient, both because they are based on crude information and because they alienate members of the community who could be highly valuable sources of intelligence. It is also deeply offensive to consider only Muslims as potential terrorists and to ignore the existence of other terrorist groups (neo-Nazis, eco-terrorists, and others); a system that proceeds in that way is not looking out for well-being so much as acting on crude stereotypes.

In the end, the best course is very likely to search everyone, as is now done with the body scanners. Airports in India manage to do a full pat down on every single passenger, respectfully and in the privacy of a curtained booth, without unduly delaying travel. But it's always reasonable for law enforcement officers to get good information and then to act on the basis of at least some generalizations from that information. That way, the public does not get used to seeing all Muslims as suspected terrorists, and does not move from the availability of 9/11 as a paradigm crime to the false conclusion that a large proportion of Muslims are criminals. Still, given the existence of violent Islamic extremist groups who do in fact pose a threat in many nations, it's reasonable for law enforcement to track and respond to that situation—preferably in whatever way is least offensive and stigmatizing.

Minarets in Switzerland, Murder in Norway

In our first two cases, fear was well-grounded, and a response to that fear, if carefully devised, would be rational. We now move to more problematic terrain, where rhetoric manufactures a fear that does not respond to evidence or argument and employs a questionably exclusionary conception of well-being.

Most mosques do not have minarets (prayer towers) attached; this is a feature only of larger mosques, usually in urban areas. Switzerland at present has only 4 minarets: in Zürich, Geneva, Winterthur, and Wangen bei Olten. It has approximately 150 mosques or prayer rooms and a Muslim population of 400,000 out of nearly eight million total residents.

Switzerland is a prosperous nation with impressive GDP, high achievements in health, and moderately high achievements in education. It ranks thirteenth in the 2010 *Human Development Report*, with life expectancy at birth of 82.2 years, one of the highest in the world, and 10.3 mean years of schooling. But it shares problems that confront most European nations. It has a very low fertility rate, approximately 1.46, and an aging population. Inevitably, it must depend on immigration to maintain economic productivity. Although economic inequality is currently low, there are reasons to fear for the future, if productivity cannot keep pace, and if new immigrants fail to achieve a level of education necessary for the skilled jobs that

43

move development forward. So worries about immigrants and their assimilation are up to a point highly rational. Switzerland, moreover, is proud of its distinctive independent ways and its record of non-alignment. Traditionally neutral, and not a member of the European Union (EU), it goes its own way in many respects, including being by far the latest nation in Europe to give the vote to women—1971! So Swiss pride in a distinctive identity is likely to be more than usually ruffled by the need to assimilate so many outsiders in a relatively short period of time. Could such assimilation be consistent with traditional Swiss distinctiveness? That is a rational concern up to a point, but also one that can quickly acquire outsize symbolic weight, changing into an ugly xenophobia.

The Wangen bei Olten minaret, constructed in July 2009, was the starting point of the current controversy: when a local Turkish Islamic community center applied for a permit to erect a twenty-foot-high minaret on top of its existing community center, local residents protested, contesting the application before a local zoning authority. Initially successful, they lost at the appellate stage. This contretemps led right-wing politicians from the Swiss People's Party and the Federal Democratic Union to launch a broader campaign against the construction of minarets. The group (which calls itself the Egerkinger Committee) insists that minarets are not religiously required, which of course is true—they are no more required than a steeple on a Christian church. It adds that the minaret is simply a symbol of an Islamic power grab. This, of course, is not true. The minaret has religious meaning—the call to prayer is issued from it; it is an optional religious symbol, just as is the church steeple. The group began a campaign to outlaw new minaret construction in Switzerland, eventually instituting a national referendum on the question, which proposed a one-sentence addition to the Constitution: "The building of minarets is prohibited." The measure passed in November 2009 with 70 percent of the vote; polls before the fact predicted a decisive defeat, evidence that people were not up front about their intentions, or were swayed by emotion at a late date.

The pro-ban campaign contained several distinct themes. First was fear for the destruction of traditional Swiss values and identity. "Before you know it," one voter remarked, "we won't be Swiss anymore." The second theme was a threat to security. An Internet video game called Minaret Attack showed minarets rising up all over an idyllic Swiss countryside, looking like missiles. At the end of the game, a message pops up, saying, "Game over! Switzerland is covered in minarets. Vote to ban them on November 29." A third theme was the rights of women. Leading feminists joined the call for a ban, arguing that the minaret was a first step toward male domination. "If we give them a minaret, they'll have us all wearing burqas," said a female voter. "Before you know it, we'll have sharia law and women being stoned to death in our streets." This despite the fact that close to 90 percent of Muslims in Switzerland are from Turkey and Kosovo and do not adhere to conservative norms of Islamic dress.

The ban was opposed by the Parliament, the Federal Council, the Catholic bishops, the Federation of Jewish Communities, and many other prominent civil society groups, all of whom argued that it was inconsistent with norms of religious liberty and mutual respect. Jewish groups reminded the public that Jews for centuries were not allowed to construct synagogues or cupola roofs.

Campaign posters played an important part in shaping public opinion. One poster shows a Swiss flag studded with black minarets that look like missiles; in the foreground stands a woman in a *burqa*. The text reads, in large letters: "Stop. Yes to the minaret ban." After some communities refused to allow the posting of that placard in public places, another poster commented on the refusal. Over a Swiss flag is the word "Censure": "Censorship." And, below, "One more reason to say yes to the minaret ban."

The campaign cleverly tapped into biological tendencies and psychological heuristics. The idea of the hidden enemy, and the startling emergence of a lethal danger, is conveyed in the video game and the first poster; the figure of the veiled woman standing in front of the "missiles" is a cagey appeal to the fear of danger emerging from hiding. The availability heuristic is here too, in the sense that the posters foreground an image of an extremely threatening type of Islam—totally covered women, a landscape taken over by hostile structures—rather than looking accurately at the varieties of Islam actually present in Switzerland. And the second poster constructs a reputational cascade, with its "one more reason to say yes": in other words, "your neighbors and friends, assessing the reasons, are already out there ahead of you, and if you're wavering, now's the time to join them."

Appeals to disgust lurk beneath the surface as well. The Swiss are proud of the clean bright beauty of their land: and the posters show black ugly objects walking all over it. Seen in one way, they look like weapons; but they can also be seen as insects, polluting the white of the flag on which they stomp.

Above all, however, the campaign is Aristotelian. People who position themselves as trusted characters (concerned citizens) construct a picture of Swiss identity involving the flag and allusion to cherished values (security, liberty, women's equality) and then construct an enemy who poses an ugly and urgent threat to what people care about. At the same time, the campaign's rhetoric constructs a "we" that excludes immigrants, no matter how long they have been in the country or how much they are contributing to the national economy.

All political campaigns use symbolism to inspire emotion. And Swiss people do have some real anxieties about the nation's future, in an era of declining fertility and economic fragility. Why, then, does this campaign raise particular concerns about fear running amok? The first problem is that it distorts facts so flagrantly, trying to make people think that all Swiss Muslims are aiming at something like a military takeover, in which women will be brutally subjugated and the Swiss countryside will be a war zone. There is no threat of scores of minarets being erected in Switzerland. The minaret is, and would have remained, a rarity. The symbolic significance of the minaret (the reason this campaign focused on something that really is not happening) is that the shape of the minaret can be made to signify a missile, thus reinforcing the idea that Muslims pose a security threat. But the minaret-as-missile metaphor is by itself a gross distortion of reality. The feminism issue is itself somewhat absurd, given the long record of the Swiss in denying the vote to women (a right that Turkish women won in 1930, forty-one years before Swiss women), and given ongoing large gaps between Swiss women and Swiss men in both secondary/tertiary education and labor force participation.[24] Real issues are being swept under the rug, and symbolic issues that have no demonstrable connection to the real issues are taking their place. Instead of engaging in a difficult but ultimately constructive debate about how to promote social cohesion and continuity in a time of immigration, and about how to move toward greater empowerment for women, people are encouraged to feel that they are making progress by engaging in a purely notional campaign against a threat that does not exist.

Moreover, this deflection of attention sets back debate on the real issues. It's much harder to achieve social cohesion in a time of necessary immigration when you demonize immigrants and represent them as external invaders, rather than as people whom you yourselves have invited in to do jobs that you need to have done, many of whom have now become your fellow citizens. And it's much harder to fight for educational and economic progress for women when people believe that all is fine in Switzerland apart from a quasi-external threat of Islamic takeover.

The Swiss minaret campaign was at least nonviolent. And so far it has had no violent consequences. We turn now to a tragedy caused by religious hatred in the apparently harmonious nation of Norway: the killings perpetrated by Anders Behring Breivik. Norway's tragedy was not the work of a psychopath. Anders Behring Breivik is no Jared Lee Loughner. Breivik writes lucidly and ideologically, despite the evidence of mental incapacity that has been found convincing by the Norwegian court. Rather like Gandhi's assassin, Nathuram Godse, he is an extremist with a paranoid view of the world, but he is capable of articulating a rationale for his deeds that is comprehensible. Indeed, just as Godse used the occasion of his trial to gain publicity for his Hindu-Right views (issuing a lengthy public statement of self-justification), so Breivik has used the occasion of his crimes to draw attention to a rationale for violence that he would like to commend to the world.

The student of fear will find much of interest in Breivik's manifesto, which invited close comparison to the *Protocols* for its depiction of a naïve Europe, heedless while under siege from a hidden enemy. Indeed, the rhetorical structure of the *Protocols* is paralleled quite closely by a number of documents in this area—including Pamela Geller's influential blog "Atlas Shrugs," the writings of Robert Spencer, and, especially, the claims of a group called Citizens for National Security, which we shall shortly examine. Let's begin, however, with the media coverage and what it said about the current climate of fear in Europe and the United States. We'll then turn to links between Breivik and more popular and influential political figures.

When the attacks in Norway took place, media all over the world were quick to link them to Islamic terrorism. Britain's *Sun* screamed, "Al Qaeda massacre: Norway's 9/11."[25] Commentators speculated that the terrorist acts were retaliation for Norway's contribution of troops to the wars in Afghanistan and Iraq. Hours after it was known that a tall blond Caucasian man, linguistically and ethnically Norwegian, had been arrested, CNN and Fox still spoke the language of "jihad." In the United States, the *Wall Street Journal* ran an editorial similar to the *Sun*'s. As facts gradually filtered in, phrases like "good disguise" or "convert" were substituted.[26] Heiner Bielefeldt, U.N. Special Rapporteur on freedom of religion or belief, condemned the coverage: "The way in which some public commentators immediately associated the horrifying mass murder in Norway last Friday with Islamist terrorism is revealing and indeed an embarrassing example of the powerful impact of prejudices and their capacity to enshrine stereotypes." U.S. media-watchdog group Fairness and Accuracy in Reporting also saw signs of a general problem: "U.S. media in general, with many exceptions, promote this view that terrorism equals Islam." The director of Harvard University's Outreach Center at the Center for Middle Eastern Studies also condemned the coverage, saying that it discouraged a subtle and accurate understanding of the diverse roots of terrorism.[27]

These media trends are above all cases of the availability heuristic leading us astray: ever since the cataclysm of 9/11, Americans have seen that day as the paradigm of bad world events and have a strong

tendency to read other events in the light of that one. Sudden violence is terrorism, and terrorism is Al Qaeda. And of course the reputational cascade is also at work, as reputable media figures spread
a view that is then taken up by many other people, whose views, in
turn, eventually cycle back again, affecting media coverage of new
events.

Particularly relevant here is the congressional inquiry into radical
Islam initiated by Representative Peter King, chair of the House
Homeland Security Committee, in March 2011. These hearings represent a step in a reputational cascade, since they both respond to
fears expressed in the media and, by attaching the prestige of Congress to those fears, further encourage fear. There is, of course, nothing unreasonable about investigating threats of terrorism, and radical Islam is one source of such threats. It would have been both
more efficient and more conducive to balanced rational debate to
investigate this threat along with others—for example, the threat
posed by the vaguely Christian parts of the militia movement that
gave rise to the Oklahoma City bombings. Such an inquiry might
even have performed a public service by delving into the world of
paranoid blogging about a Muslim takeover out of which Anders
Behring Breivik emerged. Who knows: such an inquiry might even
have stopped Breivik in his tracks, since it would quickly have uncovered evidence that even some very radical right-wing groups on
the Internet refused him membership because they found his ideas
about violence scary. The English Defense League, for example, a
nationalist group with neo-Nazi tendencies for which Breivik expressed admiration, has condemned the attacks, though it has also
warned that similar attacks are only to be expected if pro-immigrant
policies are permitted to continue.[28] Another anti-Islamist lobby
group, Stop Islamisation of Europe (SIOE), denied Breivik's attempt

to join their Facebook group over his neo-Nazi ties.[29] All of this might have been very useful if discovered in advance. Still, King can be forgiven for not entering this terrain, since the groups in question are based in Europe rather than in the United States—although the Internet makes them in effect ubiquitous. What is not responsible is to suggest to the public that the threat of violence comes only, or even primarily, from Islam. As the *Washington Post* points out, the Oklahoma City event was the single deadliest terrorist attack on U.S. soil before 9/11, and the most "remorseless and violent terrorist organization in the nation" during the past century has been the Ku Klux Klan.[30]

Still more irresponsible are statements made by King that suggest that the entire American Muslim community is suspect, not just a radical fringe. He has repeatedly alleged that Muslim-Americans in general have failed to cooperate with law enforcement. And he once made the outrageous claim that "80 to 85 percent of mosques in this country are controlled by Islamic fundamentalists."[31] Indeed, it is strident statements such as this, and inquiries that pillory a single community, which may over time produce the phenomenon King decries. When a group is subject to stigmatization, its cooperation with law enforcement tends to decrease. A poll conducted in both New York and London by two law professors (Aziz Huq of the University of Chicago and Stephen Schulhofer of New York University) and one psychology professor (Tom Tyler of New York University) shows a growing perception of discrimination among Muslims and indicates that this may over time have a significant negative effect on cooperation.[32]

Right after the Breivik attack, and thus several months after the King inquiry, a group surfaced calling itself Citizens for National Security, whose claims were brought to Washington by Representative Allen West (R-Fla.), who endorsed the group's work in a press release in the Cannon House Office Building on Capitol Hill. The claims of the group lie very close indeed to the rhetoric of the *Protocols*. It alleges that Muslims in America form a "fifth column" subverting American institutions from within. It claims to have a list of 6,000 American Muslims who have links to the Egyptian Islamic group called the Muslim Brotherhood. Citizens for National Security would not release these names, but it did release an elaborate flow chart of alleged extremist influences, in the context of litigation over the Islamic charity called the Holyland Foundation.[33] The group said that it was difficult to compile the chart, given the Brotherhood's "intentional denial and deception campaign through intentional complexity." The vagueness of the charges, the sweeping conspiracy theory, and the claim that Muslims characteristically conceal and deceive—all this might have been taken right out of the *Protocols*, but for the fact that human beings are prone to such fear games, without the need for direct causal influence.

Another aspect of the reputational cascade bears mentioning here. The FBI, on whom we rely to investigate terrorist activity in the United States, seems to have been trapped in the cascade, and of course contributes to it in turn through its monitoring choices. In the aftermath of the Breivik incident, it emerged that the FBI has been assigning, as recommended reading about Islam, a book by extremist Robert Spencer, *The Truth about Mohammed: Founder of the World's Most Intolerant Religion*. Spencer, co-founder, with Pamela Geller, of "Stop the Islamicization of America," has been, along with Geller, a leader of the protest against the Muslim community center planned for the area near "ground zero." Both Spencer and Geller were repeatedly cited by Breivik in his manifesto. Their group has been termed a "hate group" by the distinguished Southern Poverty Law Center. They certainly are not to blame for Breivik's actions, which they both have condemned. Nor is their mention by Breivik a reason the FBI should not assign their works. The problem is that the work is paranoid and deeply unreliable, quite similar to the Breivik manifesto in the level of paranoid thinking it involves.

Did the FBI assign Spencer's book as part of an inquiry into U.S. extremism? Unfortunately, the answer to that question is clearly "no." The background reading was accompanied by a PowerPoint presentation by the FBI's Law Enforcement Communications Unit that trains new Bureau recruits. These slides missed a golden opportunity to provide recruits with a historically informed and nuanced understanding of the varieties of Islam, the different national origins of U.S. Muslims, and the different world cultures in which Muslims live today. Since most Americans think of Islam as existing mainly in the Middle East, in predominantly Arab societies, despite the fact that Indonesia and India have the two largest Muslim populations in the world, both with democratic institutions, and that India (with its neighbor Bangladesh) is a major source for American Muslims, it is quite disturbing to find that the PowerPoint presentation itself refers to Islam as a religion of the "M.E." (Middle East) and tells recruits that to interrogate Muslims they need to know that "the Arabic mind" is "swayed more by words than ideas and more by ideas than facts" (whatever this means!). It also tells recruits that Muslims "engage in a circumcision ritual"—as if this were some primitive custom, in a nation in which more than half of male newborns are circumcised, and in which ritual circumcision is a familiar Jewish custom. Recruits also "learn" that Islam "transforms [a] country's culture into 7th century Arabian ways."[34]

Needless to say, we need an FBI that is competent, and "instruction" like this is a disgrace. As former agent Mike German comments, "In order for FBI training to be effective it has to present useful, factual and unbiased information. This material fails on all three criteria." In response to journalists' inquiries, the FBI now states that the PowerPoint presentation is no longer being used and that Spencer's book is no longer assigned. Other aspects of the current curriculum remain unclear. At least an invitation to Brigitte Gabriel, a strident anti-Muslim writer similar to Spencer and Geller in level of nuance and accuracy, has been withdrawn. Still, public vigilance is important. A growing profession of "terrorism consultants" has sprung up who address a variety of law enforcement agencies about this topic, earning hefty honoraria. Some of these people purvey hyped-up or downright false information, fueling fear rather than competent law enforcement activity.[35] Unfortunately, something about the current atmosphere (including current media culture) creates a market for the sensational, so a consultant eager for bookings has incentives to pursue hype rather than nuance.

One depressing conclusion that emerges from this story is that the suspicion and mistrust of academic scholarship by the FBI that began during the McCarthy era have never really ended. British intelligence during World War II succeeded, and saved the nation and the free world, because it recruited the nation's best scholars, young and old. (Philosopher J. L. Austin, serving in MI6, was among those whose ability and leadership were crucial.) At that time, the United States followed Britain's lead: philosopher of language W. V. O. Quine was part of the U.S. Navy team that deciphered encoded messages, reaching the rank of lieutenant commander. Today, Austin and Quine have been replaced, as intellectual guides, by the likes of

Robert Spencer and Brigitte Gabriel. Our world is far less safe as a result.

One final aspect of the media coverage (in this case literal covering) of Breivik is an odd admission by Pamela Geller on her blog "Atlas Shrugs," which has as its main purpose the "unmasking" of an alleged Muslim conspiracy for domination. We know that Breivik cites Geller, but Geller cannot be blamed for that. However, the nexus may be more complicated. Geller has a lot of correspondents who chat with her about the Muslim threat to the world. In 2007, she published an email from Norway that ended a rant against Muslims with this: "We are stockpiling and caching weapons, ammunition and equipment. This is going to happen fast." In her comment section to the post at the time, she said that she had deleted the sender's name to prevent the person from being investigated and prosecuted. After Breivik's attack, the offensive line was removed from the 2007 post. Still, someone had saved it, and it is on the public record.

Was the correspondent Breivik? If so, by running the post anonymously to shield the sender, Geller prevented law enforcement from investigating this terrorist threat. Rather than shielding him, she should have reported him. And if it was not Breivik, the same is true—and, in addition, we have to worry that there is some other violent person out there (or persons, since the post uses "we") who may possibly stage an attack in the future. In either case, Geller owes the police all the information she has.[36]

Fear's Narcissism

Fear is primitive. We saw this even in physiological terms: fear is connected to primitive brain processes that are shared by all vertebrates, and human fear, while in many ways more complex, continues to partake of these shared animal origins. We might say that the nervous energy of Remarque's young soldier, as the world around him shrinks to his own shaking body, is little more than that animal response—and it is indeed primitive, including only his body and his survival. The needs of others have to "tear" him "with a jolt" away from that immersion in himself. That does not mean that fear is not valuable and often accurate—but its view of the world is exceedingly narrow. Unlike grief and sympathy, it has not yet conceded the full reality of other people. And in its partnership with disgust human fear is in some ways worse than animal fear: for animals don't fantasize that other groups of animals are foul and that they themselves are pure and non-animal. So human fear combines animal narrowness with a peculiarly human shrinking from animality—in other groups of people, where animality is always imagined to be.

Even when fear is socialized—made part of culture and rhetoric—it is never really "moralized" in Mill's sense. It is always relentlessly focused on the self and the safety of the self. That narrowness of focus is a prominent thread running through the cases of fear that we've studied. Swiss voters were encouraged to see themselves as threatened and to focus on narrow issues of personal identity and security—rather than being encouraged to turn outward to the task of building a society that would appropriately include all its members. Immigrants, rather than being seen as full people, were seen from the narrow perspective of the ego, as missiles attacking the homeland. Similarly, the fear-inspired media response to Breivik immediately saw that event, whose true nature was as yet unknown, as a replay of the trauma of 9/11, and therefore, once again, as all about the self and what threatens the self. This egocentric reading prevented genuine curiosity.

In these and many other cases, both episodic fear and anxiety, or chronic fear, are simply more narcissistic than other emotions. All emotions look at the world from the perspective of the individual experiencing the emotion and that individual's set of goals and concerns—rather than "from nowhere," from an ideal point of impartiality. Thus we grieve for those we know, not for those we don't know. We feel compassion for a person whose story is made vivid to us, not for a bodiless abstraction. So all emotions have a narrowness problem and threaten complete impartiality. Fear, however, goes further, for it threatens or prevents love.

The poet Dante depicts all vices as forms of exaggerated self-love, a "fog" that stands between us and the full reality of other people. The philosopher and novelist Iris Murdoch develops this idea much further, arguing—and showing in her novels—that people have great difficulty seeing other people as fully real and worthy of genuine concern—because they are wrapped up in themselves and see others only through the obscuring haze of their own needs and plans. If one is ever to see, or love, another person, one must undertake a process of "unselfing."[37] But in *The Black Prince*, a novel that is among her most insightful, Murdoch makes a further claim: anxiety, or chronic fear, is the basic form of the excessive self-concern that damages love:

> Anxiety most of all characterizes the human animal. This is perhaps the most general name for all the vices at a certain mean level of their operation. It is a kind of cupidity, a kind of fear, a kind of envy, a kind of hate. . . . Fortunate

are they who are even sufficiently aware of this problem to
make the smallest efforts to check this dimming preoccupation. . . . The natural tendency of the human soul is towards the protection of the ego.[38]

Fear is a "dimming preoccupation": an intense focus on the self that
casts others into darkness. However valuable and indeed essential
it is in a genuinely dangerous world, it is itself one of life's great
dangers.

3

FIRST PRINCIPLES:
EQUAL RESPECT FOR CONSCIENCE

How can we best address the current climate of fear? A good approach has three ingredients: good principles, an emphasis on non-narcissistic consistency, and a cultivation of the "inner eyes," the capacity to see the world from the perspective of minority experience.

Why principles? Given the distracting and distorting potential of fear, which can so easily render particular judgments self-serving and unreliable, it seems a good idea to approach these delicate and complicated issues armed with some general principles that we can cling to as we attempt to avoid confusion and panic. If these principles are to help us address fear's tendency to self-privileging, they should incorporate a focus on the good of others, correcting for fear's partiality. Supplying principles to guide democratic political practice has been a central purpose of political philosophy, which, ever since its (Western) start in ancient Athens, has seen its goal as practical, not merely theoretical. I'll argue that philosophy really does have the sort of practical importance that the Greeks claimed for it, offering insight to every person who wants to think about these matters. So what does political philosophy have to say about religious difference and the anxieties it provokes?

The tradition I shall map out is specifically Euro-American, but we'd do well to bear in mind that similar thoughts can be found in the history of India, which developed policies of religious toleration earlier than did the West: at least by the third second century BCE, when the emperor Ashoka, himself a convert to Buddhism from Hinduism, put up a series of edicts mandating toleration throughout his empire. These policies did not endure through the entire premodern period, but they were revived and further developed in the Moghul Empire of the sixteenth and seventeenth centuries, particularly in the thought and practice of the Muslim emperor Akbar, who proclaimed toleration among all religions and created a state cult that included elements from all the major religions in his empire.[1] Akbar was a famous figure in Europe, and his ideas had a significant influence on the development of European ideas of toleration—as did the ideas and laws of the Ottoman Empire. I shall say no more about this history here, but we should remember it: our goals are fairness and understanding, and we would be thrown off from the start if we were to think, mistakenly, that the ideas of mutual respect and toleration are exclusively Western. It's particularly important, perhaps, to be keenly aware that some of their most influential architects were observant Muslims.

The specific principles I advocate are, historically, more American than European. Europeans share some of the key premises (ideas of human dignity and equality), but on the whole they have not been as eager as Americans to develop legal regimes that insist on fairness to minorities in matters where majorities make law, and even on some degree of accommodation of minority practices. Europe on the whole has relied on other strategies to deal with religious minorities: assimilation, geographical sorting (dissenters leave), and established churches with formal toleration. Such solutions are not morally adequate: the premises about human dignity and equality that Americans and Europeans share entail something like the American solution. But even if readers are not fully persuaded on this point, it is by now clear that the European solution is no longer adequate. It "worked" so long as religious minorities were few in number and so long as they could easily find a new home if they did not like their current one. (I say "worked" because this solution clearly did not do well by the Jews, who were few in number but had no attractive exit options, apart from the United States.) It was always morally wrong, I think, to require Jews to bend their conscience to the ways of the majority, but no social upheaval resulted from this wrong. The current situation in Europe is very different: declining population requires immigration, and new immigrants are numerous enough that they can't be treated to the centuries of insult that greeted the Jews, without massive social upheaval. Thus the American solution is urgently needed, even if people are not persuaded (as I think they ought to be) that it is the solution that justice demands.

Dignity, Vulnerability, Entitlement

Let's start with an assumption that is widely shared: that all human beings are equal bearers of human dignity. In other words, all human beings possess human dignity, and with respect to that dignity they are equal. People may be unequal in wealth, class, talent, strength, achievement, or moral character—but all are equal as bearers of an inalienable basic human dignity that cannot be lost or forfeited.

This idea was not always accepted. Before the eighteenth century, many people believed that lords and vassals were inherently unequal in status and dignity, and long after that many people believed that blacks and whites, and men and women, were inherently unequal. The idea of inherent human equality is very old—in the West, as old (at least) as the thought of the ancient Stoics, who did not hesitate to assert that equality transcended gender, class, ethnicity, and nationality. It is also a key idea of Christian ethics, in the form of the idea that all souls are equal in the sight of God. Nonetheless, the notion of inherent equality was widely disregarded for many centuries when it was a question of the equality of some groups of people. Today, however, it is an idea so widely accepted that it is woven into the fabric of most nations' political principles, and into the foundations of the international human rights movement.

Dignity is a difficult idea to define precisely, and we probably should not try to do so in the political realm, since different religions and different secular views have varying accounts of it, and we don't want to play favorites. (Jacques Maritain, the Catholic philosopher who became a major drafter of the Universal Declaration of Human Rights, remarks that he himself understands human dignity in terms of the idea of the immortal soul, but he would not wish to put that in a document like the Declaration, which is supposed to be a meeting place for people from many different religious and secular traditions.) We should probably avoid thinking that dignity has an obvious specific content all on its own: it seems to be a notion that gets fleshed out through its relationship with other notions, such as that of *respect* (dignity is that attribute of a person that makes the person an appropriate object of respect), and a variety of more specific political principles. It is closely connected to Immanuel Kant's idea of the human being as an end and not a mere means, and indeed that was Kant's way of fleshing out the notion of dignity.

At times in the history of philosophy, the notion of equal human dignity has been strongly linked to the human capacity for reasoning. Although the Stoics focused on practical and moral reasoning, not on theoretical reasoning, they did think that it was this capacity that raised all humans above "the beasts" and made us all of equal worth. Of course they recognized that some people are better at moral reasoning than others, but they thought that the sheer possession of this ability is such a wonderful thing that it already puts everyone who has it above a threshold of dignity, in such a way that anyone above that threshold is of infinite worth, the equal of everyone else, and deserving of equal respect. This Stoic position has a long legacy: it is, in essence, Kant's position and that of the great Kantian political philosopher John Rawls.

This attitude to the basis of dignity, while attractive in some ways, has serious problems. For one thing, it involves a sharp division between human beings and other creatures. This split has encouraged the idea that we are free to treat animals as mere tools of our purposes. That conclusion does not strictly follow from the Stoic/Kantian conception of dignity as grounded in moral capacity. Kantian philosopher Christine Korsgaard has shown that, starting from Kant's position, we can nonetheless conclude that we have strong ethical duties to nonhuman animals.[2] Indeed, she argues that a Kantian must show concern to nonhuman animals on pain of inconsistency, for it is inconsistent to recognize that we humans have duties to preserve our animal nature and to deny that these duties obtain toward similar "fellow creatures."

Still, reason-based views of dignity, historically, have certainly encouraged the idea that we needn't have respect and awe in connection with animal life.³ Furthermore, the emphasis on reason also proves problematic when we are thinking about our duties to human beings with severe cognitive disabilities. If their abilities lie beneath the threshold usually chosen, which typically involves the idea of evaluating and ranking goals and inhibiting desire in order to pursue those goals, the human being in question will be judged of unequal worth. Of course most people have long believed that individuals with severe cognitive disabilities are of lesser inherent worth, but today those prejudices are, rightly, rejected. Anyone who cares about the current attempt to treat people with disabilities with equal respect in the political realm has reason, then, to question a theory of human dignity that places so much emphasis on reason as the source of our humanity.

It seems problematic anyway. Other things also contribute to our humanity: the capacity to perceive, the capacity to move, the capacity to feel emotions, the capacity to love and care. Why shouldn't we say that as long as one or more of these capacities is present, and the person is born of at least one human parent, that person is fully equal in human dignity?⁴ That is what I and some other contemporary philosophers do say.⁵ These criteria would exclude a person in a permanent vegetative condition, and the extreme case of an anencephalic human. But it would include people with a wide range of cognitive disabilities.

As for nonhuman animals, it seems appropriate to say that they have their own types of dignity, and that these forms of dignity also demand respect. Since nonhuman animals do not engage in religious practices, however, we may bracket those concerns for the remainder of this book. Some species do move very close to religion. The grief behavior of elephants, for example, has a ritual aspect, and Barbara Gowdy's marvelous elephant novel *The White Bone* imagines a full-blown religion for elephants on the basis of this evidence. So it's not ruled out that we will learn that some species have religious behavior. If that does emerge, then those species too deserve an appropriate type of protection for the exercise of that ability.

So we have the first premise in our argument: all humans have *equal dignity.* We now add a second premise that is very widely shared, concerning the task of government. Whatever else governments do, they may not violate that equal dignity, and in general they ought to show *respect* for our equality and dignity. The whole idea that governments may not violate basic human rights is an elaborated form of this premise. But what is it to treat people with equal respect, in areas touching on religious belief and observance?

We now add a further premise: that the faculty with which people search for life's ultimate meaning—frequently called "conscience"— is a very important part of people, closely related to their dignity, or an aspect of it. (In the Stoic tradition and the parts of Christian ethics that are strongly influenced by it, "conscience" is conceived of as basically the essence of human dignity, since it is the core faculty of practical reasoning and evaluation. In the view I'm developing, however, which does not lean so heavily on rational abilities, it seems best to say that for the people who have it, it has a close relation to their dignity.) In other words, to violate conscience is to conduct an assault on human dignity.

We then add one further premise, which we might call the vulnerability premise: this faculty can be seriously impeded by bad worldly conditions. It can be stopped from becoming active, and it can even be violated or damaged within. (The first sort of damage, which seventeenth-century American philosopher Roger Williams compared to imprisonment, occurs when people are prevented from conducting outward observances required by their beliefs. The second sort, which Williams called "soul rape," occurs when people are forced to affirm convictions that they may not hold.)

The ancient Stoics did not accept the vulnerability premise. They thought that the core of our dignity was so firm within us that it was utterly impervious to the world's assaults. To be prevented from being active was no big deal: they called the action a mere "after-birth" and placed their whole emphasis on effort and intention. Nor did they think that the ethical faculty could be damaged by anything that other people did to it. Having taken such positions, they had no way of showing why slavery was bad. They wanted to criticize it, and the great Roman Stoic philosopher Seneca did energetically try to maintain that it was a terrible thing to use physical violence or sexual coercion against slaves. But he could not explain why these things are wrong, since he was determined to maintain that the only truly important aspect of a human being was utterly unaffected by those acts. And he saw clearly that he could not conclude that the institution of slavery was itself wrong: for, he reasons, what does that sort of coercion matter, since what matters is the freedom of the soul inside the person? It is because we do not agree with Seneca—because we accept the vulnerability premise—that we think that slavery matters and is a hideous wrong.

Accepting the vulnerability premise does not mean saying that external events can remove human dignity (short of death), or that they can render human beings less than fully equal. It's a delicate line to tread, for we want to say that something terrible has happened to a person who is enslaved, or a person who has been raped. But we don't want to say that this event has reduced them to a lower than fully human status. So what does it mean to violate human dignity, if it does not mean to reduce or remove it? Thinking of rape is helpful here, for we do think that rape does a terrible thing to the whole life of the woman who is raped, affecting her emotions, her health, her plans and projects. It may make her temporarily or permanently incapable of valuable forms of striving. But we also think that women are not made less than fully equal by being raped. (People used to think that way, of course. Even the great poet Dante puts Piccarda Donati in the circle of Paradise farthest from God—for all eternity—because she was raped.) Indeed, it is because of their inherent equality that rape and its terrible toll are rightly seen as such serious crimes. It's easier for me to explain this combination of views than it would be for a Stoic or a Kantian, because in my view even an utter collapse of the ability to make choices—short of death or a permanent vegetative condition—does not remove inherent human dignity. But even a Stoic or a Kantian can say that dignity remains above the threshold pertinent to equality, even when important moral and cognitive abilities are damaged. And of course if dignity really is eclipsed, by either death or a permanent vegetative condition, that is a wrong to the person who has been killed.

The vulnerability premise shows us that the conditions of political and social life matter, where equal respect for conscience is concerned. The Stoic attitude would have been that conscience is always completely free even if a person is in prison, or enslaved or even being tortured on the rack. But we have rejected that idea. The vulnerability premise, then, means that giving equal respect to conscience requires tailoring worldly conditions so as to protect both freedom of belief and freedom of expression and practice. It also suggests that freedom should be quite ample: being able to whisper prayers in your home is hardly enough for genuine religious liberty, and we judge, rightly, that a society like China, which forces many religious people to keep their religious beliefs and acts hidden, has not adequately protected religious freedom, even though we know that many Chinese people do hold religious beliefs, and very likely act on them in the privacy of their homes, insofar as they have privacy.

If we combine the vulnerability premise with the equality premise, we get the principle that liberty should be both ample and equal —a principle very like John Rawls's idea that justice requires the "maximum liberty that is compatible with a like liberty for all." Thus the framers of the U.S. Constitution concluded that protecting equal rights of conscience requires "free exercise" for all on a basis of equality. The state constitutions of that time made it clear that the commitment was to ample liberty, not just equal liberty, for they permitted only a few extremely urgent public considerations, particularly those of peace and safety, to trump the religious claim. Most legal traditions today agree, and they also hold that it is important to protect reasonably ample conditions of religious free exercise even when, for good reasons, society has severely curtailed other aspects of a person's liberty. (Thus most legal traditions hold that prisoners have rights of religious exercise, and that those rights are equal—an idea that raises complicated questions about how far government is required to go in giving prisoners of minority religions the material circumstances and the physical objects they need to exercise their religion.)

Lockean Neutrality versus Accommodation

But what do these abstract principles really mean? What is truly equal liberty in religious matters? What type of state efforts to respect religious pluralism does a commitment to ample and equal liberty require? And what limits might reasonably be placed upon religious activities in a pluralistic society, compatible with that commitment? From now on I shall focus on the Anglo-American legal/

political tradition, and especially its development in U.S. constitutional law, because in that tradition these ideas are worked out with a useful clarity. Europe and other modern democracies (India, for example) have very similar ideas. The U.S. experience is particularly illuminating in part because so many of the early settlers migrated to the colonies in search of religious liberty and then had to confront the question of pluralism head on, since the new settlers who arrived seeking religious liberty were highly diverse, including Puritans, Baptists, Quakers, Mennonites, Anglicans, Roman Catholics, and Jews; although few or no Muslims were there, they were standardly included in theoretical writings on the topic of religious liberty, as were atheists and agnostics. Moreover, the colonists soon encountered the Native Americans, with their own religions.

From the beginning, colonists knew that they had to confront a host of questions that Europe did not always face or even see: simply because dissenters were so many and there was no secure majority, the needs of minorities assumed prominence from the beginning. What sort of liberty must a good society give to members of minorities whose religion the majority finds incorrect, or even sinful and bad? Should there be an established state church? What should be done about people who want to disobey some law applicable to all on grounds of conscience, who don't want to fight in the army, for example, or to testify in court on a Saturday, or to swear a religious oath as a condition of public office (as was typically required in Britain—no avowed atheist was seated in Parliament until 1886). What limits could a decent society impose on religious behavior?

The philosophical architects of the Anglo-American legal tradition could easily see that when peace and safety, or the equal rights of others, are at stake, some reasonable limits might be imposed on what people do in the name of religion, and that such restrictions, supported by urgent public interests, might still be compatible with a respect for equal liberty. But they grasped after a deeper and more principled rationale for these protections and limits. Significantly, they found the basis for their principles in the idea of inherent equality and equal rights, not in the idea of (mere) toleration, which they judged too thin, and compatible with the type of social hierarchy they had come to the New World to avoid. A typical, if unusually eloquent, articulation of this point is in a letter written by President George Washington to the Hebrew Congregation at Newport in August 1790:

> The citizens of the United States of America have a right
> to applaud themselves for having given to mankind exam-
> ples of an enlarged and liberal policy: a policy worthy of
> imitation. All possess alike liberty of conscience and im-
> munities of citizenship. It is now no more that toleration
> is spoken of, as if it was by the indulgence of one class of
> people, that another enjoyed the exercise of their inherent
> natural rights. For happily, the Government of the United
> States, which gives to bigotry no sanction, to persecution
> no assistance requires only that they who live under its
> protection should demean themselves as good citizens, in
> giving it on all occasions their effectual support.[6]

Washington here associates toleration with hierarchy: a privileged group says that we will indulge you but retains the power not to do so, should it change its mind. Instead, he prefers the idea of equal inherent natural rights, rights that give people both liberty (to practice their religion) and immunity (from persecution and bigotry, but also from the state imposition of religious requirements). And he tells the Jews that the government will not ask them to worship this way or that way; it will ask them only for their support as conscientious citizens. (As we'll later see, he was so sensitive to the claims of minority religion that he did not even construe "effectual support" to require military service of people who objected to it on grounds of conscience.)

But what, more precisely, does this idea require of government? Here the philosophical tradition splits. (To return to our point about Europe, the origins of both strands of this tradition are in Europe, although they flourished primarily in the United States.) One strand, associated with the seventeenth-century English philosopher John Locke, holds that protecting equal liberty of conscience requires just two things: laws that do not penalize religious belief, and laws that are nondiscriminatory about practices, that is, the same laws must apply to all in matters touching on religious activities.[7] One example of a discriminatory law, said Locke, was the English law that made it illegal to speak Latin in a church but permitted people to speak Latin in schools.[8] Obviously the point of such a law was to persecute Roman Catholics. Another example of a persecutory law would be a law that made it illegal to immerse your body in water for the sake of baptism but allowed people to immerse themselves in water for the sake of health or recreation.[9] It's clear that the intent of such a law would be to persecute Baptists. Locke concludes, "In a word: whatsoever things are left free by law in the common occasions of life, let them remain free unto every church in divine worship. Let no man's life, or body, or house, or estate, suffer any manner of prejudice upon these accounts."[10]

If a law is not persecutory in this way, however, and if it is within the scope of the jurisdiction of civil magistrates (that is, it does not propose to regulate religious belief or the conduct of religious activities), it may stand, even though it may incidentally impose burdens on some religious activities more than on others. If people find that their conscience will not permit them to obey a certain law (regarding military service, say, or work days), they had better follow their conscience, says Locke, but they will have to pay the legal penalty.[11]

A modern Lockean case, decided by the U.S. Supreme Court in 1993, concerned an ordinance passed by the city of Hialeah, Florida, which made it illegal to kill an animal in a "public or private ritual or ceremony not for the primary purpose of food consumption."[12] The occasion for the law was widespread public concern over ritual animal slaughter performed by members of the Santeria religion. (Since Santeria worshippers were Cuban immigrants, a large element of ethnic bias animated the religious anxiety.) Hialeah claimed that its aims were to protect the public health and to prevent cruelty to animals. Justice Kennedy, writing for the Court, and Justice Scalia, in a concurring opinion, rejected those contentions in *Lukumi*. Obviously enough, the law was ill fitted to those ends, given that the same sorts of animal killing, or even more painful sorts, were permitted for food consumption. The Court found that the ordinances "are drafted with care to forbid few killings but those occasioned by religious sacrifice." So the laws are clearly a result of "government hostility," which is just as objectionable when "masked" as when overt. The law was invalidated. This case is not simply Lockean, it is already in Locke, who wrote:

> But, indeed, if any people congregated upon account of
> religion, should be desirous to sacrifice a calf, I deny that
> that ought to be prohibited by a law. Meliboeus, whose
> calf it is, may lawfully kill his calf at home, and burn any

part of it that he thinks fit: for no injury is thereby done
to any one, no prejudice to another man's goods. And for
the same reason he may kill his calf also in a religious
meeting.[13]

A similar case of particular contemporary interest concerns Muslim police officers in New Jersey. Policemen in Newark had been forbidden to wear beards, but an exemption was offered for certain skin conditions. Two Sunni Muslim officers, Mustafa and Aziz, objected, citing their religious belief that they were obliged to grow their beards and producing evidence from the Quran to support their position. In an opinion written by Supreme Court Justice Samuel Alito when he was a federal appellate judge, the officers won their case, on the grounds that a secular exemption from the policy had already been granted.[14] This case, *Fraternal Order of Police v. City of Newark*, follows the pattern of *Lukumi*, but Alito goes further toward protection of minorities than *Lukumi* was willing to go. Although there was no explicit evidence that the police policy had a discriminatory intent, that intent was inferred simply from the fact that a secular exemption had already been granted: "[W]e conclude that the Department's decision to provide medical exemptions while refusing religious exemptions is sufficiently suggestive of discriminatory intent so as to trigger heightened scrutiny."[15] Even the Lockean tradition, then, allows courts to unmask hidden prejudice.

Another tradition, associated with seventeenth-century philosopher Roger Williams, founder of the colony of Rhode Island and copious writer about religious freedom, holds that protection for conscience must be even stronger than this. This tradition reasons that laws in a democracy are always made by majorities and will naturally embody majority ideas of convenience, in matters ranging from choice of workdays to the legal status of various drugs. Even if such laws are not persecutory in intent, they may turn out to be very unfair to minorities. In cases in which such laws burden liberty of conscience—for example, by requiring people to testify in court on their holy day, or to perform military service that their religion forbids, or to abstain from the use of a drug required in their sacred ceremony—this tradition holds that a special exemption, called an "accommodation," should be given to the minority believer. Asking a person to pay a legal penalty for following conscience is like fining that person for having a minority religion—which of course is a grave offense against equal respect for conscience.

Historically, Roger Williams's accommodationist position differed from Locke's in one further way: it extended both religious liberty and (apparently) accommodation to pagans and even nonbelievers, whom Williams refers to as "anti-Christians." In his magisterial work of 1644, *The Bloudy Tenent of Persecution*, Williams writes: "[I]t is the will and command of God that (since the coming of his Sonne the Lord Jesus) a permission of the most paganish, Jewish, Turkish, or antichristian consciences and worships, bee granted to all men in all Nations and Countries." Thus he includes Jews (who were present in Rhode Island), Muslims (who probably were not), pagan Native Americans, who were not theists in any standard sense, and, finally, atheists and agnostics, which is what he almost certainly means by "antichristian." Locke concludes that nonbelievers must be excluded from the scope of religious liberty, since their oaths cannot be trusted. Williams, however, insists that in matters concerning political and social life the Native Americans are, if anything, more trustworthy than the "white man," and perfectly capable of all the moral virtues. And he extends this as a general point:

people who do not share religious first principles can share moral virtue and be trustworthy citizens. Not all accommodationists followed Williams, but his extension of the scope of religious liberty is motivated by the same consideration that motivates his preference for accommodationism: equal respect for conscience requires that liberty be as ample as is compatible with public order and safety.

A version of the accommodationist position gradually became dominant in the colonies, as settlers tried to figure out how to live together on terms of equal respect. The colonists were familiar with a variety of problems demanding accommodation: Quakers refused to take off their hats in court; Jews refused to obey a subpoena that required them to testify on a Saturday; both Quakers and Mennonites refused military service. Roger Williams argued that the accommodationist position was the only fair position: otherwise the majority was claiming for itself a liberty much more extensive than it was prepared to grant to others. To the governors of Massachusetts and Connecticut, who imposed an established orthodoxy, he writes: "Your Selvs praetend libertie of Conscience, but alas, it is but selfe (the great God Selfe) only to Your Selves." By the time of Independence, most state constitutions provided that only extremely urgent public considerations, such as peace and safety, or protection of the rights of others, could ever be reasons to limit any person's religious liberty—the position that Williams had defended in his copious writings, although it had many sources in colonial thinking.[16]

The U.S. Constitution's First Amendment protects religious liberty in a way that does not explicitly distinguish between the accommodationist position and a weaker Lockean position: "Congress shall make no law respecting an establishment of religion, or prohibiting the free exercise thereof." The phrase "infringe the equal rights of conscience" appeared in several drafts but was replaced in the final version by "prohibiting the free exercise [of religion]." This change shows quite clearly that the framers intended to protect religious acts as well as beliefs: "rights of conscience" could be taken to refer only to the latter, but "exercise" clearly also includes the former. But we should not read the final text as meaning that the framers relaxed their focus on equality. Equality, in the former phrase, referred to rights. If the final text had said "prohibiting the equal free exercise of religion" it would have been much too weak. A law could inhibit all religions equally—for example, by saying, "No religious practice is legal in the United States"—and that would still be something we'd want to prohibit. So the absence of the word "equal" does not mean that equality was not a concern: it just means that even equal burdens on religious conscience are ruled out.

The change from "conscience" to "religion" does seem to entail that religion is legally special from the viewpoint of the Free Exercise Clause. Other forms of conscientious commitment do not get protection—at least not from that clause. As we'll see, this issue leads some people to oppose a broad accommodationist reading of the Free Exercise Clause, on the grounds that it magnified an already troubling unfairness toward nonreligious conscience.

Shortly after Independence, George Washington offered an influential statement of the accommodationist position in a letter he wrote to the Quakers, apropos of their refusal to perform military service (1789):

> The liberty enjoyed by the people of these States, of worshiping Almighty God agreeably to their consciences, is not only among the choicest of their blessings, but also of their rights. . . .

Your principles and conduct are well known to me; and it is doing the people called Quakers no more than justice to say, that (except their declining to share with others the burden of the common
defence) there is no denomination among us who are more exem-
plary and useful citizens.

I assure you very explicitly, that in my opinion the conscientious
scruples of all men should be treated with great delicacy and tenderness; and it is my wish and desire, that the laws may always be as
extensively accommodated to them as a due regard to the protection and essential interests of the nation may justify and permit.[17]

Locke would have told the Quakers that they had better obey their
consciences, but that as a result they would have to pay a fine or go
to jail. Washington treats the issue very differently. He adopts the
principle that liberty should always be as extensive as is compatible with the nation's essential interests. All people's "conscientious
scruples" should be treated with "great delicacy and tenderness,"
and this he takes to entail that the law should be as "extensively accommodated" to those scruples as is compatible with those weighty
and urgent interests.

Even before Independence, policies were evolving in an accommodationist direction. (For example, it was understood that Jews,
Quakers, and Mennonites would not remove their hats in court,
and people honored this choice, while maintaining the policy of hat
removal as a general matter.) Right after the War of Independence,
Washington makes a major concession when he permits conscience
to exempt religious minorities from a general policy of military service. Early court cases followed suit. In 1793, Jonas Phillips, a Jew,
challenged the requirement to testify in court on a Saturday. In 1813,

a Catholic priest, Father Kohlmann, was permitted to refuse to answer questions posed to him when he was under oath as a witness in
a criminal case, when he argued that the information (about the
identity of the person who had returned the stolen goods to him)
came to him in the confessional.[18] The judge in the latter case, a
Protestant, understood that to be required by law to violate the confessional (or, indeed, to go to jail for contempt of court for not doing so) would place a very heavy burden on Father Kohlmann and
would effectively abolish the sacrament of the confessional:

> It cannot therefore, for a moment be believed, that the mild and
> just principles of the common Law would place the witness in such
> a dreadful predicament; in such a horrible dilemma, between per-
> jury and false swearing: If he tells the truth he violates his ecclesias-
> tical oath—If he prevaricates he violates his judicial oath—Whether
> he lies, or whether he testifies the truth he is wicked, and it is im-
> possible for him to act without acting against the laws of rectitude
> and the light of conscience.
>
> The only course is, for the court to declare that he shall not tes-
> tify or act at all.

For many years, the provisions of the Free Exercise Clause were
understood to be binding only on acts of the federal government,
and it was not until 1940 that they were explicitly "incorporated,"
held to apply, as well, to the acts of state and local governments.[19]
From this time on, minority requests for accommodation prolifer-
ated. Over a long period of time after "incorporation," the Supreme
Court applied an accommodationist standard, holding that government may not impose a "substantial burden" on a person's "free exercise of religion" without a *compelling* state interest" (of which
peace and safety are obvious examples, though not the only ones).

The landmark case articulating this principle, *Sherbert v. Verner,* concerned a woman who was a Seventh-Day Adventist and whose workplace introduced a sixth workday, Saturday. Fired because she refused to work on that day, Sherbert sought unemployment compensation from the state of South Carolina and was denied on the grounds that she had refused "suitable work."[20] The U.S. Supreme Court ruled in her favor, arguing that the denial of benefits was like fining Mrs. Sherbert for her nonstandard practices: it was thus a denial of her equal freedom to worship in her own way. There was nothing wrong in principle with choosing Sunday as the general day of rest, but there was something wrong with not accommodating Mrs. Sherbert's special religious needs.

For the accommodationist (and typically for the Lockean as well), the relevant unit theoretically is the conscience of the individual. Thus, if someone has a nonstandard interpretation of his or her religion, it cuts no ice to say that the majority of that religion's members do not agree. But in practice it helps to have a track record, and the public, shared views of a group supply that. For example, though individuals who object to military service have been given exemptions without being members of a group such as the Quakers or the Mennonites, the burden of proof is high: the individuals have had to supply an extensive account of their beliefs, something that gives unfair advantages to the articulate and educated.[21] Still, the theoretical point is important for religions such as Islam that contain many different views about what is required, and its spirit is attractive: if an individual sincerely believes that wearing a *burqa* is required or that killing in war is always morally forbidden, it does no good to point out that many co-religionists disagree.

The accommodationist standard is difficult for judges to interpret, and very few plaintiffs won cases before the U.S. Supreme

Court after *Sherbert:* the Court tended to find either that the burden
on liberty was not "substantial" or that there was in fact a "compelling state interest" on the other side. One important case where
plaintiffs did prevail was *Wisconsin v. Yoder,* in which members of the
Old Order Amish won the right to withdraw their children from the
last two years of legally mandatory public education in order to pursue community farming and other activities that were, they argued,
essential to the continuity of their religious tradition.[22] It should
also be emphasized that the accommodationist stance shaped the
cases that made it to the Supreme Court: often plaintiffs prevailed
at a lower level and the case was not appealed further. Thus it is mistaken to say (as many do) that the accommodationist position never
had much bite.[23] It remained controversial, however.

In 1990, that tradition received a major setback in *Employment Division v. Smith,* and U.S. law reverted, in part, to the Lockean position.[24] The case is pertinent to our concern with religious fear, because its topic was the use of drugs, a topic on which Americans are
very easily scared. Al Smith, a Native American, was a recovering al-
coholic who worked as an alcohol and drug counselor for a variety
of groups in his home state of Oregon, with considerable success.
He came to believe that participation in Native-American religion
was a key to his own spiritual development and to his continued re-
covery, and he became convinced that it would also be helpful to
other Native people struggling with alcoholism. His church uses
the drug peyote in its sacred ritual, which reconstructs traditional
Native-American ceremonies that have roots going back over a
thousand years. Peyote is a hallucinogen, but participants who use
it in the ceremony describe its effect as very mild, amounting to increased concentration and focus. Smith at first abstained, because

Alcoholics Anonymous (AA) philosophy forbids the use of any mind-altering drug. Eventually, however, he tried it on several occasions beginning in the 1970s and found that it did not lead him back to alcohol; in fact, he reported that he felt he had become a wiser and better person for having used it.

In 1982, he got a new job as a counselor in a program in Douglas County; he was praised as an outstanding counselor. Although he continued to use peyote from time to time in the ritual, he never talked about it at work—until a new employee joined Smith in the ceremony and talked enthusiastically about his experience. Both men were fired. The state of Oregon denied Smith unemployment compensation on the ground that he had committed "a willful violation of the standards of behavior that an employer has the right to expect of an employee." Peyote was then illegal under Oregon state law. Smith and the other employee went to court to challenge the law.

Ultimately, they lost in the U.S. Supreme Court. Although a concurring opinion written by Justice O'Connor uses the *Sherbert* standard and concludes that the state has met the burden of showing a "compelling state interest," the majority opinion, written by Justice Scalia, announces that the standard to be applied henceforth (and also in the past, in a highly controversial reading of the precedents) is the Lockean standard. The question to be asked is whether the law is "a neutral law of general applicability." If it is, there is no constitutional right to an exemption. Government may not ban the performance of a physical act that is generally legal when that act is performed for a religious reason (and here Scalia gives some of Locke's actual examples and others in the same vein). But the fact that some people's reason for wishing to disobey a generally applicable law is religious does not excuse them from compliance. Scalia concludes that a system of judicially administered exemptions would be tantamount to "courting anarchy."

Smith raises two independent questions: What is the best legal standard? And who ought to administer it? It's important to see that Scalia's opinion does not directly address the first question, in the sense that the justice is prepared to countenance accommodations passed by legislative majorities. Indeed, he is also prepared to mandate accommodations judicially when the state already has a program of individualized exemptions in place, as with the unemployment cases: in such cases, not to grant the exemption on religious grounds looks persecutory and becomes a Lockean type of violation. Scalia focuses on the second question, and his main complaint about accommodationism is that judges are not competent to administer an open-ended system of individualized exemptions to generally applicable laws: he sees such a system as "courting anarchy" by undermining the rule of law.

On the other hand, he indirectly addresses the first question, by denying that plaintiffs have a constitutional *right* to accommodations: their plea for accommodation must now depend on the whim of legislative majorities. Indeed, he emphasizes this point: leaving the protection of minority religious practices to the political process will "place at a relative disadvantage those religious practices that are not widely engaged in; but that unavoidable consequence of democratic government must be preferred to a system in which each conscience is a law unto itself or in which judges weigh the social importance of all laws against the centrality of all religious beliefs." Thus Scalia concludes that the best *legal* standard is the Lockean one, which is compatible with order and the rule of law in a way in which the accommodationist standard ("each conscience is a law unto itself") is not. Where legislative majorities vote an accommodation, then accommodation becomes law, and the orderly rule of law is not threatened.

In dissent, Justices Blackmun, Brennan, and Marshall reassert the *Sherbert* accommodationist standard and emphatically deny that minority liberty need always be at risk in majoritarian democracy: "I do not believe the Founders thought their dearly bought freedom from religious persecution a 'luxury,' but an essential element of liberty—and they could not have thought religious intolerance 'unavoidable,' for they drafted the Religion Clauses precisely in order to avoid that intolerance."[25] Here we see the real difference between the accommodationist and the Lockean: the former asserts as a basic right what the latter understands as a privilege that must be negotiated through the political process.

Smith caused considerable public outrage.[26] Religious groups of many kinds, liberal and conservative, Christian, Jewish, and secular, protested the change of direction it signaled. In 1993, by overwhelming majorities in both House and Senate, Congress passed the Religious Freedom Restoration Act, or RFRA, which restored the protective *Sherbert* standard through legislation. President Clinton signed the bill into law. Because the statute was a deliberate end-run around *Smith*, it is not surprising that the Court was not amused. In 1997, in *City of Boerne v. Flores*, the Court declared RFRA unconstitutional as applied to the states, holding that it exceeded the power of Congress.[27] RFRA remains constitutional, however, as applied to acts of the federal government. And a later statute, the Religious Land Use and Institutionalized Persons Act of 2000 (RLUIPA) introduced the more protective standard for issues involving not only federal land use regulations but also inmates in prisons or mental institutions. Meanwhile, many states adopted RFRA-like provisions in their state constitutions, or interpreted their constitutions to require an RFRA-like standard.[28]

Four Supreme Court cases mark out the shape of the recent debate. The first two that are significant are *Lukumi* and *Fraternal Order of Police,* which, as we have seen, follow a Lockean line, post-*Smith* (and indeed articulate Justice Scalia's understanding of the Lockean framework), but still interpret neutrality generously, to require an absence of discrimination between religious and secular practices. Next is a prison case under RLUIPA (and upholding its constitutionality): *Cutter v. Wilkinson,* a unanimous decision protecting the rights of minority-religion prisoners to food and religious equipment (for example, Hanukkah candles) that were necessary to practice their religion and that were similar to those already granted Christian prisoners (thus raising no additional issue of peace or safety).[29] RLUIPA had been challenged on Establishment Clause grounds as giving special favor to religion, but the Court gave a fine accommodationist answer: it is only because government action has created conditions that disfavor minority prisoners and favor those of the majority that corrective action, restoring equality, needs to be taken.

Finally, there is *Gonzales v. O Centro Espirita Beneficente Uniao Do Vegetal,* the 2006 case of a small Brazilian sect that uses a hallucinogen named *hoasca* in its sacred ritual. By this time, in response to the political influence of Native-American groups, the sacramental use of peyote had already been legalized by Congress, amending the Controlled Substances Act. The Brazilian sect, however, had only about 130 members and no political clout, so its members turned to the courts, and to RFRA, still in force as applied to acts of the federal government. In a unanimous decision, the Supreme Court granted the request of the group for an exemption parallel to that which Congress had granted the Native Americans. Writing for the Court, Chief Justice Roberts rejected the government's claim that there is a compelling state interest that justifies the denial of an accommodation. The exemption, he wrote, is parallel to that already granted to the larger group, and no evidence shows health dangers from the merely sacramental use of the drug. As for the question whether courts are competent to authorize accommodations:

> RFRA . . . plainly contemplates that *courts* would recognize exceptions—that is how the law works [citing the provisions of the law]. . . . Congress' role in the peyote exemption—and the Executive's—confirms that the findings in the Controlled Substances Act do not preclude exceptions altogether. RFRA makes clear that it is the obligation of the courts to consider whether exceptions are required.

This is classic accommodationist reasoning. No evidence of hostile intent was offered, and none would have been plausible. The Brazilian sect was not unpopular; it was simply unknown. The law, as amended for Native Americans and not for the Brazilians, was obtuse, not really persecutory. But it showed the common problem: in a democracy, larger groups get better treatment. Chief Justice Roberts insists that one role for courts is to right this balance, restoring equality.

How should we assess these two traditions, in the light of our basic principles of equal respect for conscience and the vulnerability of conscience? The first thing we ought to notice is that the two are not exactly opponents: they differ in degree rather than in ultimate values, and they lie on a continuum. Both traditions are concerned with ample and equal liberty. The Lockean's concern for equality manifests itself in its unwillingness to permit persecutory laws, or even laws that, like the police regulation that barred Muslim beards, betray a persecutory intent that is probably not conscious, through their obtuse willingness to countenance secular but not religious exemptions. Once we reach the point of seeing that persecution may be a result of obtuseness rather than malice, we are already on the terrain of the accommodationist. Thus the police policy that denied an accommodation for the Muslim officers was not drafted with the concerns of Muslims in mind, and the exemption for the skin condition was not implicitly a denial of a religious exemption, which, very likely, nobody had thought about. So the policy is much less persecutory than the Hialeah ordinance on ritual slaughter. From here it is a short step to the drug laws that exempt a drug (alcohol) used by the majority (and ritual use of which remained legal even during Prohibition), and fail to exempt a drug (peyote) used by the minority. Probably the Oregon drug laws were not drafted with religious concerns in view, and no malice can be inferred from their failure to exempt the sacramental use of peyote. (Indeed, recall that the U.S. Congress promptly legalized this sacramental use, after *Smith,* through amendment to the Controlled Substances Act.) Nor are laws concerning workdays made in order to penalize minorities; they are made because they are convenient. But there is obtuseness in the majority's way of pursuing convenience, and this obtuseness is harsh to central concerns of minorities. That was true of the Muslim police officers, and it is true of Mrs. Sherbert and Al Smith. The difference, then, between the class of cases where Justice Scalia and his fellow Lockeans are prepared to strike down a law or policy as non-neutral and the class of cases deemed accommodations is not sharp or principled; the cases lie on a continuum. When we add to this the fact that even Justice Scalia is prepared to countenance judicial exemptions where a system of individualized exemptions is in place (as in *Sherbert*), and that even he was willing to join a unanimous Court in *Gonzales v. O Centro Espirita*—thus restoring fairness between large and small minorities by granting the small minority a judicial exemption to match the legislative exemption the larger minority had already won—the two traditions seem to differ more in the number of such exemptions they countenance than in their type or basis. When we contrast the United States with Europe, it is revealing to see that it is in this subtle point of difference that the U.S. controversy resides, whereas European approaches often neglect even the demands of the weaker Lockean position. In that sense it might seem excessive to delve into the nuances of this debate—and yet it is revealing, for it shows how the U.S. argument has unfolded and what considerations it has taken to be essential.

Can we, nonetheless, argue that one of these traditions is more adequate to capture the idea of equal respect than the other? I believe that the accommodationist principle is superior to Locke's principle, because it reaches subtle forms of discrimination that are ubiquitous in majoritarian democratic life. All societies make choices regarding holidays, workdays, drug and alcohol restrictions, and a host of other matters touching on people's religious observances. The choices of a majority are usually supported by some type of reasoning; thus they will pass a weaker "rational basis" test, although they might not pass a "compelling state interest" test. They may, however, be extremely harsh to minorities, rendering their liberty unequal. To grant them accommodations on grounds of conscience, in areas ranging from employment to military conscription to sacramental alcohol or drug use, is to restore a standard of equal liberty.

Accommodation has its problems, however. One, emphasized by Justice Scalia, is that a system based on individualized exemptions is difficult for judges to administer. Creating exemptions to general laws on a case-by-case basis struck Scalia as too chaotic, and beyond the competence of the judiciary. Thus, although he thought that accommodations created by legislation would be permissible—such as the change in our Controlled Substances Act that legalized the sacramental use of peyote—he was opposed to granting such exemptions judicially, except where (as in *Sherbert*) a system of individualized exemptions was already in operation. To Scalia's worry about "anarchy" we can add a concern about fairness: under a system of judicial accommodations, minorities will prevail to the extent that they are both willing and able to use the legal system to their advantage. The ACLU's willingness to offer legal aid to many religious minority plaintiffs considerably reduces this concern but does not completely eliminate it. And judges may by temperament or education be more empathetic toward majority than toward minority viewpoints. The difficulty the Court has had understanding the claims of Native-American religion is a clear example of this problem.

Another problem faced by the accommodationist position is that it has typically favored religion and disfavored other reasons people may have for seeking an exemption to general laws—family reasons, for example, or reasons having to do with personal commitments to art, or even to a secular ethical creed. To some extent, it is possible to deal with these other commitments in other areas of law—through a capacious free speech principle, for example, and through laws protecting family leave. But not all problems can be handled this way. People may have bona fide ethical reasons for refusing military service that do not fit the definition of religion; they may seek to use illegal drugs for reasons of personal enlightenment. Isn't it unfair to them, and a burden on nonreligious ethical views of life, to treat their request for accommodation asymmetrically?

Some scholars think this a sufficient reason to deny accommodations for all, and thus revert to the Lockean position: if the system of accommodations cannot be made fair for all, it should not exist.[30] They thus return to a position that is both less ample and less equal in regard to religious liberty, but on grounds that are not without their merit. Other scholars seek a broader definition of "conscience" that would include many nonreligious cases of conscience.[31] The Court has moved in this direction in two draft cases during the Vietnam War, upholding conscientious objections for two plaintiffs who were not conventionally religious.[32] Still others prefer a hybrid standard: a broad definition of conscience for military conscription, but a more traditional limit to the religious for drug laws.[33] One factor influencing this group of scholars is that being asked to kill, if one's religion is pacifist, is a particularly severe and terrible burden; to be denied a chance to use drugs seems less grave, a deprivation of enlightenment but not a requirement to do wrong. Another factor in favor of a mixed policy is administrability. So long as conscientious objectors are not permitted to object to this or that war, but must be consistently pacificist, a system of individualized exemptions seems workable. A similar system for drug laws would indeed be "courting anarchy," and could not coexist with meaningful enforcement. If one thinks drug laws a good idea in the first place, one will not be inclined to favor drug accommodations, apart from a narrow set of sacramental cases with a clear religious track record.

In short, there are strong arguments on both sides: the Roger Williams position has not yet shown that it can defeat the Lockean position. The current American state of affairs, in which RFRA prevails for federal issues and in some states, while the Lockean position prevails in other states, though with room left for legislative accommodations, reflects the complexity of the issues and the tough choices the two positions pose. It also reflects, however, the narrow gap that currently separates the two positions, in their operational form, as well as in the extent to which both positions respond to people's most serious concerns about equal respect.

As we shall see, we do not need to resolve this issue definitively, because the recent European cases all involve discriminatory laws that fail to pass even the weaker Lockean test—although in the special case of French secularism this will take some time to show.

Contemporary Issues: Impartiality, State Interests

In the contemporary world we need policies that follow the insights embedded in these principles, showing equal respect for all citizens by providing both ample and equal liberty, indeed the greatest liberty that is compatible with equal liberty for all and the preservation of vital public interests (such as peace and safety). We have serious questions about whether religion should be singled out for special protection, as it is in the accommodationist tradition, and concern for even-handedness to atheists and secular people is one very strong reason for preferring the Lockean policy. U.S. law at least preserves impartiality under the Establishment Clause, which has been interpreted to reject not only state favor shown to one religion over other religions but also favor shown to religion over nonreligion, or to nonreligion over religion. Thus, a policy at the University of Virginia that used student fees to subsidize a wide variety of student activities and clubs, including political, environmental, and other organizations, but denied funding to religious groups, was ruled unconstitutional.[34] If we prefer an accommodationist account of the Free Exercise Clause, we had better remember to turn to the

Establishment Clause for balance in this way, ensuring that religion and nonreligion are symmetrically treated much of the time, at any rate.

Another problem that remains for accommodationists is to give a coherent account of the elusive notion of "compelling state interest." Peace and safety are two canonical interests recognized since before Independence, but even these need more precise delineation: how urgent must the threat to peace and safety be, and what sort of safety is pertinent? People easily feel threatened by others whom they don't know. That, after all, is a core problem of social and political life. So what evidence of danger needs to be presented before we determine that a danger is dangerous enough to justify an abridgment of liberty? Knowing our fallibility, we should set the bar quite high.

What other public interests count as compelling interests? U.S. jurisprudence under the Free Exercise Clause has been *ad hoc* about this, simply reacting to arguments that are put forward. This may be a suitable way for a judicial system to operate, but for us, trying to grasp some basic principles to guide our thinking, it would be helpful to have something a bit more articulated. I have once suggested that the protection of a group of basic human entitlements that I call the "Central Human Capabilities" would always supply government with a compelling interest that could serve to limit actions taken in the name of religion: life, health, bodily integrity, and so forth.[35] That list helps us understand, for example, why we might favor laws that limit parents' rights to withhold lifesaving health treatments from their children on religious grounds. (If adults are duly informed and able to avail themselves of treatments and choose to forgo them, then we should conclude that they have the capability but have chosen not to exercise it.) This whole topic needs further investigation and articulation. We'll have more to say about it in Chapter 4.

Establishments and Equality

What about religious establishment? This is an enormous topic that we cannot treat fully here. But we can say at least this: that religious establishments raise equality issues relevant to our basic underlying principles. When a nation has an established church, it may easily create a regime of unequal liberty. Even if it does not aggressively limit liberty for minorities, it may well make minorities jump through hoops that the majority does not have to jump through. In Finland, for example, one of the world's most benign and tolerant institutions, the established Lutheran Church, owns all the cemeteries. If a Jew wants to bury a loved one, the Jew has to apply to the Lutheran Church for permission to use an area within a Lutheran cemetery. That's quintessential modern Establishmentarianism: power and tolerance. The others get their rights at the sufferance of the majority. Even if the majority is nice and always says yes, there is something unequal about the situation.

Even the bare statement that a given religion is the established one, without any tangible consequences, appears to threaten equality, by creating an in-group and an out-group. Opposing a bill in 1785 that would have taxed all citizens of Virginia for the support of the Anglican Church, James Madison, primary architect (later) of our Bill of Rights, said this:

> If "all men are by nature equally free and independent,"
> all men are to be considered as entering into Society on
> equal conditions; as relinquishing no more, and therefore

retaining no less, one than another, of their natural rights. Above all are they to be considered as retaining an *"equal* title to the free exercise of Religion according to the dictates of conscience."

The Virginia Assessment Bill was actually very benign. People who were not Anglicans could specify that their tax be assigned to their own church; Quakers and Mennonites didn't have to pay at all; people who did not like any particular church could ask that their portion be dedicated to a fund for "teachers of religion." Still, Madison thought that the bare announcement that the Anglican Church was the default option and the official state church was a threat to equality. It put minorities on notice that their equal rights were enjoyed at the sufferance of the majority, thus making those rights not fully equal. So establishment is in its way a denial of *equal* liberty.

We can also look at the relationship between the two ideas from the other side: the denial of an accommodation for the free exercise of one's own religion is a type of de facto establishment. It means that the majority's religion has been written into law and minorities have been denied the same opportunity to legalize their own practices.

Belonging to a Nation: Citizens and Immigrants

The ethical principles we've investigated leave us with some unanswered questions, since the choice between the two traditions is a difficult one. Nonetheless, the two traditions agree more than they differ. Both accept the underlying ideas of equal respect and human vulnerability, and both are opposed not only to outright persecution but also to indirect persecution through refusal to grant religious minorities what is granted to the majority. Whichever tradition we ultimately favor, both give law a shape that is friendly to internal dissidents and new immigrants. As we'll see, many policies that are currently favored in Europe would not survive even Lockean scrutiny—and this is in a sense no surprise, for both traditions, in the form in which we've examined them here, were nourished by the experience of a new country made up of religious dissenters of many types, and enriched by new immigrants throughout its history. Americans settled in a dangerous land, and they soon saw that prosperity, and perhaps even survival, required cooperating with people who differed by religion and also, often, by dress and public behavior. Everyone was, in effect, a minority. (Although a vast majority were Christian, there were many types of Christians, and a lot of "seekers," as Roger Williams described his own discontent with established religion. At the time of Independence, only 17 percent of the colonists were members of any established church.) This led to the cultivation of a spirit of openness and even humility that is actually valuable everywhere, whether there is a secure majority or not.

Another significant difference between the United States and Europe, where religious equality is concerned, is a fact we've already observed: European nations tend to conceive of nationhood and national belonging in ethno-religious and cultural-linguistic terms. Thus new immigrant groups, and religious minorities, have difficulty being seen as full and equal members of the nation. All these nations are the heirs of romanticism, with its ideas of blood, soil, and natural belonging. All have or had some type of religious establishment. (One may include the nonstandard case of French laïcité, which is the establishment of nonreligion.) Part of the difficulty all these nations had in admitting Jews to full civil rights was their view that citizenship was grounded in religious and ethnic belonging—so Jews could not fit, unless they converted and assimilated. Even if by now European nations have granted that immigrants and religious minorities can become full citizens, their background view of citizenship, combined with the public fact of religious establishment, makes it difficult for them to take this idea to heart. Certainly these nations have the greatest difficulty seeing why the accommodationist position makes sense, even if they do understand the Lockean strategy. Their difficulty seeing the case for accommodation is connected to their difficulty seeing why establishments threaten equal dignity.

As we've seen, there is another option, realized in a wide range of nations around the world: to define national belonging in terms of political ideals, in which immigrants can fully share, despite not sharing the ethnicity, religion, or customs of the majority. Such nations have a far easier time seeing how people who adopt minority ways of dressing, speaking, and worshipping can nonetheless be fully equal citizens. And they are likely to ponder far more quickly the next step: what is it to create fully *equal* rights of conscience, when majorities arrange things in their own interest? The insights of the accommodationist tradition are intuitive, a natural response to the perceived imbalance between majorities and minorities. If we have decided to reject religious establishments on equality grounds, we should also look skeptically on situations in which majorities make laws affecting religious observance in their own interest, in ways that render minority liberty unequal.

Differences of tradition explain why nations find the solutions they do, but they don't justify them. Nations always have options: they can accentuate some features of citizenship and deemphasize others. A nation is a narrative, a story of what has brought people together and what keeps them together, a story of shared sufferings, joys, and hopes. That story is always dynamic and can be retold in ways that foster inclusion—or, if fear gets the upper hand, exclusion. If modern nations find the principles embodied in these two traditions of religious liberty appealing, they can take action to make it more likely that their citizens will embrace them.

The two traditions we have examined are not automatically self-implementing. We need to be able to think well about what a burden on another person's religious free exercise is, and this means learning to look at the world from the perspective of that religion, rather than simply seeing its demands as bad or as an affront to majority values. We also need to think well about how strong a variety of public interests in homogeneity are, for we often err by thinking homogeneity more important than it is, or by seeing dangers to peace and health in a minority practice when we don't notice them in the practices of the majority. (The differential treatment of alcohol and other drugs is but one example of this majority-biased form of risk-assessment.) We need to realize that we might be wrong about both burdens and interests, and that the reason we might be wrong has to do with an underlying failure to welcome and respect people who are different.

Whichever intellectual position we favor, then, we need to cultivate a spirit of curiosity, openness, and sympathy, and a generosity to our neighbors that extends beyond our own self-concern. (Roger Williams addresses his writings to "the Merciful and Compassionate Reader," and Locke refers to a spirit of "charity, bounty, and liberality.") In the world imagined by both Williams and Locke, the majority does not say, "I'm the norm, now you fit in." It says, "I respect you as an equal, and I know that my own religious pursuits are not the only ones around. Even if I am more numerous and hence more powerful, I will try to make the world comfortable for you." It is the spirit of a gracious hostess. A good hostess needs a good imagination.

4

THE MOTE IN MY BROTHER'S EYE: IMPARTIALITY AND THE EXAMINED LIFE

In Plato's dialogue *Euthyphro*, Socrates meets Euthyphro in front of the courthouse, where he himself has been replying to the charge that he is a corrupter of the young. What is Euthyphro's business with the court? Euthyphro explains that he is filing a prosecution against his own father, for the murder of a migrant worker who served on their estate. (Ancient Athens had no public prosecutor. All charges were brought by private individuals, and someone with no relatives around would normally go unavenged.) Aren't you afraid that it is an offense against the gods to prosecute your own father? asks Socrates. But Euthyphro proclaims that he has exact knowledge of what is pious and what is impious. Asked by Socrates to deliver that valuable knowledge, he puts himself first: "Piety is the sort of thing I am doing now," he jauntily replies. As he is questioned more and more closely by Socrates, we see that Euthyphro has actually thought very little about the concept with which he seeks to defend his actions. He quickly gets ensnared in a net of contradictions, and the reader soon feels that the basis of his action is shaky indeed.

Laches and Nicias are two of the most renowned generals in the

Athenian army. Both are celebrated for their skill and courage in battle. But when in *Laches* Socrates questions them about what courage is, they fare no better than Euthyphro. They have not thought things through, and they cannot even distinguish consistently between true courage and foolhardy rashness. They end up admitting that true courage requires knowledge of what is worth fighting for and what is not—but that element of knowledge seems signally lacking in their own grasp of their own profession. Does this matter? Well, the reader is well aware that some years after the dramatic date of their conversation with Socrates, Athens was involved in one of its greatest military disasters, the Sicilian expedition, a devastating part of the Peloponnesian War, in which the ineffectual leadership of Nicias proved a key element of the collapse.

People often make decisions heedlessly, without sufficient deliberation and self-examination. They don't sort things out in a coherent and comprehensive way, asking what they really want to pursue and stand for. As a result, their decisions are often distorted by limited experience, by tradition and peer pressure, by fear—and, as Euthyphro's case shows, by self-interest and self-protective bias. Euthyphro may have a good case in favor of prosecuting his father—after all, the murdered man has no kin to bring a charge on his behalf—but there is something alarming about the zealous arrogance with which Euthyphro rushes ahead, undeterred by the prospect that he may get his own father killed. He even defines piety as just the sort of thing he is doing, a move that precludes meaningful self-examination.

Inconsistency is a problem for decision-making even when it is just a matter of slack and incomplete thought. Socrates believed that a democracy could not possibly do its business responsibly without committing itself to "the examined life"—to deliberation

THE NEW RELIGIOUS INTOLERANCE

that involves a sincere attempt to come to a consistent view of the most important policy questions. (His complaint becomes more vivid if we bear in mind that all offices in the Athenian government were filled by lottery, with the exception of the office of general—and the *Laches* shows that even the few people selected for that expert task don't give a good account of their goals and values.) But, as the *Euthyphro* shows, inconsistency often goes hand in hand with something worse than sloppiness—with arrogance and a narcissistic desire to shield the self from criticism and the fair demands of others. People have a way of making special cases of themselves, exempting themselves from criticisms that they all too readily bring up when they look at what other people are doing. The version of Socratism that animates Christian ethics focuses on this sort of selfish inconsistency: "And why do you take note of the mote that is in your brother's eye, but pay no attention to the large plank that is in your own eye? Or how will you say to your brother, 'Let me take that mote out of your eye'—while, behold, a plank is in your own eye?" (Matthew 7.3–4).[1]

Criticizing others for something you are also guilty of—what a ubiquitous human failing. The Gospel is saying that people have a strong tendency to self-blindness and to insulating their own faults from critique. Why? Selfishness? Arrogance? Fear? Maybe all of these? At any rate, the inconsistency looks much worse than the mere sloppiness of Laches and Nicias, because it involves unfairness, pointing the finger at someone else and refusing to be similarly vulnerable.

Immanuel Kant made this problem a keystone of his ethical thought. In Kant's view—which is influenced both by Socrates and by Christian ethics—we need philosophical self-examination not because we are stupid or lacking in basically good ethical ideas but because each of us has a selfish propensity to "quibbling," to exempting ourselves from principles we apply to others. Therefore, a good way of testing ourselves is to ask whether the basis of our action could be recommended as a law for everyone.

When we test our principles in this way, we find a variety of contradictions. The person who decides to break a promise has not thought about what the world would be like if everyone broke promises. Quickly, it would become a world in which the institution of promise-making would no longer exist. In such a world, the very advantage this person hopes to gain by defecting would no longer be available—so his intention is self-subverting. The person who decides not to give anything to relieve the misery of others fails, in a similar fashion, to consider what the world would be like if the whole idea of compassionate philanthropy ceased to guide people's conduct. This case is not quite like the case of promise-breaking, since that world certainly could exist and the person living in it could still do what he proposes to do, denying aid to others. But the person would almost certainly dislike that world, since in it she could not expect any aid if she needed it.

Both cases involve, then, a kind of "free rider" behavior in which people are taking advantage of a system that they don't themselves support. This kind of inconsistency is a little different from the kind described in the Gospel, but it has a similar flavor: a selfish and self-focused person is exempting herself from rules that apply to others, indeed rules that she herself applies to others. The root of this behavior, moreover, looks similar: a failure to treat others as full equals, a desire to use them for one's own ends. Interpreters of Kant have many questions about how his "Formula of Universal Law" is connected to his "Formula of Humanity," which asks each of us to treat humanity, both in ourselves and in others, as an end

and never as a mere means. But at a general intuitive level the connection is obvious. The problem with the person whose principle
can't pass the test of universal law is that she is using others for her
own ends, rather than treating them as ends in themselves, in other
words, as people of equal dignity whose goals and purposes are to
be respected as of equal importance with her own. She is manipulat-
ing them. And making instrumental use of other people is also what
the Gospel objects to: proclaiming the vices of another (enforcing
general rules of virtue and vice) while slipping through the net oneself, simply not applying those rules to oneself.

Inconsistency and Self-Insulation in
Talk about Religious Liberty

Socrates identified a problem that is ubiquitous in human affairs:
unexamined, inconsistent thought. Kant and the Gospel focus on a
narrower part of this general problem, one that we can see in some
of Socrates' conversations (with Euthyphro in particular), but one
that he does not make theoretically central. Kantian-Christian inconsistency is no mere intellectual failing: it is a deep ethical failing,
indeed, we might see it as the deepest and most basic ethical failing
of all, the failure to acknowledge the equal reality of others.

This failing crops up in many areas of life, but it certainly occurs
all too often when religion is the issue. Religion is central to people's sense of themselves. So the tendency of the Gospels—to nar-
rate people's propensity to accuse other people of failings of which
they or their own group are guilty—is particularly likely to turn up
in that area. That was one of the points Jesus was making, clearly:
the Pharisees are often charged with hypocrisy of this sort. And the
charge of self-serving hypocrisy resonates throughout the Jewish

tradition out of which Jesus emerged. No complaint is more common in the Old Testament than the complaint that people are exempting themselves from requirements they impose upon others. And the related Kantian tendency to make up rules and principles that could not possibly stand the test of reflective consistency, rules that are covert devices for using other people as mere means, is so common in religious matters that it need hardly be illustrated. Indeed, this theme, as we've seen, was prominent in early writers about liberty of conscience. "Your Selvs praetend libertie of Conscience," wrote Roger Williams to the governors of Massachusetts and Connecticut, "But alas, it is but selfe (the great God Selfe) only to Your Selves."

Consider an example that John Locke discussed: a rule that makes it illegal to immerse one's entire body in water for the sake of baptism but allows people to go on immersing themselves in water for the sake of health or recreation. And consider the similar example discussed in *Lukumi*: a law that makes it illegal to slaughter animals in a ritual sacrifice but allows the continued slaughter of animals in the food industry. Both of these rules clearly violate the morality of the Gospels, for they call something bad when it's done as other people do it, while carefully preserving our space to go on doing the same thing ourselves. (Of course it might have been possible to show that there is a relevant difference between what the majority is doing and what the minority wants to do, but both Locke and the Supreme Court find no escape route for the hypocritical majority.) Both rules offend, as well, against Kant's idea of universal law. Their proponents adopt a maxim—"Stop people from immersing themselves in water!" or "Stop people from killing animals!"—that the majority is unwilling to apply to itself. Kant's point is that these are not just bad arguments; they are forms of deeply objectionable selfishness. At their heart they say, "I am special, I am above others, and I can use them as I like."

People made such self-serving arguments in the days of Locke; they make them today, as the Scalia case showed. When fear is running high, such arguments are all the more likely to be made and accepted: thus Locke's majority felt real fear of the antinomian Baptists, and the citizens of Hialeah, in the Scalia case, found Santeria religion scary and foreign. Now we'll see that arguments with this problem turn up all over the place in current debates about Islam (and, more generally, new religious minorities).

The *burqa* has currently been banned in three European countries: France, Belgium, and Italy. Other nations such as Spain, Holland, and Britain show significant support for a ban. Although this is not (yet) a focus of debate in the United States, it raises issues that can easily be transferred to U.S. cases, such as laws banning "Sharia law," or proposals to forbid mosque construction. Let's therefore focus on the *burqa*, since arguments made there can be adapted to other cases.

The *burqa* is rarely worn: a very small proportion even of observant Muslim women wear it, and many scholars of Islam, as well as religious leaders, hold that it is not religiously required; indeed, many think that even the headscarf is not required. But for those who wear it, it is usually understood as religiously required, and this is the issue that ought to concern us. Religions typically have many subdivisions, and liberty of conscience protects the conscience of the individual, not that of the majority of the larger group to which that individual belongs. Thus it would be inappropriate to tell an Orthodox Jew that it's fine to go to work on Saturday because a large proportion of American Jews are willing to do so. That is not the point: the person's own interpretation of the religion is what counts for conscience, although, as we saw in Chapter 3, (sub)group values are often a helpful source of information for courts seeking to assess the sincerity of a person's conscientious claim.

Five arguments for banning the *burqa* are particularly common. We'll now see that all five are made inconsistently, in ways that tacitly favor majority practices and burden minority practices. They are thus not compatible with a principle of equal liberty. Hence, in turn, they are not compatible with the idea of equal respect for conscience from which that principle springs. Indeed, all are cases of seeing the mote in your brother's eye while failing to appreciate the large plank that is in your own eye: for all target situations alleged to be present in Muslim communities while failing to note their ubiquity in the majority culture. Familiar practices are insulated from critical scrutiny. Only the unfamiliar receives suspicion.

Banning the *Burqa:* Security

First is an argument about security: it holds that security requires people to show their face when appearing in public places. This argument is commonly put forward in support of a *burqa* ban. In the Netherlands, for example, Immigration Minister Rita Verdonk said that a proposed ban was supported by "reasons of public order, security and protection of citizens."[2] A second, closely related, argument says that the kind of transparency and reciprocity proper to relations between citizens are impeded when part of the face is covered. Former British Foreign Secretary Jack Straw, for example, opined in 2006 that the *burqa* threatens social harmony. "Communities," he told the BBC, "are bound together partly by informal chance relations between strangers, people being able to acknowledge each other in the street or being able to pass the time of day."[3]

He suggested that these interactions are not possible if the face is covered. (More recently, however, Straw, as justice secretary in the former Labour government, strongly opposed a *burqa* ban, saying that it is not a fit area for the criminal law, although he continued to request that women having appointments in his office remove their facial veils before visiting him.)[4]

The problem with the security and transparency arguments is that they are applied inconsistently. It gets very cold in Chicago—as, indeed, in many parts of Europe. Along the streets we walk, hats pulled down over ears and brows, scarves wound tightly around noses and mouths, no problem of either transparency or security is thought to exist, nor are we forbidden to enter public buildings such as department stores, airports, and banks so insulated. When we are out in the hot sun, many of us also cover up, with much the same effect. My season tickets to the White Sox face right into the sun until around 5 P.M. At a day game in July or August, I wear long sleeves (light breathable fabric), long pants (ditto), a baseball cap (I would wear a bigger floppy hat if it didn't block people's view), and the largest sunglasses I have—and I sometimes feel the need to wrap a scarf over my nose and mouth, or at least to keep my hands there.

Moreover, many beloved and trusted professionals cover their faces all year round: surgeons, dentists, (American) football players, skiers, and skaters. Winter athletes typically wear a full face covering with slits only for the eyes, similar to a *niqab*. Some professionals are even more covered than the typical *burqa* wearer. My endodontist (the dental specialist who performs that dreaded dental procedure known as a root canal), needing an extremely accurate view of a very small space, wears not only the face mask that all dentists wear but, in addition, a form of headgear that covers the eyes totally with a type of eyeglass that magnifies from his point of view, but that also makes it impossible for me to see his eyes at all. I'm sure endodontists in Europe are similarly equipped, and I'm sure that nobody wants them to remove that remarkable eyeglass. It's bad enough having a root canal, without having one administered by someone who can't properly see your tooth. If I could see that dentist's eyes, I would not trust him near my mouth.

In general, then, what inspires fear and mistrust in Europe and, to some extent, in the United States is not covering per se, but Muslim covering.

But, it will be said, we are living in an era of terrorism, and in the war against terror it is legitimate to suspect women wearing the *burqa*. This is a widespread view in the United States, and probably in Europe as well. All I can say is that if I were a terrorist in the United States or Europe, and if I were not stupid, the last thing I would wear would be a *burqa*, since that way of dressing attracts suspicious attention. Criminals usually want to avoid attracting suspicious attention; if they are at all intelligent, they succeed. In the Middle East, it might possibly be a clever strategy for a terrorist to don a *burqa*. It is, however, a dumb strategy in the United States or Europe. If I were a terrorist, I think I'd dress like Martha Nussbaum in the winter: floor-length Eddie Bauer down coat, hat down over the eyebrows, extra hood for insulation, large sunglasses, and a bulky Indian shawl around nose and mouth. Nonetheless, I have never been asked to remove these clothes, in a department store, a public building, or even a bank. In the summer, again if I were an intelligent sort of terrorist, I would wear a big floppy hat and a long loose caftan, and I think I'd carry a capacious Louis Vuitton bag, the sort that signals conspicuous consumption. That is what a smart terrorist would do, and the smart ones are the ones to worry about. Indeed, unpleasant though it is that elderly people in wheelchairs are sometimes subjected to intrusive searches, experts defend the practice by appeal to the likely strategies of clever terrorists.

So what to do about the threat that all bulky and nonrevealing clothing creates? Airline security does a lot, with metal detectors, body imaging, pat downs, and so on. U.S. Cellular Field in Chicago, where my beloved White Sox play, searches all bags (though more to check for beer than for explosives, thus protecting the interests of in-stadium vendors). Private stores or other organizations that feel that bulky clothing is a threat (whether of shoplifting or terrorism or both) could institute a nondiscriminatory rule banning, for example, floor-length coats; they could even have a body scanner at the door. But they don't, presumably preferring customer friendliness to the extra margin of safety. (Some public schools do have metal detectors and searches of various sorts, and they seem to think that this enhances safety—though the threat that concerns them is of guns and knives, not explosives.) What I want to establish, however, is the invidious discrimination inherent in the belief that the *burqa* poses a unique security risk. Reasonable security policies, applied to similar cases similarly, are perfectly fine.

A reasonable demand would be that a Muslim woman have a full face photo on her driver's license or passport. With suitable protections for modesty during the photographic session, such a photo could be required, and I don't think that this requirement would be incompatible with equal liberty. Moreover, I've been informed by my correspondents that most contemporary Islamic scholars agree: a woman can and must remove her *niqab* for visual identification if so requested. Thus I am in agreement with a Florida judge who ordered Mrs. Sultaana Freeman to remove her *niqab* for a driver's license photo, concluding that the requirement of a full-face photo "does not unconstitutionally burden the free exercise of religion."[5]

The case is a difficult one, because Mrs. Freeman offered to provide DNA and fingerprints for identification.[6] Moreover, Florida has a state version of RFRA, so the state must show a "compelling" interest in order to burden religion. On balance, however, the judge has a reasonable position—provided that the requirement is applied consistently. Some Christian sects also refused drivers' license photographs, seeing them as forbidden idolatry, and these believers have been allowed exemptions by two appellate circuits and one state supreme court.[7] Such inconsistencies are troubling, and each state or appellate circuit must strive to craft a consistent and impartial policy. Meanwhile, the idea that hair must be shown in the photo, thus offending a far greater number of women who wear the headscarf, has been rejected, rightly, by virtually all U.S. districts, who have interpreted local requirements to mean that the face must be shown only up to and not beyond the hairline.[8]

By now, however, we know that the face is a very bad identifier. At immigration checkpoints, eye-recognition and fingerprinting technologies are already rapidly replacing the photo. When these superior technologies spread to police on patrol and airport security lines, we can do away with the photo, hence with what remains of the security argument.

Sometimes people argue that even if a *burqa* ban would be both overinclusive (banning dress worn by harmless peaceful women) and underinclusive (failing to ban many forms of attire that terrorists might choose), still, it is a good proxy for what is truly dangerous, and this sort of profiling is perfectly legitimate. We can certainly debate the empirics here, and we should. But within reasonable limits we do think that airports are entitled to use some types of profiling in determining whom to search. This, however, is not what we are contemplating. We are contemplating not extra searches but an outright ban on all public wearing of a type of clothing that some sincere believers think religiously mandatory. In the context of such a severe burden, the fact that the proposed ban is greatly under- and over-inclusive for security purposes is highly relevant.

Let's consider a parallel example: Chicago's short-lived Gang Congregation Ordinance, which prohibited "criminal street gang members" from loitering in public places. Under this law, if a police officer "reasonably believes" that a person "loitering" in a public place (defined as being there "without apparent purpose") is a gang member, he can order both that person and other people with whom he is "loitering" to disperse. Anyone who does not promptly obey has violated the ordinance. Suppose, for example, that blue and black are the colors associated with a particular gang. (That is often how officers identify putative gang members.) Then if a teenage boy wearing blue and black is hanging out with a group of friends, all are subject to the ordinance and may end up being both jailed and fined.

The U.S. Supreme Court declared the law unconstitutional on due process grounds, saying that it was both impermissibly vague and an arbitrary restriction on personal liberties.[9] The ordinance was both under- and over-inclusive in much the same way as the *burqa* ban: it burdened a huge amount of harmless conduct (wearing blue and black), and it failed to target a lot of harmful conduct (such as gang activity by people smart enough to circumnavigate the ordinance by not wearing gang colors). Like the *burqa* ban again, it led to objectionable ethnic profiling: if Martha Nussbaum wore a blue dress with a black handbag, no officer would look twice. Only young men would be targeted, and for the most part only minority men. The *burqa* ban does somewhat better on the vagueness criterion: it's pretty clear what is legal and what illegal. But on the count of arbitrary restriction of personal liberty it does no better. Indeed, it very likely does worse, since there was strong evidence of a correlation between gangs hanging around a place and crime in that place, but the proposed bans are not supported by any similar correlation between the presence of Muslim women in a public place and crime in that place. Once we add that the liberty in question is religious liberty, which usually gets more stringent protection than mere personal taste in clothing, the case against the *burqa* ban looks easier to make than the case against Chicago's law.

A further point should now be made. If our goal is really to maximize security, surely it makes sense to include and not alienate moderate Muslim citizens in our societies. They, after all, are invaluable sources of information about threats to safety posed by Islamic radicals. If they feel that the law is theirs and they are fully respected, they will often give enormous help. If policies show disrespect to all Muslims, or treat an article of religious dress as a per se security problem, they are likely to clam up and stay aloof from police and investigators. Inclusion is not just a gesture of respect, it is also a strategy of prudence.[10]

Banning the *Burqa:* Transparency and Civic Friendship

We still need to address the variant of this argument (what I've called the second anti-*burqa* argument) that focuses on the *transparency* proper to relations among citizens. I have already begun to reply by pointing to the many contexts in civic life—especially in the winter, or in the heat of the sun—in which we do make contact with fellow citizens while the face is to some extent covered. We can now add two further points. The first is that long-standing traditions in many cultures hold that eyes are the windows of the soul. Contact with another person, as individual to individual, is made more through eyes than through nose or mouth. Babies seek eye contact and are more interested in a face if eyes are turned to them than if they are averted. And so it proves in daily life. Once during a construction project that involved a lot of dust in my office, I (who am prone to allergies and vain about my singing voice and the state of my hair) had to cover everything but my eyes while talking to students for a longish number of weeks. At first they found it quite weird, but soon they were asking me how they could get a mask and filter scarf like the ones I was using. My personality did not feel stifled, nor did they feel that they could not access my individuality. To be sure, some versions of the *niqab* do cover the eyes to some extent—but no more than is the case with sunglasses. We usually don't find ourselves unable to have a conversation with someone wearing sunglasses, although the mirror type, completely blocking the view of the eyes, are often found distracting and off-putting.

More generally, people quickly adjust to the modalities of communication that are possible for them. People who are blind notoriously develop hyper-acute auditory skills and are usually able to recognize individuals by their voices—as, of course, are people who contact one another regularly by telephone. In addition to eye contact, the *burqa* certainly permits voice recognition, as well as recognition of characteristic bodily postures and gestures. I see no reason to think that people cannot quickly adjust to new ways of recognizing individuality, as the situation requires.

One more thing we should notice, as we search for consistent ethical principles that we can live by, is that people often have difficulty talking to people who look odd, and there's an unfortunate human tendency to blame this difficulty on the person who looks odd rather than on oneself. People with facial deformities are hugely stigmatized in most cultures. People with both mental and physical disabilities are often excluded from conversation. Indeed, children with disabilities used to be hidden away from "normal" children in a separate room, not integrated into mainstream classrooms, partly on the ground that "normal" children found it difficult to interact with them. Many communities had "ugly laws" that forbade people with conspicuous disabilities from appearing in public. Chicago, for example, passed an ordinance in 1881 that provided that "[n]o person who is diseased, maimed, mutilated or in any way deformed so as to be an unsightly or disgusting object or improper person to be allowed in or on the public ways or other public places in this city, or shall therein or thereon expose himself to pubic view, under a penalty of not less than one dollar nor more than fifty dollars for each offense."[11] This law was repealed only in 1974.

Nowadays, people with mental illness, who may behave or look unusual, are still stigmatized in this way, although the stigma attaching to other disabilities has lessened somewhat. Today, an instructor in a university classroom (to choose just one example) knows that she can't exclude a person with major disabilities such as blindness or Tourette's Syndrome, because those things are accepted categories for toleration and inclusion. So if she finds it hard to talk to such a person, she will blame not the person but herself, and she will try to do her job better. With mental illness it often goes the other way, and the student is blamed for odd or disruptive behavior, but it is increasingly recognized that this is unjust and that students with mental illness should be reasonably accommodated. I think talking to someone wearing a *burqa* is about as difficult, for the unhabituated, as talking with someone who is blind or who has Tourette's, and less difficult than talking to someone with mental illness. All too often, however, the difficulty is still blamed on the woman wearing the *burqa*, rather than on oneself.

Let me illustrate this perceptual issue with two cases from my own law school. Although the law school has for some time conformed to the standards for disability inclusion, in terms of wheelchair access, elevators, and so on, we have few students with serious disabilities. Two years ago, a very brilliant law student graduated at the top of her class. She used a wheelchair, was legally blind and always accompanied by a guide dog, and breathed through a tube. At first, people tended to think she would struggle and might not finish. Not only did she finish; she also proved a star in the law school musical: in a play reading at my home she both served as director and played the role of Hermia in *A Midsummer Night's Dream*—hilariously and with marvelous poise.

Some years earlier, we hired a young scholar of constitutional law who has a neurological condition that causes his limbs and head to make sudden and unpredictable movements. He has told me that under the old Chicago law he would not have been permitted to appear in public. I think it's fair to say that some visitors don't expect much from him when they meet him for the first time—and it's fun to see them recalibrate as they realize that he is one of the most brilliant, knowledgeable, and lovely human beings they could meet. Years ago, they would not have had the opportunity to make such a readjustment, nor would they have felt that such an effort was warranted. Being forced by law to be consistent can expand the moral imagination.

Banning the *Burqa:* Objectification

A third argument, very prominent today, is that the *burqa* is a sign of male domination that symbolizes the objectification of women: it encourages people to think of and treat a woman as a mere object.

A Catalonian legislator recently called the *burqa* a "degrading prison."[12] President Sarkozy says the same thing: "The burka is not a sign of religion, it is a sign of subservience."[13] The first thing we should say about this argument is that the people who make it typically don't know much about Islam and would have a hard time saying what symbolizes what in the different strands and interpretive traditions of that religion. But the more glaring flaw in the argument is that modern societies are suffused with symbols of male supremacy that treat women as objects. Sex magazines, pornography, nude photos, tight jeans, transparent or revealing clothing—all of these products, arguably, treat women as objects, as do so many aspects of our media culture. Women are encouraged to market themselves for male objectification in this way, and it has long been observed by feminist thinkers that this is a way of robbing women of both agency and individuality, reducing them to objects or commodities.[14] We may think these things very bad, we may think them good, or we may withhold general assessment, feeling that we can only judge in a contextual case-by-case manner. All these responses to the phenomenon of "objectification" can be defended. What cannot be defended is to object to objectification only when (as we suppose) it turns up in someone else's culture.

And what about the "degrading prison" of plastic surgery? Every time I undress in the locker room of my gym, I see women bearing the scars of liposuction, tummy tucks, breast implants. Isn't much of this done in order to conform to a male norm of female beauty that casts women as sex objects?

If the proposal were to ban all practices that a ministry of feminism had concluded were objectifying to women, the proposal would at least be consistent, although few would endorse such a sweeping restriction of liberty or the authority it would vest in a small number of alleged feminist experts. More generally, even if we don't like an option, we typically think people should be free to make their own mistakes, within limits set by the rights of others. But the proposal is not made consistently. Proponents of the *burqa* ban do not suggest banning all these objectifying practices. Indeed, they often participate in them. For many European women, for example, U.S.-style feminism is too moralistic, too censorious. We should be more accepting of the complexities of human sexuality, Europeans often urge. Once again, then, the opponents of the *burqa* are utterly inconsistent, betraying a fear of the different that is discriminatory and unworthy of a liberal democracy. In effect, they arrogate to themselves the position of the inquisitorial ministry of feminism—but only for certain people, people whose real motives and understandings they are particularly likely not to understand clearly, not for their own sort. The way to deal with sexism, in this case as in all, is by persuasion and example, not by removing liberty.

Similar inconsistencies are common historically when a new religion and its associated cultural practices inspire fear.[15] When Mormonism appeared on the U.S. scene, mainstream U.S. culture hastened to demonize Mormon polygamy as a horrible form of enslavement, even though women in monogamous marriages of that era had no property or civil rights and no access to divorce on grounds of cruelty or desertion—while Mormon women at least got the vote in the territory of Utah in 1872. No doubt all was not rosy in Mormon marriages, but things were pretty bad in all marriages at that time. Mormons were blamed for asymmetries of power that then infected the entire institution of marriage. Somewhat later, a huge upsurge in Roman Catholic immigration produced a variant on this theme, as anti-Catholic propaganda demonized that religion as anti-woman. Paul Blanshard's hugely popular book *Ameri-*

can Freedom and Catholic Power focused on the (allegedly) weird life of nuns, with their "unhygienic costumes and their medieval rules of conduct"; it stressed the stifling of their erotic instincts and an "attitude of piety and feminine subordination that seems utterly alien to the typically robust and independent spirit of American womanhood."[16] Recognizing how the tropes of objectification and subordination have been used to denigrate other immigrant groups in our history ought to make us far more careful in deploying them today.

Of course things that are legal can still be disapproved of, and we ought to ponder ethical as well as legal norms. Most of us think, I suppose, that some vulgar and denigrating treatment of women in advertisements is bad, and many deplore the extent to which women are encouraged to undergo dangerous forms of surgery in order to retain male interest. And yet we do not usually propose banning these practices. We merely support reasonable forms of health and safety regulation and the limits suggested by today's law of obscenity. So too with the *burqa*: we may criticize (though we ought to know what we are talking about first), while yet opposing a legal ban. The principles I've defended hold that equal respect for persons requires equal conditions of liberty. But they do not require equal personal approval of all religious practices. Legality is not approval. Many things are legal that most of us would consider deplorable: unkindness, stinginess, intemperance, incivility, narcissism. And in a society based upon equal respect for persons, people with one religious or secular view remain perfectly free to disapprove of some other religion's practices, or even of all religious practices and religion itself. Respect is for the person and is fully compatible with intensely disliking many things that many people do.

In a society dedicated to equal liberty, then, people remain perfectly free to think and to say that the *burqa* is an objectionable garment because of the way in which it symbolizes the objectification of women. Still, such a person ought at least to think about consistency, and I believe a duty of civility suggests that she ought at least to try very hard to understand. One should listen to what women who wear the *burqa* say *they* think it means before opining. One should also think about nosiness. In most cases it's just rude to offer unsolicited opinions about the way a person is dressed, and one risks offense even if one knows the person quite well.

Civility is an ethical virtue, and I'm suggesting that in this case it requires restraint that goes beyond simply not seeking to make a practice illegal. Law does not contain all of morality. But it's also important to point out that good laws are not immutable and must be sustained by attitudes of respect, civility, and friendship. If constitutional protections for liberty are obeyed with grudging reluctance or even animosity, they very likely won't last long. So asking people to go several steps beyond the law and to greet one another with a degree of friendliness and respect is something a good lawgiver will seek to do. Roger Williams dedicated his book on the law of religious liberty to "the merciful and compassionate reader."

If a religious practice violates the rights of nonconsenting people, or if it foments hatred against others, things are different. In the former case, legal constraint is perfectly reasonable. In the latter, freedom of speech should not be abridged except in the case of an imminent threat of public disorder, but we all may and should condemn the expression of hatred. The U.S. Supreme Court held that neo-Nazis were free to march in Skokie, Illinois, and to express their views, but it was very appropriate for others to criticize them publicly because of the hatred they expressed. The white hooded garment of the Ku Klux Klan, too, is plausibly seen as a symbol of racism, and though it would be wrong, I think, to make it illegal, it is permissible to criticize it.

It would be difficult to argue that the *burqa* is comparable to the hood of the Ku Klux Klan. A more apt comparison is the way in which some Reform Jews view the religious dress of ultra-orthodox Jews: they may find it old-fashioned, a bit repressive, intellectually misguided (since they reject a legalistic interpretation of Jewish tradition), but on the whole they will think it nosy to denounce such choices unless a friend has asked them their opinion. To speak against the *burqa*, then, though not illegal or deeply immoral, is probably nosy and rude, especially when one knows little about Islam.

One religion that makes me cringe is an evangelical sect that requires its members to handle poisonous snakes (the subject of long litigation). I find that one bizarre, I would never go near it, and I tend to find the actions involved disgusting. But that does not mean that I don't respect its followers as bearers of equal human rights and human dignity. Because they have equal human rights and human dignity, they get to carry on their religion unless there is some compelling government interest against it. (The long litigation concerned just that question. Since the religion kept nonconsenting adults and all children far away from the snakes, it was not an easy question. In the end, a cautious government decided to intervene.[17]) To criticize the religious practice—if one has decided that it does not endanger nonconsenting people—is nosy and rude. But we all have views about other people's religions, which we ponder ourselves and discuss with our friends.

Respect for persons, then, requires not the stifling of all critical discussion but equal space for people to exercise their conscientious commitments, whether or not others approve of what they do in that space. Furthermore, equal respect for persons is compatible, as I said, with limiting religious freedom in the case of a "compelling state interest." In the snake-handler case, the interest was public safety. Another government intervention that was right, in my view, was the judgment that Bob Jones University should lose its tax exemption for its ban on interracial dating.[18] Here the Supreme Court agreed that the ban was part of that sect's religion, and thus that the loss of tax-exempt status was a "substantial burden" on the exercise of that religion. Still, the Court decided that society has a compelling interest in not cooperating with racism.

The U.S. government has itself been guilty of inconsistency in its use of the compelling interest standard. Never has our government taken similar steps against the many Roman Catholic universities that restrict their presidencies to priests, hence males; but in my view they should all lose their tax exemptions for this reason. If there is a relevant difference between the two cases, it needs to be articulated.

Why is the *burqa* different from the case of Bob Jones University? First, of course, government was not telling Bob Jones that it could not continue with its policy, it was just refusing to give the university a huge financial reward in the form of tax relief, thus in effect cooperating with the policy. A second difference is that Bob Jones enforced a total ban on interracial dating, just as the major Catholic universities (Georgetown excepted, which now has a lay president) have imposed a total ban on female candidates for the job of president. Thus everyone who is part of the institution is coerced. The *burqa*, by contrast, is not mandated by an institutional rule. Indeed, few Muslims believe that it is required of all Muslim women, and even those who do believe it is required do not (at any rate in Europe) make it a condition of university entrance or other institutional entry: so it's more like the case of some student at Bob Jones (or any other university) who decides to date only white females or males because of either personal choice or familial and parental pressure. Sadly, most people in most places prefer to date only people from their own group.[19] And many religions back them up, opposing intermarriage. This may be morally short-sighted, but it does not seem like a case for government intervention.

Let's consider one more case. The Indian Constitution bans the Hindu practice of "untouchability" in all forms.[20] Untouchability, much like racial segregation in the U.S. South, was a cruel and nonconsensual practice of stigmatization and noncontact imposed by force, and frequently by violence, on a large and relatively powerless minority, who as a result led lives of great political, educational, and economic inequality. In that case, as in the case of U.S. racial segregation, legal intervention was justified, despite the restriction on liberty involved. Both practices played an extremely cruel and harmful role in denying meaningful equality to millions of people and had an overwhelming impact on the shape and conduct of public life. They were basically systems of rights-violations. Governmental intervention to protect the equal rights of all was justified. I'll later suggest that the ban on Muslim head-covering in Turkey was in some ways comparable to these cases and was probably justified, at least at one time. The wearing of the *burqa* in Europe and the United States, an individual practice of small groups of people governed by minority religious norms, is not seriously comparable to these cases.

This brings us to our next argument.

Banning the *Burqa:* Coercion

A fourth argument holds that many women wear the *burqa* only because they are coerced. This is a rather implausible argument to make across the board, and it is typically made by people who have no idea of the circumstances of this or that individual woman. We should reply that of course all forms of violence and physical coercion in the home are illegal already, and laws against domestic violence and abuse should be enforced much more zealously than they are. Do the arguers really believe that domestic violence is a peculiarly Muslim problem? If they do, they are dead wrong. According to the U.S. Bureau of Justice Statistics (BJS), intimate partner violence made up 20 percent of all nonfatal violent crime experienced by women in 2001. The National Violence against Women Survey, cited on the BJS website, reports that 52 percent of surveyed women said they were physically assaulted as a child by an adult caretaker and/or as an adult by any type of perpetrator. There is no evidence that Muslim families have a disproportionate amount of such violence. Indeed, given the strong association between domestic violence and the abuse of alcohol, it seems at least plausible that observant Muslim families will turn out to have less of it.

Suppose there were evidence that the *burqa* was strongly associated, statistically, with violence against women. Could government legitimately ban it on those grounds? The U.S. Supreme Court has held that nude dancing may be banned on account of its contingent association with crime, including crimes against women, but crucial aspects of the opinion are vague, and it is not clear that the analysis is correct.[21] College fraternities are very strongly associated with violence against women, and some universities have made all or some fraternities move off campus as a result. But private institutions are entitled to make such regulations about what can occur on their premises; public universities are entitled to limit the types of activities that will get public money, particularly when they involve illegality (underage drinking). But a total governmental ban on the male drinking club (or on other places where men get drunk, such as soccer matches) would be a bizarre restriction of associational liberty that few would defend.

One thing that we have long known to be strongly associated with coercion and violence against women is alcohol. The amendment to the U.S. Constitution banning alcohol was motivated by exactly this concern. It was on dubious footing in terms of liberty: why should law-abiding people suffer for the crimes of abusers? But what was even more obvious was that Prohibition was a total disaster, politically and practically. It increased crime and it did not stop violence against women.

Similarly, college and university administrators today generally deplore the fact that the drinking age is currently twenty-one rather than eighteen, because they believe that the higher age actually increases binge drinking and coercion of women. The reason is that at present alcohol consumption is secret and illegal rather than legal and therefore potentially regulable and supervisable by university officials.

Moreover, even during Prohibition religions that required the sacramental use of alcohol received an exemption. And federal law today exempts religious use of alcohol from the drinking age. So the correct analogue would be a ban on the *burqa* that exempted those who wear it for religious reasons—which is to say virtually all users.

What is most important, however, is that anyone proposing to ban the *burqa* must consider it together with these other cases, weigh the evidence, and take the consequences for their own cherished hobbies. Some people might sincerely propose to use legal restriction to get at the worst abuses, even if that would involve restricting liberty: but they will have to present a credible case that the practices they are targeting are really the ones associated with the worst abuses. What shall we ban? Frat parties? The sale of alcohol? Violent pornography? All these putative bans have their defenders, although both prudence and an interest in liberty suggest that we should not go there. What would be difficult indeed would be to show that the *burqa* poses a danger to women comparable to the danger associated with these practices.

But what about children and adolescents? Surely they do not have much choice as long as they are living with their parents, so family pressure to wear religious dress is likely to be difficult to resist.

This question opens up a huge topic, since nothing is more common in the modern family than various forms of coercive pressure—to get into a top college, to date people of the "right" religion or ethnicity, to wear "appropriate" clothes, to choose a remunerative career, to take a shower, "and so each and so on to nolast term," as James Joyce once said.[22] So where should government step in? Certainly it should step in when physical and/or sexual abuse is going on, which is very often. Where religious mandates are concerned, intervention would be justified, similarly, in cases in which the behavior constitutes a gross risk to bodily health and safety. So courts have typically held with respect to Jehovah's Witnesses who refuse their children life-saving blood transfusions, and with respect to Christian Scientist parents who refuse their children needed medical care. (Note that the parents remain perfectly free to choose to forgo treatment themselves.) Legal intervention also seems justified if a nonconsensual procedure permanently impairs some major functioning. Thus it is reasonable to argue that female genital mutilation practiced on minors should be illegal if it is a form that impairs sexual pleasure or other bodily functions. (A symbolic prick is a different story.) Male circumcision seems to me all right, however, because I do not see solid evidence that it interferes with adult sexual functioning; indeed, it is now known to reduce susceptibility to HIV/AIDS. Other forms of bodily alteration of children—ear piercing, for example, or orthodonture, or plastic surgery repairing an ear that is alleged to stick out too much—are not legally regulable because they do not impair a major functioning.[23] In every case, what is really going on is my two-sided balancing test: is there a substantial burden on the parents' religious freedom? And, if so, does a compelling state interest justify the imposition of this burden?

Now to the *burqa*.

The *burqa* (for minors) is not in the same class as genital mutilation, since it is not irreversible and does not endanger health or impair other bodily functions—not nearly so much as high-heeled shoes risk doing. If it is imposed by physical or sexual violence, that violence ought to be legally punished. Otherwise, however, it seems to be in the same category as all sorts of requirements, pleasant and unpleasant, that parents impose on their children: wearing "respectable" clothing, going to the "right" school, getting top grades, practicing the violin, dating only people of the "right" religion, getting into a top college. Some practices of this type do appear to violate laws against child cruelty. Thus when law professor Amy Chua admitted in a popular book that she had forced her three-year-old daughter to stand outside in the cold, and on another occasion had forced her to stay at the piano without bathroom access or water because she had not mastered a difficult passage in a piano work, one did wonder why the police were not on her doorstep.[24] That sounds to me like child abuse, and I think the police could intervene, though clearly they didn't. If the incident had occurred in an immigrant Muslim household rather than in the upper-middle-class home of two Yale University law professors, the mother hailing from a minority known for its laudable work ethic, the police might have shown more concern for that little girl, and in this case they would have been right. If similar coercive tactics were used to get a child to wear a *burqa,* then, the case would be open to intervention. But most cases are not like this, and (where any type of coercion is involved, as often it is not) are more like emotional blackmail of an all too familiar, indeed ubiquitous, type. Parents who motivate their children by emotional blackmail are often blameworthy, but to bring the police in on all such occasions would surely be to countenance too much legal intervention in the affairs of the family.

At times, the coercive pressure may express hatred of a group of citizens. My father, for example, threatened to disown me if I appeared in public in a group that contained African Americans; he later refused to attend my wedding when I married a Jew. I think it would have been perfectly appropriate to criticize this coercive pressure, even for people who did not know my father, because it is always right to protest against hatred and stigmatization, as well as against pressure on children to comply with hate-motivated requirements—just as it is right to protest against the white hood of the KKK. In the vast majority of cases, however, things are far less clear, and the *burqa* is one of these times, since it does not express hatred of a group of people. So in this case, I'm inclined to think that even vocal public criticism seems nosy and rude.

I have said that protection of central human capabilities should always be seen as giving the state a compelling state interest. At the limit, where the state's interest in protecting the opportunities of children is concerned, is the denial of education at stake in the Supreme Court case *Wisconsin v. Yoder*, in which a group of Amish parents asked to withdraw their children from the last two years of legally required schooling.[25] They would clearly have lost if they had asked to take their children out of all schooling, but what was in question was these two years only. They won under the accommodationist principle, although they probably would have lost on Justice Scalia's Lockean test, since the law mandating education until age sixteen was nondiscriminatory and not drawn up in order to persecute the Amish. The case is difficult, because the parents made a convincing argument that work on the farm, at that crucial age, was a key part of their community-based religion—and yet education opens up so many exit opportunities that the denial even of those two years may unreasonably limit children's future choices. And of course the children were under heavy pressure to do what their parents wanted. (Thus Justice Douglas's claim that the Court should decide the case by interviewing the children betrayed a lack of practical understanding.)

Societies are certainly entitled to insist that all female children have a decent education and employment opportunities that give them exit options from any home situation they may dislike. If people think that women wear the *burqa* only because of coercive pressure, let them create ample opportunities for them, and then see what they actually do. Societies may legitimately, in addition, insist on teaching children about the diverse groups that live in their society, a very important part of history and civics education. Moreover, by making sure that public space is administered in a nondiscriminatory manner, they provide ample opportunities for young people to meet others different from themselves, thus expanding their range of choice. (From the point of view of my father's segregation-

ist goals, New York was a wonderful opening, where I constantly encountered "wrong" people of many different types.)

One thing that Americans and Europeans need to face squarely is
the fact that some people do actually choose lives involving authority and constraint. Given that the United States and most European
nations have had volunteer armies for some time and that Germany
just dropped its own conscription law, all citizens of these countries
have reason to be grateful for the fact that the preference for a struc-
tured life submissive to authority runs strong in their societies. And
most do treat the choices of the men and women of the military respectfully, rather than suggesting that such choices ought to be
banned. Authoritarian choices, as we may call them, do look pretty
weird to many prosperous middle-class Americans, and perhaps especially to intellectuals. I recall a phone conversation with an FBI
agent who was investigating a former philosophy graduate student
of mine who had rejected a career as a philosophy professor for a
career as a Marine officer, and who was now applying for top-level
security clearance. When she asked whether Tom had any traits that
were unusual in the graduate student community, I had to say yes:
he wanted to be a Marine. That is about the weirdest trait that a
philosopher can possibly have. But the point the agent and I saw (as
we both laughed over the contrasting values of the two professions)
is that society needs and should accommodate both types, and people should leave others plenty of room to make those choices. Above
all, though, they should not demonize some lives that involve submission to authority and extol others—unless they can find a relevant difference. (That the United States is worth a sacrifice of autonomy but religion is not? Many people believe something like
this, but it seems nosy and rude to make such judgments about
other people, unless they have asked my advice.)

Before we leave the topic of coercion, there is a reasonable point to be made in this connection. When Turkey banned the veil long ago, it was with good reason in that specific context: because women who went unveiled were being subjected to harassment and violence. The ban protected a space for the choice to be unveiled, and was legitimate so long as women did not have that choice, although it was non-optimal because of the restriction on liberty that it involved. We might think of this as a "substantial burden" justified (temporarily) by a "compelling state interest." The ban does not appear to be justified today, when women are able to circulate freely, unveiled. Nor would it be justified in today's Europe or the United States, where women can dress more or less as they please—with only the usual amount of public harassment that the ongoing reality of sexism in these nations brings with it. Currently, then, in the United States and Europe, there is no reason for the burden to religious liberty that the ban involves.

Banning the *Burqa:* Health

Finally, one frequently hears the argument that the *burqa* is per se unhealthy, because it is hot and uncomfortable. I have heard this argument often in Europe, most recently in Spain. This is perhaps the silliest of the arguments. Clothing that covers the body can be comfortable or uncomfortable, depending on the fabric. In India I typically wear a full *salwaar kameez* of cotton, because it is superbly comfortable, and full covering keeps dust off one's limbs and at least diminishes the risk of skin cancer. It is surely far from clear that the amount of skin displayed in typical Spanish female dress would meet with a dermatologist's approval. Sometimes the intensity of the sun appears to demand facial covering. I said that at a baseball game I pull down my cap and wear large sunglasses, but I also cover my nose and mouth at times from the assault of the sun.

More pointedly, would the arguer really seek to ban all uncomfortable and possibly unhealthy female clothing? Wouldn't we have to begin with high heels, delicious as they are? But no, high heels are associated with majority norms (and are a major Spanish export), so they draw no ire. In general, the state limits its regulatory interventions into clothing to making sure that items sold for children are flameproof and without harmful chemicals, and that other gross health risks are avoided. But on the whole women in particular are allowed and even encouraged to wear clothing that could plausibly be argued to create health risks, whether through tendon shortening or through exposure to the sun.

Suppose parents required their daughters to wear a Victorian corset—which did a lot of bodily damage, compressing various organs. Adult women today could wear something just as restrictive with no impediment. If people made a fuss about teenage girls being forced to wear corsets, it is likely that a ban would at least be contemplated. If corsets were mandatory for some religion, however, they would (under the accommodationist standard I favor) have to show not just a rational basis for the ban but a compelling state interest: so they'd have to show that the risk to health was considerable. The *burqa* is not even in the category of the corset. As many readers of my *New York Times* column pointed out, the *burqa* is sensible dress in a hot climate where skin easily becomes worn by sun and dust. What does seem to pose a risk to health is wearing synthetic fabrics in a hot climate, but nobody is talking about that.

All five arguments in favor of the *burqa* ban involve inconsistency. And the inconsistency is not simply a logical failing or a failing of comprehensive thought, as in some of Socrates' cross-examinations.

It is the type of inconsistency decried by the Gospels and held up to relentless scrutiny by Kant. It is the inconsistency of narcissism, of people who take others to task while making an exception for themselves. The person who argues this way is putting herself up above others and failing to respect them as equals. To that extent, she is just using them as tools of her own purposes.

In terms of our legal/political principles, all five arguments fail to pass the weak test of neutrality endorsed by John Locke and Justice Scalia. We don't even need to reach the delicate issue of religiously grounded accommodation to see that they are utterly unacceptable in a society committed to equal liberty. Equal respect for conscience requires us to reject them.

But what of the argument that, if there is even just a little something in several of these arguments, they may all assume significant weight when put together? It seems likely that many Europeans think something like this. We should certainly think hard about the possibility. I've suggested that there is really not anything at all in some of the arguments (health, for example). So that one doesn't add any weight at all to the others. But the trouble in the other cases is that the same combination strategy would add up to a far greater weight when we consider majority practices. Let's think about high heels. They are a health risk. They certainly can be said to conduce to the objectification of women. There is a good deal of psychological pressure on women to wear such shoes (which I love, don't get me wrong). They are also a security risk to the wearer, since they prevent her from running away from assailants. Or take plastic surgeries such as tummy tucks, breast implants, and liposuction. These pose a health risk that is significant, although when properly monitored as law typically provides (by a board-certified plastic surgeon), they can be reasonably safe. They also deter women from physical fitness by promising a quick fix for unfitness. They conduce to and derive from a climate of objectification. They are usually part of an atmosphere of strong psychological coercion: women may have a positive love of nice shoes, but they are unlikely to love these very difficult surgeries. Such surgeries might even be said to impede transparency and civic friendship, since they create an artificial woman-construct (a kind of body-suit not unrelated to the famous Playboy bunny costume) that may impede recognition of the real woman. So if we adopt the combination strategy, we'd end up with a stronger case for banning high heels and at least some plastic surgeries than for banning the *burqa*. In the end, then, the combination strategy does not help the defender of the *burqa* ban.

French *Laïcité:* Homogeneity and Sexuality

Let us now consider more closely the special case of France. Unlike other European nations, France is consistent—up to a point. Given its history of anticlericalism and the strong commitment to *laïcité*, religion is not to set its mark upon the public realm, and the public realm is permitted to disfavor religion by contrast to nonreligion. This commitment leads to restrictions on a wide range of religious manifestations, all in the name of a total separation of church and state. But if we look closely, the restrictions are unequal and discriminatory. The school dress code forbids the Muslim headscarf and the Jewish *yarmulke*, along with "large" Christian crosses. But this is a totally unequal burden, because the first two items of clothing are religiously obligatory for observant members of those religions, and the third is not: Christians are under no religious obligation to wear any cross, much less a "large" one. So there is discrimination inherent in the French system.

Would French secularism be acceptable if practiced in an even-handed way? According to U.S. constitutional law, government may not favor religion over nonreligion, or nonreligion over religion. For example, it was unconstitutional for the University of Virginia to announce that it would use student fees to fund all other student organizations (political, environmental, and so forth) but not the religious clubs (*Rosenberger v. Rector and Visitors of the University of Virginia*, 515 U.S. 819 [1995]). I must say that I prefer this balanced policy to French *laïcité*; I think it is fairer to religious people. Separation is not total, even in France: thus a fire in a burning church would still be put out by the public fire department; churches still get the use of the public water supply and the public sewer system. Still, the amount and type of separation that the French system mandates, while understandable historically, look unfair in the light of the principles I have defended.

Let's now consider the language of the law banning the *burqa*. It prohibits "wearing attire designed to hide the face" *(porter une tenue destinée à dissimuler son visage)*—and then there is a long list of exceptions:

The prohibition described in Article 1 does not apply if the attire is prescribed or authorized by legislative or regulatory dispensation, if it is justified for reasons of health or professional motives, or if it is adopted in the context of athletic practices, festivals, or artistic or traditional performances.

[L'interdiction prévue à l'article 1er ne s'applique pas si la tenue est prescrite ou autorisée par des dispositions legislatives ou réglementaires, si elle est justifiée par des raisons de santé ou des motifs professionals, ou si elle s'inscrit dans le cadre de pratiques sportives, de fêtes ou de manifestations artistiques ou traditionnelles.]

One's first reaction to this capacious list is that the law has tried to include every possible occasion for covering the face—except the *burqa*. Certainly, if we go down my list of parallel cases, we find that most are dealt with: skaters and skiers by sport, doctors and dentists by professional requirements, my office face mask by health, and a variety of other theatrical uses of the mask by aesthetic and traditional "performances." I am not sure what becomes of me in Chicago in the winter, but I'd be willing to bet that I'd get an exemption on grounds of *santé*. Clearly, though, you don't purchase principled consistency simply by listing as an exception to the principle everything except the one thing you really dislike.

The French have a reply to make, however. For they do not exempt any *religious* occasion or motive for covering the face. In the case of the school dress code, they did: and those "small" crosses showed favoritism to the Christian majority. (Similarly, bans on Muslim headscarves in other countries that exempt nuns in full habit are inconsistent and a form of majority favoritism.) From the point of view of our principle of equal liberty, the whole policy of *laïcité* is mistaken, since it privileges nonreligion over religion and constricts the liberty of religious expression without any compelling government interest (apart from *laïcité* itself). But we are not asking that question at this point, we are simply asking about fairness among the religions. Does the application of the ban to all religions mean that the ban, unlike the school dress code, is truly neutral? Well of course, although the word *burqa* does not occur in the legislation, we understand perfectly well that this is what it is all about. And the fact that the law is so generous with other cultural and professional exemptions shows that the French are not terribly worried about the practice as such—only when it is a religious manifestation. But still, isn't that a consistent and, up to a point, neutral application of the policy of *laïcité*?

The difficulty we have here is that no other religion has a custom of precisely that sort. So what the law has done is to single out something that is of central importance to at least some members of one religion and to apply a very heavy burden to it, without similarly burdening central and cherished practices of other religions.[26] Indeed, it seems clear that one would not be fined for making the sign of the cross over oneself in a public place, for singing a religious hymn as one walked down the street, or for wearing any type of religious apparel other than the *burqa:* cassocks, nuns' habits, Hasidic dress, the saffron garb of the Hindu priest—all of these remain unburdened. So it is neutral in one sense, but not at all neutral in another. At this point, defenders of the ban will typically allude to one of the other arguments, saying that the *burqa,* unlike these other forms of clothing, is a security risk, an impediment to normal relations among citizens, and so on. But the fact that the government does not credit these rationales is clear in that it permits so many exceptions to the ban. Even a public masquerade, at which hundreds of people cover their faces, received explicit defense in the statute. So it's clear that the government does not think that security provides a compelling interest in favor of the restriction: it's trumped routinely by very weak and even frivolous interests. Thus I conclude that the French ban is not truly neutral, any more than the school dress code is neutral. Besides the obvious objection that French secularism does not allow sufficiently ample freedom for religious observance, we may add the objection of bias.

More generally, the French law betrays a bias in favor of the familiar and dominant French way of being a human being, whatever that way is. Obviously enough, French people are heterogeneous, and the *burqa* policy was the object of much debate. Nonetheless, it is not implausible to see it as expressing some dominant social norms. As historian Joan Scott has eloquently and convincingly argued (concerning the headscarf, well before the idea of banning the *burqa* took center stage), the controversy over Islamic dress really reduces to a dogmatic insistence on a French way of being a woman, in which sexuality is casually displayed as a form of individual initiative and personal self-expression. This understanding of female sexuality is taken to be "modern," and anything else is taken to be archaic, subversive, and threatening: "[T]he opposition between French and Islamic cultures was an ideological construction that reduced complex realities to simple, oppositional categories."[27] Of course this way of thinking is profoundly flawed because it lacks genuine respect and curiosity. It gives latitude to the familiar but refuses the unfamiliar a similar concern, a similar liberty.

The nations of Europe differ in many ways, and each has a unique history that it would take an entire book to unfold in a nuanced way. Nonetheless, all share a concern for homogeneity that leads them to commit some errors in public argument that are troubling. If those nations were isolated islands in the middle of a wilderness, as the original American colonies saw themselves, it would at least be more understandable that they would seek a secluded space within which to associate with people like themselves, a sort of national analogue of the gated community. Puritan Massachusetts was in that sense a gated community, excluding dissenters and heretics—who then went to reside elsewhere. Even that arrangement was troubling, because it did not provide sufficiently ample liberty. We've said that human dignity requires not just some liberty but ample liberty. People are searching beings, and even people who begin by agreeing with one another will end up disagreeing, as they search for the meaning of life in their own ways. Massachusetts prevented them from staying, if they disagreed with the majority. The nations of Europe are uncomfortably similar to Puritan Massachusetts, denying equal space to minorities.

If all those nations had done was to have immigration policies that favored people like them, they would at any rate be doing what nations all over the world do all the time. We could think those policies problematic, and we could and should debate them; but at least the countries involved would not be treating their own citizens unfairly. Such, however, is not the current situation of Europe. All European nations are already pluralistic, because all have already admitted, indeed sought out, workers to supply important ingredients to national welfare. And the EU involves a principled commitment to the free movement of labor among the nations, including the free movement of many dark-skinned and/or Muslim people to lands dominated by blond and Christian people. To make these commitments for reasons of national welfare, and *then* to treat the people unequally, is a worse failing than the failing to admit them in the first place. Once they are admitted, the society is a plural society, and efforts need to be made to treat all members with equal respect.

Societies are certainly entitled to take measures that stabilize their core values and their political culture, in a time of increased immigration. One obvious measure, which most nations already use, is compulsory civics instruction—both in publicly funded schools and in private or religious schools that seek accreditation. Indeed, in this regard the United States has not done as well as it could, since, despite a Supreme Court ruling that reasonable civics requirements may be imposed on private and religious schools, home schooling is currently permitted with extremely lax requirements, with the result that a lot of young people grow up without understanding their society's diversity or the core values of respect and equality that hold it together.[28] Societies may also insist on nondiscrimination in public space and define that space broadly, including all retail stores and any rental structures that have more than a very small number of units. In this way, they protect public space as a space within which diverse citizens encounter one another on a plane of equality. Neither minorities nor majorities, entering these spaces, may insulate themselves from contact with those who are different. Discrimination in public space can and should be illegal, and minorities as well as majorities must obey nondiscrimination laws, so far as public accommodations are concerned.[29] Further, all nations already emphasize core values in citizenship instruction and examination. And nations can make an intelligent use of public artworks, public parks, public festivals, and political rhetoric to inspire emotions connected to core political values, a project essential to their stability, as successful leaders from Abraham Lincoln to Martin Luther King, Jr., have clearly seen.[30] All these are positive moves; none requires banning a personal and consensual religious practice, and none requires extra burdens on minorities.

Bias is ugly. Indeed, as Kant suggests, it is a good candidate for being the basic form of ethical failing. We must not tolerate bias in our laws and institutions, and we should strenuously try to avoid it in our more informal dealings with our fellow citizens. We have a chance of avoiding it only if we try as hard as we can to lead the examined life.

5

INNER EYES:
RESPECT AND THE
SYMPATHETIC IMAGINATION

To make good principles real, we need to develop our "inner eyes." This expression comes from Ralph Ellison's great novel *Invisible Man,* which begins as follows:

> I am an invisible man. No, I am not a spook like those who haunted Edgar Allan Poe; nor am I one of your Hollywood-movie ecto-plasms. I am a man of substance, of flesh and bone, fiber and liq-uids—and I might even be said to possess a mind. I am invisible, un-derstand, simply because people refuse to see me. Like the bodiless heads you see sometimes in circus sideshows, it is as though I have been surrounded by mirrors of hard, distorting glass. When they approach me they see only my surroundings, themselves, or fig-ments of their imagination—indeed, everything and anything ex-cept me.
>
> Nor is my invisibility exactly a matter of a biochemical accident to my epidermis. That invisibility to which I refer occurs because of a peculiar disposition of the eyes of those with whom I come in contact. A matter of the construction of their *inner* eyes, those eyes with which they look through their physical eyes upon reality.

Most of us look out at the world through physical eyes. But all of us (sighted and nonsighted) look through our sense-organs with an inner organ, the imagination. What disturbs Ellison's hero is that the inner eyes of white America do not see his human reality. They see "only my surroundings, themselves, or figments of their imagination." They have never stopped to ask what his life is like, what its human emotions and ambitions are. They have inner eyes, but those eyes remain uncultivated.

Nor is this failure unique to American racism. We all move through our lives, a lot of the time, wrapped in a fog of our own selfish aims and desires, seeing other people as mere instruments of those desires. Kant thought, plausibly, that we need good principles to address this ubiquitous failing. But we need something else as well, the habitual cultivation of a displacement of mind, a curious, questioning, and receptive demeanor that says, in effect, "Here is another human being. I wonder what he (or she) is seeing and feeling right now." This curiosity needs to be fed by facts: for without correct historical and empirical information we can't possibly answer such a question. But it needs something more, a willingness to move out of the self and to enter another world.

Civic Friendship and Inner Vision

The first bit of Narragansett language that Roger Williams teaches his readers is a question: "What cheare, Nétop?" And then he explains: "Nétop is friend." The imagination I'm talking about is the sort expressed in that simple greeting, which shows both factual information—Williams has learned to speak Narragansett, and urges his readers to know at least some of what he knows—and an openness of spirit that factual information by itself does not guarantee.

Our inner eyes can work well even when we are not engaging in any sort of conscious effort or indulging poetic flights of fancy. Their good operation can be a daily and routine matter, in a society that has cultivated them from the start. In the summer of 2010, I went, as I often do, to a White Sox game (the one in which my dear team took over first place). I was there with two friends from Texas and my son-in-law, who was born in Germany and now has a Green Card. So in Chicago terms, we were already a mixed multicultural lot. Behind me was a suburban dad with shoulder-length gray hair (an educated, apparently affluent ex-hippie, like the "Bobos" of David Brooks's book), who took pleasure in explaining the finer points of the game (like the suicide squeeze) to his daughter and two other preteen girls in fashionable sundresses. On our right was a sedate African-American couple, the woman holding a bag that marked her as working for the "U.S. Census Religion subcommittee" of her suburban county. In front of us were three Orthodox boys, ages around six, ten, and eighteen, their *tzizit* (ritual fringes) showing underneath their Sox shirts, and cleverly double-hatted so that they could doff their Sox caps during the National Anthem, while still retaining their *kipot*. Although this meant that they had not really bared their heads for the Anthem, not one person gave them an ugly stare or said, "Take off your hat!"—or, even worse, "Here we take off our hats." Indeed, nobody apart from me seemed to pay any attention to them.

That non-attention was very likely the result of habituated well-functioning inner eyes. What were the people around me thinking (half-consciously, without giving it much of a thought)? Few are likely to have known much about what *tzizit* mean, or about different varieties of Judaism. But they all would have recognized this as Jewish religious dress, and most would have understood that the *kipoh* was a religious requirement. So some would have thought (not very consciously), "Those boys are following their religion. Good for them." Maybe some others would have thought, "Silly archaic requirements." But then, they would also have thought, "But it's their religion and it's not my business." From the time when Quakers and Mennonites refused to doff their hats, and when both Mennonites and Amish adopted "premodern" dress, we Americans have been pretty comfortable with weird clothes, and we've become used to the idea that people's conscientious observances frequently require them to dress in ways that seem strange or unpleasant to the majority. My own reaction was probably especially complex, because I am a Jew who rejects the requirements of orthodoxy. I would not encourage a child or relative of mine to wear *tzizit* or, outside of temple, a *kipoh*. As a Reform Jew, I view these things as totemism and fetishism. But I would not offend strangers by pointing that out, nor acquaintances unless they were friends who had asked my advice.

Why do I say that this is a case of well-functioning inner eyes? Because all the people at that ballgame were used to recognizing humanity in strange costumes, especially costumes dictated by religion. They had grown up with that idea. People who look different did not immediately seem threatening, nor did they offend the majority by their refusal to adopt majority ways. The "premodern" nature of their religious observance did not seem offensive—or, if to some it did, they had the good sense and civility to keep that reaction to themselves. An essential idea about people has been grasped: that they follow their own conscience, even when that leads them not to assimilate. Many people these days (particularly, perhaps, in Europe) talk about how immigrants have to learn to fit in. But I ask: what would they have liked to see at that ballgame? What I saw, or three Jewish boys ejected from the park because they allegedly failed to respect the flag? (And note that, like most minorities, the boys did show respect in the way they felt they could, without violating their conscience.)

This story shows us something about respect: that it is blind unless the "inner eyes" are cultivated. We might have supposed that all we need are good principles, mandating equal respect for all, plus the idea that equal respect requires equal, and ample, religious liberty. But principles do not apply themselves: we first must have appropriate perceptions of the salient features of the situations before us.[1] If those boys had been seen as "subversives," as "a security threat," or even as "a threat to national identity," they would not so easily have been brought under a principle of religious liberty: the idea that some "compelling" public interest supported restraint on their conduct would then have seemed plausible. Again, had people seen them and thought, "Children are in danger here because of adults' cruel imposition of premodern values," the idea that any restriction on the boys' religious custom constituted a "substantial burden" might not have been reached.

Under the principles we've been considering, respect is for persons and not necessarily for everything they do. The idea that equal respect requires us to approve of all religions equally, or even all instances of religious conduct, is just mistaken, and the participatory imagination doesn't require approval either. It just requires seeing the other as a person pursuing human goals, and understanding in some loose way what those goals are, so that one can see what a burden to their conscience is, and whether the conduct really does contravene vital state interests. I have many problems with the type of orthodox Judaism that the boys exemplify, and if a friend asked my opinion I would give it. But the participatory imagination reminds me that they have their own lives, just as I have mine, and they are entitled to the space to pursue their own goals, on a basis of equality with me, unless some genuinely compelling public interest does intervene.

More generally, the imagination makes others real for us. A common human failing is to see the whole world from the point of view of one's own goals, and to see the conduct of others as all about oneself. Thus: "those veiled women are aggressively defying Frenchness"; or "those boys are un-American." A refusal of homogeneity is taken, all too often, as all about the majority, a kind of defiance or even assault. By imagining other people's way of life, we don't necessarily learn to agree with their goals, but we do see the reality of those goals for them. We learn that other worlds of thought and feeling exist.

I've said that the participatory imagination is, or can be, mundane and nonconscious; we are all capable of making countless daily decisions in ways that take the views of others into account, if we are once trained to proceed that way. Still, it's useful at this point to have some cases of deliberate cultivation of the imagination, in which writers of a variety of types challenge their audience to think about religious minorities in a more participatory way, rather than seeing them simply as obstacles to their own preeminence. Such cases, if they are well done, are founded on historical and sociological accuracy; but they go beyond this to enlist the reader in thinking about the world from the other's point of view.

Pitfalls of Imagining: Partiality, Narcissism

The participatory imagination (or "empathy," as I often call it) is just one ingredient in the attitudes of sympathy and compassionate concern. A good actor has an active participatory imagination with characters of many types but is likely to sympathize far more with some than with others. And a person with a vicious character may use empathy to harm, even to torture: for understanding how one's victim sees the world is often an ingredient in skillful sadism. So the participatory imagination does little good if people are not basically well-intentioned, if they do not have attitudes of concern and sympathy toward other human beings that involve genuine ethical commitments not to harm. But many people have those attitudes while still being very obtuse in their dealings with others, because they simply have not imagined the other's situation. That was why Ellison thought that his novel could perform a valuable public service: because, as he saw it, white America was not so much committed to vice as crude and obtuse. Once the world of experience of an African American was made fully real to them, their behavior would alter.

Strong experimental evidence, in fact, suggests that vivid imagining leads, other things equal, to helping behavior. For many years Daniel Batson of the University of Kansas has conducted a long series of rigorous experiments testing this proposition.[2] The classic experiment involves having subjects listen to a radio broadcast that describes the predicament of a fellow student—she has broken her leg, say, and needs someone to drive her to class. One group is told not to pay attention to the story, but only to listen to the technical qualities of the broadcast. The other group is told to imagine the story vividly and put themselves in the position of the other person. The second group reports emotional responses and is shown to engage in helping behavior in significant proportion. So empathy makes a difference (although it is of course only one factor in people's lives, and Batson has carefully set up the situation so that the help is easily performed). Batson also shows that literary narratives have effects similar to those of the radio broadcast. The subjects who helped others had to have other background characteristics: they weren't sociopaths or deeply pathological people cut off from others. But given a basic level of human decency, widely shared, the experience of vivid imagining changes a person's view of what should be done.

The empathetic imagination moves in a direction opposite to that of fear. In fear, a person's attention contracts, focusing intently on her own safety, and (perhaps) that of a small circle of loved ones. In empathy the mind moves outward, occupying many different positions outside the self. That directional difference already makes it seem valuable as an antidote to fear's narcissism. But we must be cautious: for empathy can have its own narcissism.

The participatory imagination is part of our primate inheritance. Work on primates by Frans De Waal shows that at least chimpanzees and bonobos have a capacity for perspectival thinking, seeing the world from another point of view. (Elephants also have this ability, and dogs may have it.) And work by psychologist Paul Bloom shows that human infants have this ability by the age of one year: they are able to imagine their parent or other caregiver's "take" on the situation, and to use this in getting what they want. But this capacity is still highly immature, from the point of view of morality and political fairness: it is exceedingly narrow and prone to play favorites. Nonhuman animals usually can see the world only from the viewpoint of their narrow group (although dogs can cross the species barrier, forming a symbiotic family with their human guardians). Human infants use perspectival thinking primarily to get what they want from a small circle of caregivers. Much needs to be done to enable the imagination to move outward, to embrace the situation of people at a distance. And even when the imagination does move outward, its animal origins suggest that it will be easier to relate to the predicament of people in one's own "group," whether defined by ethnicity or religion or nationality.

Even when people have become in principle capable of seeing the world from the point of view of distant people and groups, intense sympathy with those closer to the self may often block this outward movement. A well-known part of the criminal trial, in the sentencing phase, is a defendant's opportunity to present a longer life history, offering mitigating evidence that is beyond the immediate reach of the trial (pertaining, for example, to childhood abuse or trauma), and to plead for sympathy from the jury. Recently, victims of crimes have in some cases been permitted to introduce their own stories at this time, describing the suffering the criminal has inflicted on their families. Since it often happens that crime victims are closer to most jurors in class, race, and ethnicity than they are to the defendant, it seems that the intense sympathy with the stories of victims short-circuits the movement of imagination outward toward the defendant.[3] Given that the chance to appeal for mercy at the penalty phase has been held to be a defendant's constitutional right, this blockage poses a potentially grave problem.[4] Whether this problem is sufficiently serious to justify not admitting victim impact statements is a separate issue. (They pose other problems as well, favoring victims who have appealing friends over solitary and unconnected victims.) What this example shows, however, is that *if* we have decided that we need to gain an understanding of people at a distance from ourselves in ethnicity or race, we have to watch out for interference that may come from our tendency (rooted in our animal heritage) to sympathize above all with people who belong to our own group—whether that is defined in terms of kinship, or race, or religion, or nationality. More empathy is not, then, always better. We need to ask what our particular blind spots are and then to address those, in a way that is as free from distraction and interference as possible.

From now on, then, I'll be focusing on works that help the imagination break out of its narcissistic moorings close to "home," by challenging it to inhabit the reality of a life that is in some respects distant or difficult. Literary works are of course not the only source of this sort of education, but they are a good place to begin a discussion.

In order to see what is well and not well done in the realm of the imagination, it will be helpful to move away from current reality, taking our cases from a past toward which we now have some perspective, rather than from controversies in which we are currently embroiled. In these long-ago cases we can study the work done by the imagination, seeing how it gave essential life to principles of equal respect, and at the same time see which uses of the imagination led to decisive progress against prevalent suspicion and fear.

Why, in my baseball example and in two of my cases here, do I focus on the Jews? One reason is that both stupidity and viciousness were involved in the stereotypical perception of Jews of which my cases are examples. But another is that there are some more specific parallels between yesterday's anti-Semitism and today's suspicion of Muslims. In Europe for centuries, and at times in America, Jews were viewed with both fear and contempt precisely because they wanted to dress and eat differently from Christians. This problem is still endemic to European (and, less frequently, American) discussion of religious minorities. Moreover, Muslims, like Jews, are always accused of having a double loyalty, and both are seen to submit themselves to a double set of legal requirements—religious law somehow making them bad subjects of civil law.

Of course the two cases have disanalogies as well as analogies, and I do not want my discussions here to be read as mere allegories of contemporary Islamophobia. (For one thing, there is plenty of contemporary anti-Semitism still around.) I merely ask readers to ponder these cases, and then to look to see whether similar mistakes of the "inner eyes" are being made anywhere in their own societies.

Roger Williams and the Narragansett Indians

We encountered Roger Williams in Chapter 3 as a philosophical theorist of religious liberty. As the architect of Rhode Island he was also founder of the first colony (anywhere in the world, it seems) in which genuine religious liberty obtained for all.[5] Williams was, however, the sort of philosopher who cared about mental approaches and inner ways of seeing. Now we turn to one of the most remarkable aspects of his career, his lifelong friendship with the Narragansett Indians, about whom he wrote his first published book.[6]

Williams was born in England, probably in 1603, to a prosperous merchant family. He grew up in London, near the Smithfield plain, where religious dissenters had been executed for years; the executions stopped only a short time before his birth. As a young man, he attracted the attention of the distinguished lawyer Sir Edward Coke, Chief Justice of the King's Bench. On a visit back to England in 1652, writing to Coke's daughter, Mrs. Anne Sadleir, Williams recalls that the great man "was often pleased to call me his Son" and speaks of the "honorable and precious remembrance of his person and the Life the Writings the Speeches and Examples of that Glorious Light." (Mrs. Sadleir was unresponsive. A devout Anglican, she refused even to look at Williams's own writings and repudiated his gift of John Milton's *Eikonoklastes*—an indictment of the late Charles I—with the blood-curdling remark: "[Y]ou should have taken notice of gods judgment upon him who stroke him with blindness. . . . God has began his Judgment upon him here, his punishment will be here after in hell."[7] Such was the lack of curiosity surrounding him, a common norm in his time. That we speak this way less often today can be credited to the success of Roger Williams's arguments and to the political institutions his arguments helped to create.

Coke arranged for the young man's education at Sutton's Hospital, the future Charterhouse School (an elite "public school" that focused on a classical education), and then at Pembroke Hall in Cambridge University, where Williams received his A.B. in 1627. Williams quickly impressed by his remarkable flair for languages, mastering Latin, Greek, Hebrew, French, and Dutch. In this way he made John Milton's friendship: he taught Milton Dutch in exchange for receiving Hebrew lessons. This linguistic acuity would also prove a key to his most daring act of friendship.

Already critical of the Anglican orthodoxy, and appalled by violent persecution of Puritan dissenters, Williams decided that he could not live the religious life he wanted in England. He set sail for Massachusetts in 1630. At first, Williams was warmly welcomed by the leaders of Massachusetts Bay Colony.[8] Right at the start, however, he took issue with the colonists' treatment of the native inhabitants, publishing a pamphlet attacking the colonists' claims to the Indians' property. The officials of Massachusetts Bay called him into court but took no action when Williams agreed to withdraw the pamphlet. He continued, however, to teach the falsity of the colonists' property claim. During this period Williams spent some peaceful months at Plymouth, where he pursued his study of Indian life and languages, living with the Narragansett Indians for extended periods.

On the whole, the colonists viewed the natives with a mixture of fear and contempt. The Indians' paganism and their migratory lives made the colonists look down on them as primitive. Unlike Williams, these people, accustomed to European ideas of property, did not observe the regular patterns of these migrations, a linchpin of Williams's later argument that, though nomadic, they had property rights.[9] And the natives, with their painted faces and their frequent intertribal wars, also inspired fear, and fear was one crucial motivation for the colonists' interest in confiscating their lands. Indeed, the whole existence of these early European settlers was wrapped up in anxiety, since the land was wild and inhospitable, their own knowledge of it insecure. Fear and contempt are a toxic combination. In this case, they subverted any serious attempt at friendship and understanding.

By 1635–1636, the authorities saw that Williams was bent on continuing his divisive teaching. They ordered his arrest. Tipped off in advance, he fled. Looking back on the incident from Providence in 1670, he describes it this way:

> I was unkindly and unchristianly (as I believe) driven from my howse and land, and wife and children (in the midst of N. Engl. Winter now, about 35 years past). . . . I steerd my course from Salem (though in Winter snow wch I feele yet) untl these parts, whrein I may say as Jacob, Peniel, that is I have seene the Face of God.[10]

So begins the story of Rhode Island. In keeping with his sense of divine deliverance, Williams named the new settlement Providence.

A key part of the life of the new settlement was respectful friendship with the Indians. Williams had always treated them as human beings, not beasts or devils. He respected their dignity. When the great Narragansett chief Canonicus (who spoke no English) broke a stick ten times to demonstrate ten instances of broken English promises, Williams understood his meaning and sided with him.[11] When the colonists objected that the Indians could not own land because they were nomadic, Williams described their regular seasonal hunting practices, arguing that these practices were sufficient to establish property claims—a legal argument that strikingly anticipates very recent litigation over aboriginal land claims in Australia.[12] Linguist that he was, he reports having, at this period, a "Constant Zealous desire to dive into the Natives Language," and he learned several of the languages by actually living with the Indians for long periods of time: "God was pleased to give me a Painfull, Patient spirit, to lodge with them in their filthy, Smoakie holes . . . to gaine their Toung etc."[13]

When Williams arrived as a refugee, then, his dealings with the Indians had long prepared the way for a fruitful relationship. Chiefs Massasoit and Canonicus welcomed him like an old friend, because he had befriended them before he needed them and had given them lots of gifts for many years. He was already known as a good public debater in the Indian languages, "and there fore with them held as a Sachim."[14] One of the key provisions of the Charter of Rhode Island was that "itt shall not bee lawfull to or For the rest of the Collonies to invade or molest the native Indians," a provision that Williams particularly sought and, when granted, applauded, noting that hostility to the Indians "hath hietherto bene . . . practiced to our Continuall and great grievance and disturbance."[15]

Throughout his life, Williams continued these friendships. He helped the Narragansetts in their struggle against the aggressions of the Pequot tribe, daring "to put my Life into my hand, and Scarce acquainting my Wife to ship my selfe all alone in a poore Canow, and to Cut through (a stormie Wind 30 mile in great seas, every minute in hazard of Life)."[16] One gets the impression that Williams —an adventurous man, though frequently troubled by pain in his joints and limbs, very likely arthritic—enjoyed joining the Indians in these adventures with the elements. They were in many ways the truest friends he had. As he wrote to the governor of Massachusetts Bay, explaining his refusal to return, "I feel safer down here among the Christian savages along Narragansett Bay than I do among the savage Christians of Massachusetts Bay Colony."

Williams did not mean that the Indians were converts: indeed, he explains in his book *A Key into the Language of America* that he did not attempt to convert them. The Indians' behavior, for Williams, expressed the Christian spirit of love more truly than did the severities of Massachusetts. He was fond of noting examples of Indian decency and honesty, contrasting the behavior of the natives with that of the English, or of his Massachusetts neighbors.[17] "It is a strange truth," he wrote in *Key*, "that a man shall generally finde more free entertainment and refreshing amongst these Barbarians, then amongst thousands that call themselves Christians."[18] Near the end of his life, he recalled that he never denied to Canonicus or (his successor) Miantonomi "[w]hatever they desired of me as to goods or gifts or use of my boats or pinnace, and the travel [that is, travails] of my own person, day and night, which, though men know not, nor care to know, yet the all-seeing Eye hath seen it, and his all-powerful hand hath helped me."[19] Significantly, then, he imagines God as pleased by his generosity to "Barbarians." In one of his letters from England, he adds at the end: "P.S., My love to all my Indian friends."[20]

On a voyage back to England in 1643, Williams occupied his time by writing *Key*, which was published shortly in Britain. Ostensibly it is a language primer, and it does indeed contain very valuable evidence of Narragansett language, though it is more a phrasebook than an analytical grammar. The point of the book is, however, clearly more profound. It is a set of instructions to Englishmen about how to deal with natives when they meet them, and how to think about them should they not meet them. Williams supplies ample commentary on Indian customs and behavior, the general point of which is to get Christians to recognize that pagans can have moral virtues that Christians do not always attain. But even the linguistic instruction is highly significant. In telling people the phrases Williams thinks they need to know, he is really telling them what they ought to be saying to new people who look strange and inspire fear.

As we saw, the first phrase Williams teaches the reader to say is, "What cheare, Nétop"—explaining, "Nétop is friend." A combination of curiosity and amity, then, animates the recommended approach. This phrase, says Williams, "is the general salutation of all English toward them." But of course he knows that it usually isn't: by "is the general salutation" he means "ought to be the salutation," or "is the proper salutation." Next, since the first utterance he recommends is a linguistic hybrid, he tells the English that they really ought to do more to learn the language, or at least some of it: "They are exceedingly delighted with Salutations in their own Language." This simple recommendation is also profound: if you want to deal well with people, try to learn at least some phrases in their language, going part way to meet them.

This advice is followed by a short list of things the traveler might try out first:

Neèn, Keèn Ewò	I, you, he
Keén ka neen	you and I
Asco wequássin,	
Asco wequassunnúmmis	Good morrow.
Askuttaaquompsìn?	How doe you?
Asnpaumpmaûntam	I am very well.
Taubot paumpmaúntaman	I am glad you are well.
Cowaúnckamish	My service to you.

Recall that this book was published in England and thus read by people a tiny minority of whom would ever have occasion to use any of these phrases—and you see that what the book provides is a general meditation on human attentiveness and courtesy. Williams's list is crucial because he is showing the reader that a book about others really ought to be about them and their language, their ways of looking at the world. The list also exemplifies courtesy and respect. English travelers probably would not have reached for those phrases first in dealing with half-naked "savages" without Williams's refined awareness to guide them. The Indians were profoundly scary to the English, and it is easier to think of them simply as dangerous savages than to figure out how to deal with their humanity.

Keén ka neen, "you and I," establishes parity, like a level gaze of the eyes. And "my service to you" reminds the English that a traveler ought to be generous to hosts who are themselves receiving him graciously.

Williams shortly makes this theme explicit. After he teaches the phrase, "Why come you not in?" he comments, "In this respect they are remarkably free and courteous, to invite all Strangers in; and if any come to them upon any occasion they request them to *come in*, if they come not in of themselves." Another two-column list follows, of which I give only the English:

Warme you.
Sit by the fire.
What say you?
Is it you friend?
Come hither friend.
Come in.
Have you seene me?
I have seen you.
I thank you for your kind remembrance.
I thank you.
I thank you for your love.
. . .
I love you.
He loves you.
You are loving.
Understand you?
I understand.

Once again, in translating, Williams is also recommending: these are the first things to say when someone who has different customs, religion, and language has invited you in. They are not the things usually said first to "savages" or "infidels." The end of this remarkable first chapter is a poem about courtesy:

> The courteous Pagan shall condemne
> Uncourteous Englishmen,
> Who live like Foxes, Beares, and Wolves,
> Or Lyon in his Den.

> Let none sing blessings to their soules,
> For that they Courteous are:
> The wild Barbarians with no more
> Then Nature, goe so farre:
>
> If Natures sons both wild and tame,
> Humane and Courteous be:
> How ill becomes it Sonnes of God
> To want Humanity?[21]

This poem makes it perfectly clear that Williams does not think the English strongly inclined to courtesy, or eager to learn the phrases that courtesy recommends. But he is simply not going to allow them to speak "like Foxes, Beares, and Wolves": by shaping what they know how to say in Narragansett, he shapes a new mode of interaction.

After 150 pages, Williams does get around to the language of wrong doing and anger. He does teach the English how to say (and hear) things like "You are a lying fellow," and "I will revenge it."[22] However, lest the reader think narcissistically that error is all in the other, he immediately follows these lists with another "Observation": "I could never discerne that excesse of scandalous sins amongst them, which Europe aboundeth with." Despite their superior access to religious truth, the English are in many areas inferior when it comes to moral conduct. Williams concludes this section with another poem, whose final stanza is:

> We weare no Cloaths, have many Gods,
> And yet our sinnes are lesse:
> You are Barbarians, Pagans wild,
> Your Land's the Wildernesse.[23]

Once again, we should be clear that Williams is not uncritical of the Indians. He consistently emphasizes the fact that their religion is entirely misguided, and he is particularly critical of their custom of covering their faces with paint, which he thinks contrary to divine law. But he was far-sighted enough to recognize how abysmal the behavior of the English toward the Indians usually was: in a straight comparison, the Indians (at least as regards that relationship) come out morally ahead. Williams speaks, here, as an Indian: his "we" is they, but it includes himself.

More generally, taking issue with a group's religion, and indeed its entire way of life, does not mean failing to appreciate its people's virtues, or the lack of "humanity" involved in treating them as less than fully human. English readers of his language book learn, at the same time, how to start off on the right foot in a new relationship.

Jews in Eighteenth-Century Europe: Lessing's *Nathan der Weise*

For centuries, the Jews in Europe, like the Native Americans in the colonies, were regarded with a mixture of fear and contempt. (Indeed, we really should not use the past tense, since negative stereotypes are still widespread: the 2011 Pew survey on religious attitudes shows improvement in favorable judgments about Jews, but still, in Spain only 59 percent view Jews favorably, by contrast to a 76 percent favorable view of Christians; Britain and Russia also have large gaps, while France and Germany approve of Jews and Christians in equal measure.[24]) The situation of Jews, of course, was very different from that of the Native Americans, since Jews were understood to be highly intelligent and capable of intellectual excellence—despite the severe obstacles to education and professional success that all

European nations put in their way (if they did not expel them utterly, as did Britain between the year 1290 and the Protectorate of Cromwell in the seventeenth century). Judaism was also to a certain extent recognized as a religion akin to Christianity. Christians accepted Jewish scriptures as part of their sacred canon, though they usually believed that the morality of the New Testament had superceded that of the Old. Rarely did people fully acknowledge that Christ was a Jew of Near Eastern birth; works of art typically depicted him with European features and coloring.

Contempt for the Jews focused on their alleged greed and their association with usury (which was an artifact of other professional restrictions, though rarely recognized as such). The sense that Jews were mercenary and were incapable of spiritual refinement crept into people's understanding of the Jewish religion. At the same time, Jews were feared as the nation that had murdered Christ, and a persistent fiction known as the "blood libel" held that Jews murdered Christian children to use their blood for ritual purposes.[25] No doubt the achievements of the Jews in areas of life to which they were allowed to contribute gave still further fuel to suspicion and animosity.

As we ponder possible analogues between European anti-Semitism and today's widespread fear and contempt for Muslims, it is important to understand the key role played by Jewish separatism and non-assimilation. As Shakespeare's Shylock is made to say, "I will buy with you, sell with you, talk with you, walk with you, and so following, but I will not eat with you, drink with you, nor pray with you."[26] This refusal of a common social life, combined with conspicuous difference in dress, was understood to make the Jews unfit for normal citizenship, which Europeans (though not Americans in colonial times) understood to require homogeneity of custom.

The *Protocols of the Elders of Zion,* discussed in Chapter 2, summarizes and crystallizes centuries of prejudice. That phony but widely credited document illustrates the obstacles that any attempt to establish a politics of equal respect and sympathy in Europe would have to overcome. The idea that the Jews always lie (familiar today in its Islamic variant, as people frequently observe that the Quran tells Muslims to deceive others about their real purposes)—that Jews are acting a part when they behave like good citizens or even potential friends—undermines trust and genuine curiosity and openness. The idea that there is a conspiracy to take over the world and that all Jews are somehow a part of it, especially when they seem not to be, stifles learning while being extremely difficult to refute, since all evidence is taken to confirm it. How, in such an atmosphere, could a different set of attitudes be encouraged?

One remarkable example of clear-eyed reasoning, in the Kantian-Christian style I recommended in Chapter 4, is Christian Wilhelm von Dohm's "Concerning the Amelioration of the Civil Status of the Jews" (1781). In this influential document, Dohm undertakes to convince Germans that the Jews ought to have full civil rights—a task that required refuting various harmful myths about them.[27] Dohm's treatise stirred up a spirited debate, in which the great Jewish philosopher Moses Mendelssohn (1729-1786) played a leading part, supporting and publicizing Dohm's arguments.

Dohm addresses, first, a fear that Jews hate gentiles and will therefore feel free to commit crimes against them; he replies that if some do hate gentiles, their resentment is amply justified by their centuries of mistreatment, and is thus really the fault of the oppressors. Furthermore, Jewish scripture—which Christians, too, regard as sacred—forbids crimes very clearly and provides a fine foundation for modern citizenship, if only prejudice and ill-treatment would be removed.

Dohm also addresses the more subtle anxiety about the fact that Jews stick to their own group and don't befriend or mingle with others. This, he nicely points out, is actually true of most religious groups in all times and places, only the majority doesn't notice it is doing this, because it's so ubiquitous. As for the idea that Jews are mercenary and immersed in greed, this prejudice arises from laws that confine the Jews to money-making and would be removed by giving them equal rights and access to all the professions. Part of equal rights would be equal religious rights. Very significantly, in light of our contemporary debates about the building of mosques, Dohm then argues that part of equal civil rights for Jews would be the right to build synagogues "in all places."

Dohm is an assimilationist to a mild degree: he thinks that Jews should be required to learn the dominant language of their country, and perhaps in professional education they might even be required to be educated alongside Christians in the dominant language. Still, he devotes yet more emphasis to the need for all Christians to educate themselves, and thus assimilate themselves to a world with Jews in it, getting rid of their "prejudices and uncharitable opinions." He outlines a plan for education in pluralism that begins with childhood: young people should be taught "to regard the Jews as their brothers and fellow men who seek to find favor with God in a different way."

Dohm reasons well, and his arguments were influential. They show us what clear-eyed argument in the Kantian-Christian mode (not making a privileged case of oneself, and casting out the plank in one's own eye before impugning the flaws of another) can achieve in divided religious times. But people usually don't drop entrenched fears because they hear a good argument: in that respect Dohm was preaching to the converted, or at least to the relatively open-minded, whose inner eyes had already been cultivated to some extent.

Another work, addressed to the imagination, went further, preparing the way for Dohm's arguments to have the influence they did: the play *Nathan der Weise,* or *Nathan the Wise* (1770), by Gotthold Ephraim Lessing, one of Germany's most renowned dramatists (1729–1781). Lessing was a philosopher as well as a playwright, and his skill in argument is not irrelevant to the success of his play. A close friend of Moses Mendelssohn, he portrayed his friend's ideas (and his personality) in the character of Nathan, as was widely recognized. The play has had a towering significance in world literature, however—and is still popular in Germany today, while Mendelssohn's ideas are generally forgotten—because of the power of the poetry and narrative in which Lessing (a pioneer of bourgeois realist drama, who attached importance to the particularity of character depiction) realizes the abstract principles involved.

Throughout his career, Lessing was concerned with the situation of the Jews in Germany. An early drama *Die Juden* (*The Jews,* 1749) deals with the widespread prejudice that Jews are mean-spirited and ignoble. Lessing represents them as capable of nobility of character. The Jewish traveler is loved as a fine man before his identity as a Jew is known. When it is revealed, the Baron has to conclude that Jews can be fine people, and we understand that prejudice against Jews would probably have prevented him from seeing that fact had the traveler's identity not been concealed. But Lessing then turns the screw in Dohm-like fashion: the traveler responds that he has now just learned that Christians can be generous, and it would be a good thing if all Christians behaved as well as the Baron. The majority is used to thinking the minority ignoble, and feels it is behaving magnanimously when it is prepared to make exceptions to this generalization. The minority, however, feels that the whole imposition of stereotypes is ungenerous, and that it is the rare person who is prepared to look at the individual with a glimmer of imagination.[28]

In *Nathan*, Lessing's aim is far more ambitious: to map out, and to realize in people of flesh and blood, a general idea about how people different in religion should interact in a decent society. Set in Jerusalem during the time of the Crusades, the play concerns not two but three religions. There are Christian knights who have come to Jerusalem to convert and conquer; there are, naturally, Muslims, including the twelfth-century sultan Saladin (1138–1193), a ruler renowned throughout Europe for his wisdom and chivalry; and, finally, there is a family of fictitious Jews who live in Jerusalem, on good terms with the Muslims: the merchant Nathan is the head of this household. Nathan's wife and seven children have been burned some years before in a pogrom, but he is bringing up Recha, a young orphan, as his stepdaughter. The complex plot has many aspects, including some comic relief and some romance.

The center of the work, however, and a part that has become independently famous, is a scene between Saladin and Nathan, in which, pressed by the monarch to tell him which religion is true, Nathan responds with a parable.[29] A valuable ring had been passed down in a certain family, the father always giving it to the son whom he loved best, regardless of birth order, until it came to a particular father, who had three sons whom he loved equally, and who seemed equally worthy. In moments of weakness he promised the ring to each of the three. As death neared, he didn't know what to do, so he asked a famous artist to make two duplicate rings. The artist succeeded so well that from that time forward nobody could tell which ring was real and which was imitation.

The sons fell to fighting and took their case to a judge. The judge said that, given that the father was no longer around, he could not settle the question, but: one property of the true ring is that it makes its wearer beloved. So all three had better live so as to be beloved, and that way the one with the true ring might be discovered. Of course each must strive to aid the ring with his own efforts: "With gentleness and heartiest friendliness, / With benevolence and true devotedness to God." Maybe at the end of time some other judge will finally be able to settle the matter.

Nathan tells Saladin that this is similar to the situation of the three major religions in society. Each person thinks he has the true one, but they are so similar, as guides to life, that it's impossible to adjudicate the question. What, says Saladin? Aren't the three very different in clothing, food, and drink? Sure, says Nathan, but not in their core and their ultimate basis. For one thing, all get their warrant from historical texts that are intrinsically slippery. At the end of time the rivalry among them might be cleared up, but as for the present time, what we can all do is to live with generosity and brotherhood toward one another, loving all humanity and trying to make ourselves worthy of being the heirs to the true religion, whatever it is. This exchange cements a close friendship between Saladin and Nathan.

Eventually it emerges (as a very complicated story unfolds) that the three faiths are also linked by previously unknown family ties: Recha (Nathan's foster-daughter) and the young Christian knight turn out to be the nephew and niece of Saladin's brother Assad. "Now you have to love me," jokes Saladin. And of course the point is that we are all blood brothers at some remove, and ought to have to one another the attitude of kinship that the play's plot, and the parable of the rings, suggest.

Nathan der Weise was a huge success when it was first produced, and it really did influence attitudes. Its popularity has continued, and it has entered the canon of German literature. It continues to influence attitudes today. Taught as a required text in all German and Austrian schools at around the age of fourteen, it has become a catalyst for classroom discussion of religious friendship and the treatment of Muslims and other subgroups. Its philosophical argument can be found in many sources; but the appealing portrayal of complex personalities and the power of poetry have been able to get under people's skins even when they are not terribly interested in philosophical first principles.

The story has its flaws. For example, even Nathan does not appear to be able to imagine the possibility that, at the end of the day, there could be more than one acceptable way to pursue spiritual understanding. Nor does anyone suggest that polytheists, agnostics, and atheists can also join the company of the morally virtuous. But the basic idea is also Roger Williams's: when we encounter people who differ in religion, we ought to focus on ethical virtues of generosity, kindness, and love, leaving the question of religious truth to one side in our civic interactions.

Jews in Nineteenth-Century Britain: George Eliot's *Daniel Deronda*

Britain had—and to some degree still has—a long history of anti-Semitism, recently documented in Anthony Julius's relentless and brilliant book *Trials of the Diaspora*.[30] Because the Jews were expelled

in 1290, and their unofficial readmission began only in the Protectorate in the mid-seventeenth century, a lot of British anti-Semitism
was based on sheer fantasy. (Indeed it is thus a particularly pure case
of the fact that prejudice against a group always involves fantasy: as
Ellison says, if the inner eyes aren't cultivated people see only aspects of themselves.) Astonishingly, then, the public who reacted to
Shakespeare's portrait of Shylock had never seen Jews and could assess Shakespeare's portrayal only by comparing it to other literary
and traditional constructions. Once readmitted, Jews continued to
be the target of both legal prohibitions and social ostracism for a
very long time; the "blood libel" played a key role in making Jews
objects of fear as well as contempt, and fictional portraits of Jews,
from Shylock to Dickens's Fagin (*Oliver Twist*, 1838–1839), show them
as lacking in key virtues of charity and generosity.

During the mid-nineteenth century, these attitudes began to shift
gradually. The claim that Jews should not be admitted to political
office because they could never be good citizens—a claim that re-
curs with depressing regularity concerning almost every new religious group—no longer commanded universal assent. The influential writer Thomas Babington Macaulay subjected that argument
to withering scorn in an article published in the *Edinburgh Review*
in 1831:

> If all the red-haired people in Europe had, for centuries,
> been outraged and oppressed, banished from this place,
> imprisoned in that, deprived of their money, deprived of
> their teeth, convicted of the most improbable crimes on
> the feeblest evidence, dragged at horses' tails, hanged, tor-
> tured, burned alive, if, when manners became milder, they
> had still remained subject to debasing restrictions, and

exposed to vulgar insults, . . . what would be the patriotism of gentlemen with red hair? And if, under such circumstances, a proposition were made for admitting red-
haired men to office, how striking a speech might an
eloquent admirer of our old institutions deliver against so
revolutionary a measure! "These men," he might say,
"scarcely consider themselves as Englishmen. They think
a red-haired Frenchman or a red-haired German more
closely connected with them than a man with brown hair
born in their own parish. If a foreign sovereign patronises
red hair, they love him better than their own native king.
They are not Englishmen—they cannot be Englishmen—
Nature has forbidden it—experience proved it to be impossible. . . . [I]f they ask for leave to exercise power over a
community of which they are only half members—a community, the constitution of which is essentially dark-
haired—let us answer them in the words of our wise ances-
tors, *Nolumus leges Angliae mutari.* [We are not willing to
change the laws of England.]"[31]

This argument is in one sense a good Socratic-Kantian argument:
it asks people to have consistent standards about qualifications for
public office and not to withhold full civil rights by appeal to a characteristic that is irrelevant to the capacity to be a loyal and good
citizen. But it also ducks one key issue, for it assumes that being
Jewish is merely skin-deep, that a person's religion really is as superficial as hair color and can as easily cease to be a mode of organization of a person's life. In the example, red hair is important only because of the prejudices of others. But Jewishness, like other religious
identities, has an importance for many if not most of its possessors

that goes beyond the stereotypes that make it a source of social disadvantage. Macaulay is, in essence, an assimilationist of a far stronger type than Dohm: he thinks Jews will in effect stop being Jews as soon as Englishmen stop maltreating them. But he would not say the same of Christianity and Christians: so his imagination has not done enough work. He has not tried to imagine the distinctive ways of life that Jews lead in Britain, and why those ways, and the identity they compose, matter. That task requires both learning and imagination; it was performed with distinction by the great novelist George Eliot in her 1876 novel *Daniel Deronda*.

In 1858, Jews were allowed to sit in Parliament: the key oath was revised so that reference to "the true faith of a Christian" was made optional. Lionel de Rothschild, covering his head and swearing, "So help me, Jehovah," became the first Jewish member of Parliament. (The first atheist was seated only much later, in 1886.) Benjamin Disraeli, baptized at the age of twelve, but a Jew in culture and public perception, served as prime minister from 1874 to 1880. (Britain has never since had a Jewish prime minister.) But social attitudes change slowly, and Jews were still perceived in terms of a variety of demeaning stereotypes. As Eliot wrote to American writer Harriet Beecher Stowe:

> Can anything be more disgusting than to hear people
> called "educated" making small jokes about eating ham,
> and showing themselves empty of any real knowledge as
> to the relation of their own social and religious life to the
> history of the people they think themselves witty in in-
> sulting? They hardly know that Christ was a Jew. And I
> find men educated at Rugby supposing that Christ spoke
> Greek. To my mind, this deadness to the history which

has prepared half our world for us, this inability to find interest in any form of life that is not clad in the same coat-tails and flounces as our own lies very close to the worst kind of irreligion. The best that can be said of it is, that it is a sign of the intellectual narrowness—in plain English, the *stupidity* which is still the average mark of our culture.[32]

Eliot describes a social situation, but she does much more. In characteristic fashion, she links moral error with laziness of the imagination. What is wrong with the "educated" English is that they don't have any curiosity about people different from themselves; they have never gone out of themselves to inhabit, in thought, a different way of life. But this "stupidity" is, she says, akin to "the worst kind of irreligion." Why? Because the same narcissism that makes us think that we can go through life with other people without making any effort of the imagination is also a central form of moral error, the form that makes laws only for ourselves, and denies the reality and equality of others. In one deft paragraph, Eliot shows why good ethical principles are incomplete without imagination.

Eliot's own interest in the Jews led her to learn Hebrew and to go through a massive task of self-education, which she recorded in her journals, with an awe-inspiring list of the readings she had completed.[33] So too her hero. Daniel Deronda began, she tells us, by thinking of the Jews as an antiquated sect, following the quite narcissistic custom of the English of thinking of Judaism as all about them, the Christians. Judaism is just an archaic form of Christianity:

> The Chosen People have been commonly treated as a people chosen for the sake of somebody else; and their think-

ing as something (no matter exactly what) that ought to
have been entirely otherwise; and Deronda, like his neigh-
bours, had regarded Judaism as a sort of eccentric fossil-
ized form, which an accomplished man might dispense
with studying, and leave to specialists. . . . This wakening
of a new interest—this passing from the supposition that
we hold the right opinions on a subject we are careless
about, to a sudden care for it, and a sense that our opinions were ignorance—is an effective remedy for *ennui,*
which unhappily cannot be secured on a physician's pre-
scription.[34]

Deronda is not curious about Jews at the outset, but his mobile
imagination prepares him to become curious, the moment it is set
in motion. But his whole life is soon to undergo a profound transformation. A chance encounter with Mirah, a young Jewish woman
in search of her family, propels him into the Jewish world, where he
begins an odyssey of learning and friendship that culminates in the
discovery that his own origins are Jewish. Rather than being, as he
believed, the illegitimate child of the aristocrat who raised him, he
is the son of a Jewish opera singer who left her family and community to pursue her career, entrusting her (legitimate) child to the
aristocrat to bring up. This discovery of his identity, however, is a
plot device—and a creaky one, since it distracts the reader's attention from the main story, which is one of curiosity, imagination,
and friendship, by suggesting that all of Deronda's morally admirable traits are but the superficial expression of a blood tie.

Putting this problem to one side, we may focus on the theme that
Eliot makes central: the unshackling of the mind. Made "stupid"
by the prejudices around him, Deronda has a great advantage over

most of his contemporaries—he thinks and feels: "His early-wakened sensibility and reflectiveness had developed into a many-sided sympathy." His "plenteous, flexible sympathy" includes a highly developed capacity for "seeing things as they probably appeared to others."[35] At this point in his life, Eliot emphasizes, this perspectival tendency has led Deronda to be chronically indecisive, incapable of strong partisanship because he can always see the point of view of the other side. As he matures, he becomes more capable of combining sympathy with effective commitment. But sympathy is the best preparation for his encounter with a different tradition. In effect, his attitude is that of the inquiring novelist: he wants to learn, travel, get the facts, but he also wants to immerse himself in relations with real people whom he sees as highly varied individuals. Thus from the beginning his relationships with Mirah, Ezra Cohen, and the tubercular intellectual Mordecai are uncluttered by any view that they must be all the same because they are all Jewish.

As Anthony Julius argues, *Daniel Deronda* marks a new era in the literary portrayal of Jews in England, not simply because of its favorable attitude and genuine curiosity, but for five specific reasons: (1) It contains no conversion narrative and no marriage across religious lines. (This feature is the flip side of what I have called the "creaky" nature of the story of Deronda's birth, but Julius is right to see its positive side.) (2) It breaks with a tendency to represent Jews as always and centrally Jewish and all alike in their Jewishness, by showing us a wide range of Jewish types, including Zionists, philosophical liberals (in the Philosophers' Club), antireligious defectors (Deronda's mother), and even a totally amoral scoundrel (Mirah's father). (3) It shows love to be fully at home in the Jewish context, thus subverting Shakespeare's famous association of Judaism with revenge, love with Christianity. (4) It focuses only incidentally on anti-Semitism, preferring to stand inside Jewish life and to see it as not wholly defined by the majority.[36] (5) Finally, it is to Christians, not Jews, that punishment is meted out: Grandcourt dies, Gwendolyn is left to a lonely and unhappy life.[37]

These achievements are all significant, and Julius is right to emphasize them. But Eliot's plan is not simply to stage a literary "coup": it is to show all these insights as the outgrowth of a certain type of imagination, which is exemplified by the novelist's own work in constructing the novel, as much as it is by her character's odyssey within it. By following the prose of the novelist, the reader is receiving a training in friendship and sympathy across cultural lines.

Daniel Deronda has some serious flaws of execution. As in her Florentine historical novel *Romola,* here too Eliot does not wear her learning lightly enough. *Romola* is (at least to me) virtually unreadable, so thick is the instruction in political and intellectual history, and so obtrusive is the author's pride in her learning,: "Look at me, I can show Machiavelli as a character in my novel, and isn't it well done!" *Deronda* has far less of this irritating air of proclaiming a superior education, and yet it is not utterly free from it. As a result, the author stands squarely at center stage in the Jewish portions of the book, and the characters themselves are less psychologically interesting than the Christian characters, whom Eliot permits to have their own errant life. Thus one is hardly sure, at the end, that one has come to know individual Jews (surely Eliot's plan), rather than high-minded abstract figures of Jews. Indeed, the rebellious mother, who appears only briefly at the novel's end, and the con-artist father, who also plays a lamentably small part, are perhaps the most successfully realized Jewish characters, because they do not have to bear the weight of showing how good Jews can be, and thus they are permitted to have an internal tension and complexity that the Cohens and Deronda lack.

One more achievement of the novel remains to be discussed. As we've seen, even British philo-Semites tended to be assimilationists. Macauley represents Jewish particularism as an artifact of persecution, and the assumption behind his analogy to red hair is that a distinctive mode of Jewish life will disappear when persecution ceases. Whether he is aware of Zionism is unclear, but his point about divided loyalties surely applies: any search for a homeland outside of one's own country of residence is also an artifact of being treated as if one had no right to be there, and can be expected to drop away when integration is achieved. As Gertrude Himmelfarb emphasizes in her excellent treatment of Eliot's encounter with Judaism, one of the most original features of *Daniel Deronda* is, consequently, its keen sympathy with Zionism. Mordecai, the intellectual and dreamer, is unable to go to Eretz Israel himself, because he is dying prematurely, so he entrusts his dreams to Deronda, who, at the novel's close, is bound for the Holy Land with his new bride, Mirah. This courageous insistence that some Jews of integrity may always resist assimilation and may indeed have a double loyalty—and that this is reason to admire their quest rather than to persecute them—sets Eliot apart from even the more liberal of her contemporaries.

There is, nonetheless, something confused about the way in which Eliot renders the issue of non-assimilation. For there is a missing, or at least a very underdeveloped, alternative: that Jews might remain in Europe, and yet still opt for a distinctive way of life, including distinctive dress, dietary customs, and worship. There is absolutely no reason a distinctive Jewish identity need be linked to

Israel, nor should any Jew be put in the uncomfortable position of choosing between assimilation and emigration. The alternative we've been pursuing all through these chapters is one of respectful friendly life together. In that sense, I feel Deronda's departure for Palestine as a capitulation. He, and Mordecai, have written off England, prematurely.

Like *Nathan der Weise*, then, *Daniel Deronda* has flaws as political philosophy, and it also has flaws in artistry. And yet, the courage of its imaginative undertaking, in a culture full of intellectual and imaginative "stupidity," is impressive, enacting the theme of moral perception that it also depicts.

Books for Young Children: Marguerite de Angeli

Williams, Lessing, and Eliot all addressed mature and highly educated readers. But attitudes to other religions are formed early. Even if they can be altered later, as were Daniel Deronda's, a pluralistic society is well advised to begin young. Children learn attitudes from parents, peer culture, television, and films, as well as (decreasingly, perhaps) from books. This section is only, therefore, an example of what can be done to challenge the imagination, and was done in the pre-television era; any constructive program for today should focus on popular media as well as on books. It should certainly not ignore books, however, since they can mold a classroom experience.

Books about minorities for young children often seem facile to adults: they are apt to avoid many truly difficult issues and to represent the minority characters in an implausibly sweet and idealized manner. The books to be discussed here are not free of this failing, and perhaps it is not even a failing, when the subculture in question has long been vilified and subjected to demeaning stereotyping. A little idealization is not so bad, as the social influence of *The Cosby Show* shows.

It is also important to bear in mind that children's literature is always on the political firing line, even if in hindsight it seems very anodyne. The 1981 Danish book *Jenny Lives with Eric and Martin*, which showed a little girl living with her father and his male partner, with her mother a frequent visitor—and doing such outrageous things as planning a birthday party and doing laundry—not only caused a scandal in Britain but also led to the passage of a law that remained on the books from 1986 to 2003, forbidding public libraries from purchasing books "promoting homosexuality" or representing "the acceptability of homosexuality as a pretended family relationship." (Part of the outrage was clearly cultural: the British public did not like the idea that the men were lying in bed barechested; despite the fact that Jenny was sitting on top of the covers, they suspected that all-too-Scandinavian nakedness lay beneath.) So what seems tepid in a children's book may actually be quite bold, given the resistance of the bigoted imagination at a particular time.

I choose just one author, as an example of how children's literature can work. In keeping with my aim to detach these studies from the heated controversies of today, I remain in the past, although in this case not the very long past. Indeed, one reason for my interest in these books is that I grew up with them. Despite being brought up in an extremely conservative upper-middle-class home in suburban Philadelphia, I somehow was given or found these books, and perhaps the charm and respectability of their author eclipsed from my parents their subversive character.

Marguerite de Angeli (1889–1987) was a prolific author and illustrator for children. During her long life, she wrote many well-known books, mostly aimed at girls around eight to twelve, the ages of most of her leading characters. Because she and her husband moved a lot and she was busy raising a large family, she published her first book at the age of forty-seven, by which time she was settled in the Philadelphia area, where many of her books are set. De Angeli's subject was minority experience, and her most common focus was religious minorities. Her heroines (and the occasional hero) included young people who were Amish, Mennonite, Swedish-American Lutheran (in the seventeenth century), Quaker, African-American, Polish-American, and, in one case, a child with physical disabilities. Her stories were low-key, but they sometimes took on large social issues, particularly in the areas of race and poverty. Her religious minorities were not the most controversial ones: there is nothing about Mormons or Jehovah's Witnesses in her work, to my knowledge, and there is no book primarily about Jews, although Jews do figure prominently as characters. Even where she dealt with a "popular" minority, such as the Amish, however, her aim was always to present the humanity in people, so that young readers would not sentimentalize them as cardboard cutout figures. Her children are usually mischievous and rebellious in some ways, and yet ultimately loving and loved. Young people can be entertained by the scrapes they get into without being alienated by them, and the point usually is to indicate that recognizable human emotions animate an otherwise strange world—about which De Angeli gives, in a deft way, a huge amount of interesting information, some of it linguistic in Roger Williams's way. (The dialect of the Pennsylvania Amish, for example, is conveyed in a simplified way, but still shows the reader that they have different ways of seeing and naming things.)

De Angeli is interested in difference, and a great part of the allure of her books is the chance to learn about customs, foods, games, and ways of talking in different groups and in some cases at different times. She did really listen to other people's voices: *Thee Hannah!*, for example, was based on the oral history given her by an elderly Quaker friend of her family who was active in the Underground Railroad. She has no interest in assimilation: her minorities are proud of their differences, or, if they rebel, they ultimately learn to take pride in what sets them apart. But at the same time she is to some extent a universalist about the heart, and this is a key to her plots: people recognize one another's humanity across lines of difference and learn to see others as friends despite their differences of race or creed. We might imagine that this is how Roger Williams would have written for children, if that idea had ever occurred to him. Let's examine just two books more closely.

Thee, Hannah!, a classic that has been read more or less continuously since its original publication in 1940, tells the story of a nine-year-old Quaker girl in Philadelphia at the time of the Civil War.[38] In this context it should be remembered that Quakers were not exactly an approved or popular minority in Philadelphia, even when I was growing up there. Their pacifism has been a problem since the days of George Washington's Letter, and it was certainly a problem during the Second World War. Later on, when I became acquainted with the book, during the Cold War, Quakers were often suspected of being "fellow travelers," and my family forbade me to apply to any Quaker-administered college, such as Oberlin or Swarthmore, on the grounds that they were "pink." The editor of the *Main Line Chronicle*, a local newspaper for which I briefly wrote a column while in high school, was constantly attacking Haverford College (also Quaker, but only for males in those days) as "pink" and anti-American, and I was frequently torn between my ambition to see my words in print and my disapproval of the editorial voice of the one paper that would print me. So Quakers were not like the Amish: they were regarded by many as a "fifth column."

Much of the book is a family drama. Hannah is a restless nine-year-old who longs for the fancy clothes that she sees all around her. Although her mother tries to explain Quaker ideas of simplicity and innerness, and although the importance of conscience as an inner "light" and "stopping voice" is also made clear to her repeatedly, she keeps getting into trouble through her taste for fashion: for a pink sash, some frilly pantalets. Readers are likely to sympathize with her at this point, since the drabness of Quaker dress will seem very constraining and pointless, and little girls like to dress up—but Hannah's mother makes an impression from the start, and we want to know more about what these people stand for.

In the key episode, Hannah is walking through the Philadelphia streets in her Quaker bonnet when she is approached by a runaway slave woman with a small child. They have traveled along the Underground Railroad, hoping to join the woman's husband, a free shipyard worker in Boston. Hannah mobilizes her family, and her parents soon feed the pair and help keep their secret. Eventually the whole family plays a part in sneaking them on board a boat bound for Boston. As they say goodbye, the black woman tells Hannah that she called out to her because she recognized the Quaker bonnet and knew that she could trust her: she was a "Friend." (And all Philadelphia children knew the word "friend" for Quakers, from its use in the names of Quaker-founded schools such as Germantown Friends and Friends Central.) Hannah for the first time feels proud of her bonnet: "It was something to be proud of just as it was—without any flowers or ribbons like Cecily's. She looked up at Mother with the 'inner light' shining through her eyes."

This story is quite predictable and simple in its way, but it does tell children about a crucial period of American history and about the role of those "pinkos" in that history—their willingness to run risks that few were willing to run, for the sake of justice and humanity. It also raises themes of simplicity versus extravagance, of conscience versus external authority, and of how religious conviction can be connected to social action, that are crucial for both Quakers and non-Quakers to ponder.

By far De Angeli's most daring book, however, is *Bright April*, a 1947 story of racism in the Germantown neighborhood of Philadelphia.[39] In fact, even much later, when I was the age of ten-year-old April, living right next door to Germantown, it was a daring book, and I am not quite sure how it got into my house, except through the established prestige of the author and, probably, my own excursions to the local public library. The story concerns race, not religion, but religion is part of it, through the role of the Jewish characters, and a parallel is drawn between racial and religious exclusion. It seems appropriate to include it here because it focuses on general defects of human imagining and how to overcome them.

April Bright is a nice ten-year-old African-American girl, the daughter of a homemaker mother and a postman who has just been decorated for twenty years' service to the U.S. Post Office. She has three siblings: one older brother, around twelve, is in school but happier when he is drumming; he works for extra income in a drug store on weekends. Her older sister is a nurse. The oldest child in the family is in the army, about to be discharged, but anxious about returning to a racially fraught society. He has received some training in architecture and has been able to use it to some extent in the army, but he wants to know what job opportunities he is coming home to. The clearest example of upward mobility is an uncle who has just been appointed to the faculty of "that famous music school in New York"—an accurate picture of the fact that some avenues of advancement were less closed to African Americans than were others.

April's family is a bit Cosbyish in its ideal decency, but it is not Cosbyish in privilege, and economic constraint is everywhere.[40] Her parents are frugal and obsessed with mending clothes, repairing the house, cleaning everything—in short, with maintaining an appearance of respectability. They are fearful of a downhill slide, as some houses in their neighborhood start to look rundown and some people don't take care of their clothes. (April even wears gloves when she goes on an outing to the dentist downtown! As a well-off white child ten years later, I was required to wear a hat when going downtown, but not gloves.) April's mother constantly tells her that they all have to have self-respect if they want others to respect them, and, indeed, a recurrent motif is that of cleanliness winning over the suspicious. In subtle ways, De Angeli depicts a society dominated by hidden disgust. April is always conscious that others are aware of her skin, wherever she goes, and that they are not sure she is as clean as they are.

Prejudice has other manifestations: her adolescent brother Tom is harassed by the police on vague suspicions when he is simply hanging out on a block where some thefts have recently taken place. Only the sterling reputation of his father convinces the authorities not to tarnish his record with a false charge. And the whole family is aware that their father was passed over for the number one position in the Post Office, despite having greater merit and seniority than the man who got the job.

Fortunately for April, she has a best friend, Sophie Meyer, whose Jewish family welcomes her enthusiastically and even tells her the story of Passover, and how it signifies freedom for all people. April's mother, for her part, encourages that friendship. She points out that Passover and Easter are historically the same holiday, and that "none of us can have freedom or peace unless we all have it." (April, then, starts life ahead of most of George Eliot's contemporaries, who do not realize that Christ was a Jew.) The theme of black-Jewish friendship and understanding is significant in the novel. It reminds children of the similar issue of prejudice against Jews, suggesting that the two forms of prejudice are parallel. It also sends a message of toleration and inclusion to the black community, where anti-Semitism has long been a problem, as well as describing the actual historical alliance of these two groups in the cause of justice.

April's schoolteacher, Miss Bell, and the head of her Brownie troop, Mrs. Cole, are both extremely astute, indeed light years ahead of their time, as they react to any nuance of prejudice in the children. Miss Bell even teaches American history with an emphasis on the contributions of minorities: April is told about Crispus Attucks, who fought in the American Revolution, and the teacher pointedly recommends to Sophie the story of Haym Solomon, who financed a great part of the Revolution. American history was not really taught this way to schoolchildren until around 2000! But by becoming part of curricula, De Angeli helped to bring that transformation about.

One fascinating aspect of the book is that while Mrs. Cole, the Brownie leader, is repeatedly depicted in the illustrations as African American, the race of Miss Bell is never revealed, and no illustration depicts her. A child is said to present her with a portrait of herself that shows "the comb in her hair, the dimple in her chin, and the little mole on her neck." But we are pointedly frustrated in our quest for the obvious, and reproved implicitly for thinking it the most important issue. The schoolchildren notice only individuating features, and they do not (yet) notice the first thing the surrounding society wants to know. We are led to believe Mrs. Bell is white simply because of the remarks made by others about how hard it is for blacks to gain access to respected professions, but we are also made conscious of the impertinence of our question, which small children know too little to make central. Thus the world of the classroom is a kind of time capsule into an ideal future where race does not define destinies. April's mother nourishes a similar futuristic view, telling April that she is a nice coffee color and that other children are a nice pink color. (I remember this as a new way of talking about skin color when my daughter was in elementary school in the late 1970s.) And Mrs. Bright condemns racists for their ignorance: they have not studied science and do not understand that human blood is all the same.

Still, the reality of prejudice keeps creeping up on April. When the girls in the troop are discussing what they want to do when they grow up, April says she'd like to go into the women's clothing business and own a department store. Two other girls (Italian American) laugh and say that someone like April could never do that. The kindly Mrs. Cole says to April afterward that society will indeed put obstacles in her way, and it is to be hoped that society will change fast enough: "'Perhaps by the time you are grown up you can go anywhere you want to go.' Then she added slowly, 'I hope so.' She was very serious and unsmiling."

The climax of the story offers a pointed assault on the politics of disgust. Because of her high score in various Brownie activities involving mastering the names of birds and plants, April is invited to an all-regional gathering of meritorious Brownies at a farm outside the city. (This provides occasion for humor, as the urban child sees rural life for the first time, reminding us of other barriers to understanding.) One of the children there—interestingly, represented as a guest rather than as a Brownie, as if she would have learned better values had she been a member—is a racist child, quite rude to April and disparaging of her presence. The teacher tells April that this child, Phyllis, has lost her mother, appealing to her imagination—so April's hurt begins to be tempered by sympathy. A big storm comes up, preventing them from going home that night, and they must all crowd together in a few rooms in the farmhouse. April is put in the same room as Phyllis. Mrs. Cole sends her to bed with the whispered Brownie motto D. Y. B. (Do Your Best). When the thunder and lightning wake Phyllis up, April is inclined to comfort her, but the sting of resentment holds her back:

> April could hear Phyllis moving about on the couch. She heard her sigh. She thought how lonely Phyllis must be with no mother. She felt sorry for her and wanted to go and comfort her. But when she remembered how Phyllis had refused to sit beside her at the table, she just couldn't, so she set her lips together and turned over, pulling the covers over her ears.
>
> The delicate smell of lavender coming from the smooth sheets, the light warmth of the blanket were comforting. April fell asleep.
>
> Some time later April felt herself gently but firmly pushed over to the edge of the cot. She half awoke as two little arms crept about her. Then came a whisper, "It's me—Phyllis. I'm cold, and I'm *so* lonesome. Can't I stay here with you?" April was awake now.
>
> "Of course," she answered, hugging Phyllis close.
>
> Phyllis was quiet for a moment, then said hesitantly, "You know, at first I didn't like you. I never knew anyone just like you before. But Flicker [the assistant scout leader, white] told me about you and how nice you are. She told how much you know about birds

and trees, too, and she says you like to read books. So do I. I read all
the time, even when I'm drying dishes. I prop the book up on the
shelf against the salt box. I like fairy stories best. Do you?"

She didn't wait for April to answer, but went on as if she couldn't
wait to get it all out at once: "When I touched your hand that time,
I felt how nice and smooth it was. I saw that your dress was just as
fresh and clean as mine, too." She stopped for a moment, then went
on, "I like you now." She breathed a deep sigh and went sound
asleep!

An illustration on the facing page shows four girls dressing in the
morning; the three white girls, all short-haired, look admiringly at
April, who is braiding her long black hair. All wear spotlessly clean
white slips.

This is a complex and fascinating episode. On the one hand, De
Angeli sounds the note of universal humanity, as Phyllis is brought
around by learning of April's similar love of reading and birds, and
by the discovery that her skin feels the same; April, on her side, is
brought around by Phyllis's loneliness. The recognition is powerful
because it is so physical: Phyllis sleeps in April's bed, clinging to her.
On the other hand, the episode provides a vivid reminder of the
disgust-fantasies that create divisions between people: Phyllis is surprised that April's skin feels "nice and smooth," and she is even
more surprised that her dress is clean: evidently ideas of sliminess
and filth simmer just beneath the surface. We see that all the obses-
siveness about cleanliness in the Bright household is amply warranted: one slip from that ideal dirtlessness, those fictionally ironed
and gleaming dresses and even underwear, and cross-racial understanding would have been impossible.

Understanding is that frail. In one way it is based upon truth: human bodies are all similar, and black skin is indeed smooth and warm. The last sentence of the book has April's mother saying that Phyllis rejected her at first because she didn't know the truth. "We must know *the truth*, always, even when it hurts. The Bible says, 'Ye shall know the TRUTH, and the truth shall make you free!'"

And yet, there is a further layer of complexity in this appeal to truth: for Phyllis's newfound friendliness is based, in another sense, on fiction, on the denial that children's bodies and clothes get dirty. The dominant group can sweat and ignore the evidence of that sweat, the minority must arrange to be sweat-free, to be almost bodiless, in their white starched underwear. (It looks starched, at least: and yet this can only be fantasy, since nobody sane would starch a slip.)

All this is subtly presented to children who will not yet fully take it in, but they will have a lot to think about and talk about—or to be silent about, as the case may be. In my case, I read that book right around the time my father (raised in the deep South) got furious at me for offering an African-American girl in the neighborhood (the daughter of live-in servants, or else she would not have been there) a drink of water in our kitchen: he indicated that it was a kind of contamination of the drinking glasses. So I had to make sense of De Angeli's case study of irrational fear in relation to a living example. Most white children in Philadelphia reading that book would have been in a similar situation, although their parents, not being from the South, might have been more polite. I am sure that this course of reflection led me to understand that my father lived in a strange world of fantasy that was surprisingly immune to science and truth, values that he held dear at other times. Needless to say, these reflections could only have been spurred, at that age, by an engaging story; abstract argument would have had little force.

De Angeli by now is one of thousands of writers who investigate racial, ethnic, and religious differences for children, although at the time she was part of a far smaller group. She was often unchallenging, choosing "safe" and pleasing religious minorities rather than those against whom prejudice and fear were really directed. Especially in her account of racial prejudice, however, she goes beyond the rest of her work, and beyond her time, providing a template for thinking about a wide range of prejudices, and how they might be overcome if we address them in childhood, in a way that focuses on the common embrace of the body.

All of our examples show "stupidity" being overcome by the sympathetic imagination, which achieves what clear-eyed argument by itself would probably have been unable to achieve. Sympathy involves empathetic participation, but it goes beyond it, assessing the values involved in the situation and criticizing aspects of hierarchy and social obtuseness that cause stigmatization and unfair suffering for the minority characters. To be valuable in the moral life, sympathy, as all four of our authors emphasize, must begin with factual truth. All four authors, therefore, do a good deal of historical and cultural research, showing the reader that this type of realistic curiosity about how another group of people lives and thinks is essential if the imagination is to work well. For, as our stories show, the imagination often works poorly: either "stupidly," as when it does not take any interest in anything unfamiliar, or, even worse, in a manner propelled by narcissistic fantasy, as when people who are sure that they are humans with souls imagine Indians as mere savages, or see African Americans as mere animals, foul and filthy, fit to be their instruments rather than their equals.

In effect, our authors have a triple task: first, to present true facts; then, simultaneously, to lure people's imaginations into that world and entice them to care about the people they find there; finally, to convince readers that the people there are not actually disgusting or evil but deserving of friendship and respect.

For all our examples are really about civic or political friendship. Roger Williams understood this well, when he put "What cheare, friend?" at the top of the list. What they all demand is the bare bones of friendship: curiosity, listening, responsiveness, a willingness to acknowledge a full life and world over there, outside ourselves. Friendship is rarely uncritical, and friends may well differ in their evaluations and argue, sometimes fiercely. But to remain friends they must take the first step of trying to see the situation from the other point of view. They must avoid the error of making a special case of themselves. And that means that they must avoid seeing the world through the narcissism of anxiety.

Good political principles and consistent arguments work well only against the background of morally informed perceptions, and these perceptions need the imagination. Only the "inner eyes" can tell us that what we're seeing is a full human being, with a range of human purposes and goals, rather than a weapon assailing our safety, or a disgusting piece of garbage.

With the three pillars of our approach in place—ethical consistency, specific principles of religious liberty, and an approach through the imagination, let's now return to contemporary issues, asking where our principles lead us in a complicated recent case.

6

THE CASE OF PARK51

One of the most difficult and divisive issues in recent U.S. debates over religion has been the question of establish-
ing an Islamic-initiated multifaith community center, containing a
prayer space, several blocks from "ground zero," where the devastating 9/11 attacks left an open space that is now, after ten years, being
filled by a memorial to the victims of 9/11. From quiet and initially
uncontroversial beginnings in early 2009, the Park51 project took
on national visibility and became an extremely polarizing issue. Although some progress has been made in recent days toward clarification and reconciliation, the use of the controversy as a campaign
topic in New York's special election for Congress on September 13,
2011 (for a district that does not even contain the relevant area of
the city), shows its ongoing resonance.

Ground zero has become a quasi-sacred space, a place of mourn-
ing for the lost and of meditation on the fragility of America and
America's way of life in the face of the threat of global terrorism. So
it is a place of fear as well as of grief. This fear, to the extent that it
focuses on the 9/11 terrorist attacks and the threat for the future
that they suggest, is entirely rational.

Ground zero is not in the middle of nowhere. Lower Manhattan is a rapidly growing area of the city, with a large and diverse population of both residents and workers. Unlike some parts of Manhattan, the area around ground zero is not restrictively zoned, and all kinds of establishments flourish there.[1] Only two blocks away, on Church Street, is an off-track betting (OTB) facility. Just around the corner, on Murray Street, is New York Dolls, a strip club. Just down the street from ground zero is another strip club, the Pussycat Lounge. Liquor stores, restaurants, and many other types of retail establishments abound. The area is usually thronged with people—workers, customers, residents.

Quite a few buildings in the area suffered damage in the 9/11 attacks. One was the Burlington Coat Factory, a nineteenth-century structure that was no longer in use after the attacks. In January 2006, it was purchased by developer Sharif El-Gamal, a thirty-seven-year-old Muslim businessman with a Lebanese father and a Polish Catholic mother, who has long lived in the area.[2] (The larger block of land, 45–51 Park Place, is owned by Con Ed, and El-Gamal currently leases it from the utility.) There were already two mosques in the immediate area. One could hold only sixty-five people and had to schedule multiple services to accommodate everyone. The other, on Warren Street, five blocks from ground zero, had been in operation for years, but space was limited, and the Muslim working population of the area was rapidly growing, so there was need both for more prayer space and for other facilities useful to the community. That mosque held 1,500 people, but it was still overflowing, and people were praying on the sidewalk. For seven years, El-Gamal and others had been looking for a suitable site, and when the Burlington building was abandoned in 2006 he saw an opportunity. Finally, in January 2009, as CEO of the development company SoHo Properties, he was able to purchase the building. Initially he entertained other possibilities for the space, such as a condominium complex. Meanwhile, in May 2009, the Warren Street mosque lost its space, and so the need for worship space only grew.

El-Gamal, who had taught his kids to swim at the Jewish Community Center on the Upper West Side, conceived the idea of a similar facility in Lower Manhattan, open to all faiths, which could house a wide range of activities for people of the community: classes, athletics, programs for kids—while also containing a Muslim prayer space. He began holding Muslim prayer in the abandoned building, which now also hosts yoga classes and lectures. His idea was that such a center could contribute to the revitalization of Lower Manhattan: "I can't say this often enough. We work in lower Manhattan, we care about lower Manhattan and we're here to provide services to lower Manhattan."[3] But an ancillary consideration he mentions was that the location could also accommodate people from other boroughs, since it is easily reached from Manhattan, Brooklyn, and Staten Island. He has always stated explicitly and resolutely that he "will not tolerate any kind of illegal or un-American activity and rhetoric. Radical and hateful agendas will have no place in our community center or in the mosque. We are building this center for New York City, because we're New Yorkers. We're Americans. We have families and futures here."

El-Gamal was himself involved in the 9/11 disaster. Like many residents of Lower Manhattan, he went to the site and spent two days handing out water to first responders and victims. One of his close friends, a woman he describes as "a Muslim and a New Yorker," was severely injured in the blasts. Fortunately, she was dug out of the rubble and survived, and she went straight to work assisting others. El-Gamal recalls, "We understand the horror of that day because we lived it. Terrorists attacked our city and our country, and terrorists have continued to threaten our city and our country. We're proud of the many Muslims who have worked with our fellow Americans to keep our city and country safe. . . . Hundreds of Muslims died on that day. New Yorkers of all faiths and no faiths died together. There are also hundreds of Muslims in our police force and fire department and many Muslims who volunteered to help the injured and the hurt."[4] Indeed, he often mentions that it was the tragedy of 9/11 that led him to reconnect to his faith. To my knowledge, despite the eagerness of the project's opponents to tar its supporters with the brush of radicalism, nobody has ever impugned El-Gamal's record on religious matters, his motives, or his history of service to the community. (He did admit to a 1994 arrest for patronizing a prostitute, and he was once charged with assault for allegedly punching in the face a tenant who was late with the rent, although he denied having done so and the charges were eventually dropped. These matters did not attract significant public attention.[5])

El-Gamal did not state his intentions clearly at the outset; in fact, he began to develop his plan with no fanfare and with little consultation. But he made one crucial decision: he chose an imam of a nearby mosque, Feisal Abdul Rauf, to be the religious leader of the proposed center and the imam of the mosque that would be a part of it. Rauf, born in Kuwait, is a Sufi Muslim. Sufism is a spiritual movement within Islam that has historically been strongly linked to interreligious cooperation and has always been against aggression or radical political agendas.[6] In India, for example, Sufi Muslims often made common cause with liberal Hindus, as in the reign of Moghul emperor Akbar, when the Sufi poet Kabir wrote verse beginning, "Kabir is the child of Allah and of Ram," to indicate the kinship of all religions in the human spirit. In more recent times, the Bauls of West Bengal, who derive from both liberal Hindu and

Sufi Muslim traditions, were philosopher Rabindranath Tagore's models for a new "religion of humanity" based on love and inner devotion.[7]

Both Rauf and his wife, Daisy Khan, are international figures, very active in movements for interreligious cooperation and respect.[8] Rauf has written three books on Islam and contemporary society, including *What's Right with Islam Is What's Right with America*. He has criticized radical Islam very strongly, describing the terrorist bombings as anti-Islamic and Islamic conservatism as in the "Dark Ages." Among his friends is former Secretary of State Madeleine Albright, and he has appeared publicly with Bush administration Secretary of State Condoleezza Rice and Bush adviser Karen Hughes. During the controversy, he wrote an eloquent account of his beliefs and goals that makes it clear that the objectives of his Cordoba Initiative, a multinational, multifaith organization that he founded in 2004, are to counter Islamic extremism and, more generally, to "cultivate understanding between people of all religions and cultures," goals that in and of themselves are noble and unobjectionable.[9]

Rauf has sometimes been controversial, however, in part for his interest in raising funds from Saudi Arabia, but also for his somewhat grandiose ideas about how large the center would be and the world-historical role it would have. He has also made some provocative statements. In an interview on CBS's *60 Minutes*, he called the United States an "accessory" to the 9/11 attacks, without explaining this shocking statement clearly.[10] Later he and his wife clarified that he was referring to the role of the United States in earlier years, in supporting the Taliban in Afghanistan against the Soviet-backed government, and in financing Osama Bin Laden. That's a plausible point to make, and it is true that U.S. support for the Taliban, originating out of zealous anticommunism, played a role in strengthening the hand of radical Islam in the region.[11] However, Rauf did not exercise good judgment in making such an inflammatory statement without utter clarity. He also ignited controversy by refusing to comment on whether he considers Hamas a terrorist organization—although eventually he did utter an unequivocal condemnation of Hamas's acts of terrorism. Rauf has also blamed the U.S. sanctions against Iraq for the deaths of thousands of Iraqi children.

In short, although Rauf had served lower Manhattan as an imam for a long time, he was clearly a figure on a larger world stage, a leader with admirable values but one who had shown questionable judgment in some instances. With his selection the project appeared to change course, from a local to a much more international enterprise. He announced that the new center would be part of the Cordoba Initiative and would therefore be named Cordoba House. The name, he later explained, harked back to Cordoba, Spain, in the Middle Ages, when the city was a place where Muslims, Christians, and Jews lived together cooperatively, forging a syncretistic culture. But of course the mention of Corboda signaled to many people the Muslim conquest of Spain in the eighth century, and thus the idea of Muslim domination over Christians. It's pretty surprising that Rauf did not think of this, and we see here another instance of questionable judgment. Even the cultural co-existence of Muslims, Jews, and Christians in Cordoba might be questioned, since it was on terms of Muslim political domination and incomplete religious equality. Cordoba was just an unfortunate name choice, even in the best construal. El-Gamal has always preferred the neutral and humble name Park51. Rauf also envisaged a thirteen-storey structure, considerably more imposing than the modest structure originally envisaged by El-Gamal.

Rauf's involvement and his distinctive vision also raised the question of why the center needed to be located in a controversial spot. It really didn't, if its purpose was to establish a monument to peace and cooperation. That could be done anywhere, and Rauf admitted as much very late in the day. At the time, he defended the location by saying that the center "sends the opposite statement to what happened on 9/11."[12] But he later conceded that the statement could be made elsewhere.

El-Gamal's original plan, by contrast, was far more rooted in local necessity: Muslims simply didn't have space to pray in the area, and he owned the building and was already using it for prayer, as well as for other activities. So he was proposing simply to expand on the existing activities by offering much more to the entire Lower Manhattan community. The old Burlington building didn't absolutely have to be the spot for that undertaking, but it would have to be someplace nearby; he had acquired a suitable property there, and it was already in use.

The plan for the center was publicly announced by the two organizers, without a lot of prior consultation with the local community or with the national Islamic community. Initially, there was no controversy. The FBI issued a statement praising Rauf's role as a liaison to the Muslim community after 9/11. The Jewish Community Center expressed pleasure that it had been chosen as a model for El-Gamal's plan. When Daisy Khan first announced the plan on national TV, on conservative pundit Laura Ingraham's guest-hosted segment of the *O'Reilly Factor* on December 21, 2009, the project was welcomed. Ingraham said: "I can't find many people who really have a problem with it. Bloomberg is for it. Rabbis are saying they don't have a problem with it. . . . I like what you're trying to do and Ms. Khan we appreciate it and come on my radio show some time." Khan replied, "Yeah, we need the support of people like you seriously." "Alright, you take care," said Ingraham. Ingraham later changed her tune utterly, joining the opposition, but this beginning was peaceful.[13]

The opposition can be traced above all to right-wing blogger Pamela Geller, who runs an organization called "Stop the Islamicization of America" and writes a popular blog called "Atlas Shrugs" (alluding to the Ayn Rand novel) from her home. The blog, which was a favorite of Norwegian assassin Anders Behring Breivik (hardly Geller's fault, but an accurate indication of the blog's content and audience), focuses on the alleged threat of a Muslim takeover of the United States. Geller quickly took the line that the proposed center was a place for radical organizing and that its very existence would be a triumphalist statement by Muslims, insulting to the victims of 9/11 and their families. One typical Geller headline was "Monster Mosque Pushes Ahead in Shadow of World Trade Center Islamic Death and Destruction." (No friend of evidence, Geller once suggested in all seriousness that President Obama's father was Malcolm X; she has also alleged, totally without evidence, that the president used to have a girlfriend who was a "crack whore." And she has consistently repeated the canard that the president is a Muslim.) Along with anti-Muslim author Robert Spencer, Geller launched a campaign to stop the "9/11 Mosque."[14]

Not too surprisingly, debate ensued, as Fox News gave prominent coverage to Geller's writings. National media celebrities such as anti-Muslim author Brigitte Gabriel and politicians such as Sarah Palin and Newt Gingrich joined the fray, their denunciations countered firmly by the somewhat surprised developers and by New York Mayor Bloomberg. As discussion became more heated, polls showed a lot of resistance to the proposed project, even among New Yorkers, although misinformation was so widespread that it was quite difficult to tell whether those opposed really were against the actual plan. Meanwhile, the proposal passed its first test in late May 2010. In a heated four-hour meeting, Community Board 1, which must approve all plans for that area of Lower Manhattan, voted for the plan twenty-nine to one, with ten abstentions. Religious leaders and relatives of survivors were among those who testified at the hearing. One commonly expressed view was that the construction of a mosque was insensitive to families of the 9/11 victims. C. Lee Hanson, whose son was killed in the attacks, said, "The pain never goes away. When I look over there and I see a mosque, it's going to hurt. Build it somewhere else."[15] With this objection as with many others, one can't tell to what extent it is based on misinformation. Does "When I look over there" mean "look from ground zero"? If so, Mr. Hanson is misinformed. He would not see the center from there. And does the sight of a mosque cause pain because he thinks that 9/11 was caused by Islam as such? Because he thinks that this particular mosque is to be a breeding ground for terrorists? Again, if these are his thoughts, they are based on incorrect information. It's hard to know.

The next hurdle was to debate a proposal that would have granted the building "landmark" status, so that it could not be demolished to build the center. That proposal, first made twenty years ago, had long been shelved, but opponents of the center reopened it. The motion failed in August, by a 9 to 0 vote. Meanwhile, in early June over 1,000 people turned out for a protest, carrying signs with slogans such as "No 9/11 Mega Mosque," and a statement by a Tea Party supporter that the proposed center would serve "for the worship of terrorists' monkey god." Pamela Geller somehow paid for an anti-center poster to be displayed on New York City MTA buses in some areas of the city. The poster showed the 9/11 attacks, complete with smoke and airplane flying into the side of the towers, juxtaposed with a drawing of the proposed "mosque." When the MTA initially refused to use the posters, she sued, and the MTA gave way. Other posters she financed offered Muslims advice on how to give up their religion. Since that time, "leaving Islam" posters have also appeared in other cities.

Over the summer, the protests gained ground, as some responsible leaders spoke out in opposition to the plan. Abraham Foxman, chair of the Anti-Defamation League, and Carl Paladino, a Republican candidate for governor, focused on the issue of insensitivity: the organizers should defer to the wishes of New Yorkers and build the project somewhere else. Mayor Bloomberg, by contrast, dug in: "To cave to popular sentiment would be to hand a victory to the terrorists," he said on August 2, right after the landmark commission vote allowed the project to continue.[16] He was joined by Congressman Jerrold Nadler, whose district includes the disputed area. On August 13, President Obama made what appeared to be a statement of support, but only a day later he said that his remarks were not an endorsement of the wisdom of going forward with the project.

The controversy simmered on. The landmark commission was then sued by the American Center for Law and Justice, representing a firefighter who survived the 9/11 attacks. The suit charged the commission with violations of its own procedures. The plaintiffs also filed a motion in State Supreme Court in Manhattan for an injunction to stop the construction. (Since construction had not begun and funds had not even been raised, this one was a bit premature.)[17]

The next major development came in mid-January 2011, when El-

Gamal announced that Imam Feisal Rauf and his wife would no longer speak for the project. The split, which grew out of longstanding tensions and differences, left Rauf as a member of the advisory board, but he is no longer the center's imam. El-Gamal announced that no imam would serve as the project's public face. A new imam, Shaykh Abdallah Adhami, was still selected as an associate—but he was quickly relieved of his duties on February 5, 2011, after it emerged that he had made insensitive remarks about homosexuality. (What he said was: "A small, tiny percentage of people are born with a natural inclination they cannot explain. You find this in the animal kingdom on some level as well." A gay Muslim filmmaker commented that this is not as bad as what he has heard from many Muslim leaders, and is itself a sign of progress.[18])

And that is basically where things stand. El-Gamal is busy fundraising for the project, bloggers and politicians are still arguing about it, and it has even been a major issue in the tight race for a congressman to replace Anthony Weiner. Republican candidate Bob Turner made the claim that Democrat David Weprin wants to "commemorate the tragedy by building a mosque on ground zero," a statement both inaccurate and inflammatory. He won the election on September 13, although this issue seems to have been minor compared to others. Meanwhile, on the tenth anniversary of the 9/11 attacks, there was a small anti-Muslim demonstration (about 1,000 people), but far larger was the show of interfaith unity and amity in the official observances, organized by the mayor.

Now we can step back to reflect about how this narrative fits with the philosophical and legal arguments developed in earlier chapters. First, we'll look at the grasp of basic facts, then at the values manifested in reactions by various parties. Finally, we'll bring our three-part approach to bear and assess those factual and evaluative perceptions.

Common Errors Made in the Debate

The debate has been full of misinformation from start to finish, so we must begin there. Philosophical principles can do nothing without correct facts, and in some cases the factual record was seriously distorted:

1. A mosque is being put up "on ground zero." As we can see, the proposed center is, first of all, an interfaith community center, not primarily a mosque, although it will have a prayer space. And it is three blocks from ground zero and not visible from there. Moreover, Muslim prayer has been going on in that building for several years, and another longstanding mosque is only five blocks away. Pertinent, too, is the fact that this area of Lower Manhattan is no sacred space, as shown by the presence of the OTB parlor and two strip clubs.

2. The center is intended to convey a triumphalist message, showing that Muslims defeated the United States on 9/11. As we can see, this is just the reverse of the truth: both Rauf and El-Gamal are moderates who strongly condemn radical Islam in all its forms, and they have guaranteed that such opinions will have no place in the proposed center. Rauf's aim is a symbolic display of interreligious cooperaton; El-Gamal's is more local and humble, simply a center that will serve longstanding needs of the Lower Manhattan community. The name Cordoba, though certainly an unfortunate choice, was intended to convey mutual cooperation

and respect. This error is due to a much larger one: the equation of all Islam with its most radical and violent strains, and a complete failure to understand what Sufism has represented in the history of that religious tradition.

3. The center is scheduled to open on the tenth anniversary of 9/11. This myth, purveyed by Pamela Geller and eventually broadcast on Fox News, has no foundation at all in reality. Quite apart from the controversy, it would have taken many years to demolish the existing building, raise the funds for a new structure, and then design and construct the building. The organizers had not even raised the funds by the tenth anniversary of 9/11, and they never announced any target date.

4. The center would be a cell for radical Muslim organizing. Again, unless one simply decides that all statements made by the organizers are false, this won't happen: El-Gamal has insisted that such strains of Islamic opinion will have no place in the center. Once again, this error takes place against a larger background of error: interdenominational differences and indeed conflicts are simply not appreciated, and the canard that Muslims always lie may also be playing a baneful role.

Two Questions, Not One

We can hardly analyze the issues without first figuring out what the question is. Although discussion of the proposed community center has often blurred the issues, at least a good deal of it has not. Much public debate, and at least some of the debate by politicians and pundits, has accurately kept separate two issues that are significantly distinct. First, do the developers have a constitutionally protected right to build an Islamic center, including a mosque, on this property? Second, is it wise (sensitive, helpful, well advised) for them to go ahead with this plan in the light of the controversy that has erupted? Some thoughtful opinion pieces have suggested that, though the answer to the first question is yes, the answer to the second is no, in the light of the expressed suffering of survivors of some of the victims (although survivors of other victims disagree, and although the developers themselves include survivors and friends of Muslim victims).

These two questions are importantly distinct in many areas of constitutional life. The fact that the First Amendment has been held to protect Nazi marchers as they demonstrate in a Jewish neighborhood hardly means that it is wise or just of them to carry out their march, or wrong of others to object and to protest. The fact that offensive speech of many types is protected by the First Amendment hardly means that it would be good or wise for a newspaper to agree to publish such speech—speech demeaning to racial or religious groups or to women, for example. This issue often gives rise to confusion. For example, in the case of the controversial Danish cartoons that offended Muslims, people invoked free speech as if that decisively settled the issue of whether a given newspaper ought to publish those cartoons. But of course newspapers do not publish everything they have a constitutional right to publish. Considerations of offense are usually relevant to such decisions. Had the *New York Times* published a racist cartoon that gave offense to African Americans, nobody could say that the paper did not have a constitutional right to do so, but the editor in charge would probably have lost his job, and rightly.

It is, then, a perfectly coherent position to say (as Sarah Palin and Harry Reid have in different ways said) that the developers clearly have a constitutional right to proceed, but that the wisdom of the decision should be questioned. Many believe that position to be correct. We cannot, however, assume that the mere existence of strong negative sentiment on the part of a lot of people means that it is unwise to proceed.

On one view of society, the strong negative sentiments of average people are trumps: people can even pass laws forbidding acts that disgust and deeply offend them, even though those acts cause no harm to nonconsenting parties. Such was the position of Britain's Lord Devlin with regard to consensual homosexual acts, a view that by now our society has repudiated, holding that personal rights of intimate sexual conduct are protected even if lots of people don't like to think that these things are going on. But there is a difference between that case and our case: the sexual acts of others are viewed as protected from interference in part because they take place in seclusion, and therefore do not impinge on the lives of others, except through the imagination. In other words, to the extent that they inflict pain, it is what John Stuart Mill called a "purely constructive injury." People don't see it or interact with it, so they are pained only because they imagine it and don't like what they imagine. The case of Park51 is not quite like that, because people will have to see that building, in some degree of proximity to ground zero. They will walk by it on their way to work or to the 9/11 memorial. So, at first blush anyway, it does not seem that the injury is "purely constructive."

Even here, however, we need to probe further. The proposed building, as we saw, would not actually be visible from ground zero. Two and a half blocks, in a crowded area of Manhattan, is a long way, and if the person were simply walking around, without rhetorical intervention, she would have no particular reason to think of the two places as intimately linked—any more than she would have seen a link between ground zero and other neighboring buildings, such as strip clubs and betting establishments. So the offense may be "purely constructive" after all: people are reacting to the words "ground zero mosque," so often used in this connection, and not to the reality of New York life that would ultimately exist were the plans carried out—and that exists already, since the Burlington Coat Factory building has been used for Muslim prayer for some time.

Another way in which the offense has a "constructive" aspect is that people imagine what is likely to be going on inside that community center, and their ideas play a huge role in their feelings. Just as neighbors of a gay couple imagine not love and affection similar to their own, but vile, forbidden anal acts that spread contagion into the community—so the objectors may be imagining what bloggers harp on, namely, triumphant, contemptuous celebrations of the "defeat of America" on 9/11, money-raising for radical Islamist organizations all over the world, and so forth. To the extent that people's pain is based on these pictures of what they think is going on, rather than on the reality before their eyes, the harm seems, once again, to be of the "purely constructive" sort, and what would be relevant would be to ascertain clearly that no such security-threatening activities are going to go on there, and that the expression of religious hatred is far from being the center's purpose, indeed is (or so far appears to be) completely antithetical to its purpose.

Suppose the objectors say that they are motivated not by any particular picture of what would take place inside the proposed center, nor by any false view of the physical layout, but only by the sheer distance from ground zero, which anyone can see: what then? Well, they will have to be clear about how much distance they think is enough, since there has long been a mosque operating five blocks away, and they are not objecting to that: so they need to make clear that they are objecting to the difference between two-and-a-half and five blocks. They would also have to explain why their objection holds against a community center and prayer space but not against strip clubs, a liquor store, and the off-track betting parlor. Well, let's suppose that they come up with some reply to this question. Would the strong view of the public, and especially of families of victims, carry the day then?

The problem is that people often object to things that they see, and their objections do not always carry the day, even in the court of public opinion (since everyone grants that they rarely carry the day in a legal sense). Lots of people object to seeing interracial couples expressing affection in public, holding hands and walking with their arms around each other; even more people object to seeing same-sex couples expressing affection in public in such ways. We may all agree that they have a legal right to express affection, in ways that do not violate nudity or public indecency laws: but do we think that, in ethical terms, it would be wiser for those couples to conceal their affection? Opinion is divided here, but, on the whole, we do not think this way, because we think that the opinions involve an unfair sort of discrimination: straight and monoracial couples get privileges that other types of couples do not. So it's not clear that we ought to defer, ethically, even to the very sincere pain of people at what they see before their eyes. We have to look more deeply into the whole question of what constitutes an ethically legitimate source of offense and what does not.

There's another, more intangible issue we need to bear in mind in such cases. Constitutional principles are separate from ethical norms, and they cannot be altered by majority vote. But they still need the sustenance of public sentiment at some level. If people live on a daily diet of religious or racial hatred, they will likely lose the will to sustain and enforce good constitutional norms. Weimar Germany fell prey to the spread of vicious anti-Semitism, and many other societies have lost their good principles, over time, because of vicious sentiments that ran roughshod over a sense of principled fairness. That is why I've argued that good principles need the imagination: they don't fully sustain themselves, in the absence of particular ways of seeing and feeling, which had better be sufficiently widespread to give those principles stability. It was for this reason that early defenders of religious liberty, such as John Locke and Roger Williams, spent a good deal of time talking about the attitudes with which people ought to approach one another, commending delicate and respectful attention, generosity, and friendliness.

This means that a sharp separation between the ethical and the constitutional question is not always wise. Where we are concerned with fellow citizens who are not expressing hatred or denigration of others (as those Nazi marchers were), but are simply going about their daily religious lives, allowing attitudes of offense to determine our actions may ultimately risk eroding our commitment to principles of equal respect for the equal rights of all. Roger Williams is right to say that if we think the principle of religious liberty a fine one, we have reason to cultivate civic friendship.

With these questions in mind, let's look at some of the prominent opinions expressed in the controversy. We'll then be able to turn back to our philosophical principles to see how they help us.

Opinions: Error and Insight

Hundreds of views have been expressed on both sides of this controversy, but we can make a sampling of some highlights, asking how well reasoned they are, and how alert to the distinctions I've introduced. Later, we'll look more deeply at the ways in which the debate revealed both grasp and lack of grasp of the three elements of good judgment that I've recommended.

Pro: Bloomberg, Nadler, Friedman

Mayor Bloomberg has been from the beginning a supporter of the planned center. He makes an argument that is both constitutional and ethical. Often he has alluded to the planners' constitutional rights. But he has also affirmed the wisdom and goodness of building the center. Early on, on December 9, 2009, through a spokesperson, he said, "The idea of a cultural center that strengthens bonds between Muslims and people of all faiths and backgrounds is positive."[19] As controversy heated up, his statements became more extensive. At a press conference in July 2010, reacting to Sarah Palin's remarks about the pain such a center would cause, he stated:

> I think our young men and women overseas are fighting
> for exactly this—for the right of people to practice their
> religion and for government not to pick and choose
> which religions they support, which religions they
> don't. . . . Everything the United States stands for and
> New York stands for is tolerance and openness, and I
> think it's a great message for the world that unlike in
> other places where they might actually ban people from
> wearing a burqa or they might actually keep people from
> building a building, that's not what America was founded
> on, nor is it what America should become.[20]

Bloomberg begins with constitutional principles, but he then suggests, plausibly, that those principles include a spirit of fairness:

government should not treat different religions differently. That idea of fairness, in turn, is connected to a deeper underlying attitude of openness and acceptance. Contrasting the United States with Europe, he suggests that allowing the center to be built (where, of course, a Christian church could be built without comment) is an expression of an attitude of acceptance and friendliness that is "what America was founded on." Thus he argues, quite plausibly, that principles of religious liberty are sustained by an ethical attitude that is well known in our history but that has become fragile, giving rise to a risk that the United States would move in the direction Europe has recently taken, a direction that he views as exclusionary and unfair. Allowing the proposed center to go forward would make a statement about basic American ethical values that nourish and sustain our political culture. Bloomberg is altogether refreshing in his apparent willingness to lead, rather than worrying about the next election. For this reason, he was able to say something coherent and even profound.

Bloomberg's position is that of most of the defenders of the proposed center—those, that is, who make an ethical argument for it as well as a constitutional argument. Congressman Jerrold Nadler expressed a very similar view, saying that he found the singling out of Muslim Americans for "animus and hate" on account of their religion to be "shameful and divisive," and going on to make the ethical argument that New York has understood for centuries the positive value of diversity, tolerance, and understanding.[21]

A different defense of the center, with an interesting angle, was made by journalist Thomas Friedman in his column in the *New York Times*. Friedman argues that the mingling of diverse ethnic and religious groups that is characteristic of New York (he begins with his experience at a recent Broadway show) is the secret of American creativity and innovation, in many areas ranging from dance and music to business. The "sheer creative energy that comes when you mix all our diverse people and cultures together" is America's "most important competitive advantage. . . . We live in an age when the most valuable asset any economy can have is the ability to be creative—to spark and imagine new ideas, be they Broadway tunes, great books, iPads or new cancer drugs." Creativity, he argues, requires being exposed to divergent ideas and people. So building the proposed center makes a statement to the world that we love and embrace diversity:

> When we tell the world, "Yes, we are a country that will even tolerate a mosque near the site of 9/11," we send such a powerful message of inclusion and openness. It is shocking to other nations. But you never know who out there is hearing that message and saying: "What a remarkable country! I want to live in that melting pot, even if I have to build a boat from milk cartons to get there." As long as that happens, Silicon Valley will be Silicon Valley, Hollywood will be Hollywood, Broadway will be Broadway, and America, if we ever get our politics and schools fixed, will be ok.[22]

Friedman doesn't write very well (the mixed metaphor of melting pot and milk cartons is a particular mess), and he vastly overrates the current state of the Broadway theater. But there is an insight here. Unlike Mayor Bloomberg, he is making an economic, not an ethical, argument: it's in America's economic interest to welcome people of diverse origins with the sort of creative ferment that New York often displays. But at the same time he expresses a love of openness and diversity that is powerfully ethical. (In many ways his argument is reminiscent of Salman Rushdie's writings about India, which involve a similar embrace of the energy generated by diversity, and a repudiation of an ideology of homogeneity and purity.) And, like Walt Whitman's poetic praise of America's diversity, his essay evinces a spirit that undergirds legal principles and gives them vitality.

Con: Palin, Reid, Cohen, Foxman, Gingrich, Peretz, Cohen

Opinions against the center were quite varied, and so we need to examine more of them. Although Sarah Palin is often perceived as radical and irresponsible, and sometimes is so, her comments on this topic have actually been quite sane and appropriate, though perhaps not entirely persuasive. "Peaceful Musims, pls refudiate," she tweeted. She expanded: a large, publicly visible Islamic structure close to ground zero "feels like a stab in the heart to, collectively, Americans who still have that lingering pain from 9/11." Again, "Peace-seeking Muslims, pls understand, Ground Zero mosque is UNNECESSARY provocation: it stabs hearts. Pls reject it in the interest of healing." Palin explicitly insisted that the group has a constitutional right to build the center; she based her opposition on the idea of insensitivity: "We all know that they have the right to do it, but should they?" She can certainly be criticized for using the misleading phrase "ground zero mosque," but in general her distinction between constitutional rights and ethical sensitivity is clear, as is her welcome distinction between terrorists and "peaceful Muslims."

A very similar argument was made by Harry Reid, majority leader of the Senate: "It is time to bring people together, not a time for polarization, and I think it would be better off for everyone if it were built somewhere else." Reid insisted that the First Amendment protects the group's freedom to build the center, but he thinks that good judgment suggests moving it somewhere else.

The Reid/Palin position was widely shared. Perhaps it was most carefully expressed in an op-ed piece by Roger Cohen in the *New York Times*. Cohen, noting and deploring the rise of anti-Muslim feeling all around the world, argued that the principle of religious liberty is extremely important but also quite secure in the United States; therefore we ought to concentrate on the emotional issue. In a time of inflamed sentiments, it would be better to do whatever would promote peace and reconciliation: "The mosque project near ground zero upholds a great American principle, but it's not a sensible idea. Good sense is needed when a harvest of anger is in."[23] Cohen mentioned the related case of crosses near the site of Auschwitz, which we shall shortly discuss. And this case became central to the very similar argument of Abraham Foxman, chair of the Anti-Defamation League, opposing the construction of the center on its planned site.

What makes all these positions responsible (though not necessarily complete or correct) is that they carefully separate the question of constitutional rights from the question of good judgment. And they do not demonize Muslims. Moreover, they have a plausible case that our overwhelming objective at this time ought to be peace and reconciliation, whereas the debate over Park51 is inflaming sentiments further. They do, however, fail to discuss some complicated issues about civic friendship, which we shall later mention.

Quite different were the statements of some other contributors, but let us simply choose two. Presidential candidate Newt Gingrich framed his intervention in the context of a sweeping claim: "America is experiencing an Islamist cultural-political offensive designed to undermine and destroy our civilization." One could hardly be less nuanced. Gingrich continued: "The time for double standards that allow Islamists to behave aggressively toward us while they demand our weakness and submission is over"—thus equating the proposed center with terrorist aggression and with a demand for submission. Saying, "This is a war," he suggested that Congress should declare ground zero a battlefield site—apparently in the belief that this would make it impossible to build an Islamic center three blocks away. (And what of the strip clubs and the OTB parlor? What of the mosque in the Pentagon, one of the targets of 9/11?) Gingrich also commented that we should not allow a mosque in New York as long as there are no churches or synagogues in Saudi Arabia—as if that nation were a model of constitutional democracy that the United States ought to imitate! And he crowned it all by saying that building the proposed center was like placing a "Nazi sign" next to the Holocaust Museum. Of course these remarks—equating all Muslims with Nazis—contribute to irresponsible fearmongering against Muslims. They utterly fail to distinguish between Islam and terrorism; they fail to distinguish constitutional rights from ethical sensitivities; in short, they are a fine paradigm of irresponsible demagoguery.

Still worse was a column by Marty Peretz in the *New Republic*, which included the following:

> But, frankly, Muslim Life is cheap, most notably to Muslims. And among those Muslims led by the Imam Rauf there is hardly one who has raised a fuss about the routine and random bloodshed that defines their brotherhood. So, yes, I wonder whether I need honor these people and pretend that they are worthy of the privileges of the

First Amendment which I have in my gut the sense that
they will abuse.

One hardly knows where to start. Peretz blithely neglects the constant and insistent statements by Rauf, Daisy Khan, and El-Gamal
that terrorism is hateful and, in their view, un-Islamic. (Or is he simply assuming that Muslims always lie?) More generally, by asserting
that terrorism and "random bloodshed" define Islam, he somehow
avoids obvious realities, such as the fact that the two nations with
the largest Muslim populations in the world, Indonesia and India,
are flourishing democracies, and the equally obvious fact that Islamic leaders all over the world have condemned terrorism. Not to
mention the slightly more subtle fact that Sufism is opposed to violence of any sort. On the facts he is as bad as Gingrich and Geller,
and with less excuse, since he is a trained intellectual. (Well, Gingrich has a history Ph.D., so perhaps they are on the same plane after all.)

Yet more insidious and irresponsible is his attitude to U.S. constitutional law. Peretz's words "worthy of the privileges of the First
Amendment" suggest that he thinks that constitutional rights are
like merit badges rather than universal entitlements inherent in our
citizenship and (since they extend to noncitizen residents as well) in
our basic humanity. People are protected by the First Amendment
whether they are good or bad people, whether they love or hate religion, and, importantly, whether or not they even understand the
very idea of freedom of religion. (Thus Americans with severe cognitive disabilities have all the same basic constitutional rights as other
people.) Indeed, Peretz harks back to the hierarchy-based position
about religious toleration wisely repudiated by George Washington,
when he wrote, "It is now no more that toleration is spoken of, as if

it was by the indulgence of one class of people, that another enjoy the exercise of their inherent natural rights." In the old Europe, Washington is saying, you were tolerated if people approved of you; in the new America, religious freedom is a natural right that all Americans have in equal measure. Peretz seems to prefer the ancien regime. His column was surely a low point in American journalism by self-professed intellectuals.

Unclear: President Obama

The president began, on August 13, 2010, with a statement that certainly sounded as if he agreed with Mayor Bloomberg: not only was there a constitutional right to build the center, but it should go forward in the name of American values. In a speech marking the start of the Islamic holy month of Ramadan, he began by stating that "as a citizen, and as president, I believe that Muslims have the same right to practice their religion as anyone else in this country . . . This is America, and our commitment to religious freedom must be un shakable. The principle that people of all faiths are welcome in this country, and will not be treated differently by their government, is essential to who we are."[24] So far, he is addressing only the constitutional question, although by raising the issue of differential treatment he does move toward the ethical question, suggesting that Muslims are being unfairly singled out for opposition. He then went on, however, to distinguish the terrorists who carried out the 9/11 attacks from Islam as a religion: "Al Qaeda's cause is not Islam—it is a gross distortion of Islam. In fact, Al Qaeda has killed more Muslims than people of any other religion, and that list includes innocent Muslims who were killed on 9/11." He also noted that Muslims serve with honor in the U.S. military. In these remarks he at least strongly suggested his support for the construction of the center as planned, and he was so understood by Mayor Bloomberg and many others.

The following day, however, perhaps bowing to criticism, the president said that he had commented only on the constitutional question and had not addressed the wisdom of building the center in that place: "I was not commenting, and I will not comment, on the wisdom of making the decision to put a mosque there. I was commenting very specifically on the right people have that dates back to our founding. That's what our country is about."[25] This somewhat baffling retraction is not altogether atypical of waffling of many sorts that has defined this presidency, but it is pretty surprising, given that Obama had waited for months in silence, and then had evidently planned a major address for the start of Ramadan. To plan and make a major statement and then to "clarify" it the following day so that it no longer has the meaning that most intelligent observers had imputed to it certainly marks a failure of leadership.

Overview: Time Magazine

One thing that is badly needed in this time of inflamed opinion is a careful look at the reality of Muslim lives in America. The imagination can hardly work in a vacuum, and many Americans do not live where they meet Muslims in the course of their daily lives. In this context, *Time* magazine's decision to devote a cover story to Muslim lives in America, under the stress of rising fear, was most welcome. Called "Islamophobia: Does America Have a Muslim Problem?," the article, with many photos, came out on August 19, 2010, right at the height of the controversy. It began with an invitation to empathy:

"To experience what it feels like to be a Muslim in America today, walk in the shoes of Dr. Mansoor Mirza of Sheboygan County." The doctor, born in Pakistan but a longtime U.S. citizen, attends a community meeting in Wisconsin at which he is supporting a proposal to build a mosque in the town of Oostburg, on some land that he already owns. Quickly, scorn and hostility are expressed—even by people who during the day are his patients. People say that Islam is essentially a religion of hate. Although some speakers try to calm things down, Mirza's insistence that the mosque would be a place for quiet prayer is met with scorn. He is asked whether there would be weapons and military training in the mosque. A Christian pastor urges, "The political objective of Islam is to dominate the world with its teachings—and to have domination of all other religions militarily." The doctor is simply dumbfounded that the same people who treat him with respect at the hospital would talk like this.

The article uses this incident as a starting point to investigate the rise of anti-Muslim sentiment in the United States, presenting lots of poll data and quotations from influential leaders who have denounced Islam (Pat Robertson, Franklin Graham, son of evangelist Billy Graham, and many others)—while also pointing to the wide difference between the United States and Europe on this question and to the influential efforts of President Bush to prevent the demonization of Islam after 9/11. But the accent is on ordinary working Muslim Americans, as the article depicts the enormous diversity of that community, from so many different ethnic and national origins and religious sects within Islam. *Time* magazine actually interviewed respected scholarly authorities on Islam for the story—in sharp contrast to the journalism surrounding Park51, which did not call on such scholars (this is true even of the *New York Times*).

The article misses an opportunity, for it allows to go unchallenged the statement that most acts of terrorism are committed by Muslims, whereas the record shows that in recent years by far the largest proportion of suicide terrorist attacks has been perpetrated by the Tamil Tigers, a secular political group operating in Sri Lanka.[26] Still, as such things go, it is quite a wide-ranging and useful piece, especially because it puts on the page a range of real Muslims with lives, careers, community roots, and the desire for a normal American life. It ends with a temporary victory: the Wisconsin town's council approves Mirza's request, and he is converting a building on his property into a mosque. The article has rather the shape, in fact, of a Marguerite de Angeli book, with a happy ending that nonetheless points solemnly to large, unresolved social problems in the wings. It's not a bad place to begin thinking about the Park51 issue, which is mentioned in passing as one example of difficult times ahead.

Such was, and is, the world of public opinion. But since the Park51 developers themselves were always at center stage, shaping opinion and responding to it, it is time to assess their contributions and their deficiencies.

Errors of the Developers

The developers had a promising idea; indeed—and this was part of the problem—they had several different promising ideas. Serving the local community through a multifaith community center seems like a project worth doing. So too, in a very different way, is the project of creating a symbol of religious reconciliation and amity. Both goals clearly and explicitly involved the denunciation of violence and hatred and a determination to make sure the center would not become a home for extremist ideas. That watchfulness and explicitness were also admirable. But what, really, was the center about? Onlookers can be forgiven for being confused.

In hindsight it is obvious, as El-Gamal has conceded publicly, that large errors were made in the initial phases of the project. First, the developers should not have gone public with the plan until they had a much clearer agreement about what the proposed center would be. Rauf and El-Gamal had overlapping but distinct agendas, reflected in the different names that they used for the proposed center: Cordoba House in the case of Rauf, Park51 in the case of El-Gamal. Rauf's plan was big and world-historical, and it did seem to make central reference to 9/11: he sought to establish a large, splashy center for religious harmony and toleration that would show the whole world that Muslims can join with others in an atmosphere of amity and inclusion, right on the site where both non-Muslim and many Muslim New Yorkers were murdered. Although he clearly blundered with the choice of "Corboda House," which was widely construed as a reference to Muslim conquest, what he says he meant, and to all appearances did mean, was to use the city of Cordoba, where Muslims, Christians, and Jews lived in harmony and cultural syncretism, as a grand (and possibly grandiose) symbol of the cultural aims of the project. Unfortunately, he did not clarify this issue until very late in the day—explaining that he had not wanted to comment publicly while traveling abroad, a defense that itself raises the further question why he had thought it appropriate to travel abroad for such a lengthy period rather than attending to local issues.[27]

El-Gamal's aims were far more modest and local: first and foremost, to meet the need of the lower Manhattan Muslim community for more space for both prayer and recreational activities. At the same time, he sought to set up an interfaith community center that would be useful to all the people of Lower Manhattan, or to any New Yorkers who chose to join in, much in the style (as he has repeatedly emphasized) of the Jewish Community Center on the Upper West Side (a parallel he often cites, recalling that this was where his kids had learned to swim), or the 92nd Street YMCA, whose Christian origins have been almost forgotten, given its service to the entire community.

Rauf was the one who wanted a thirteen-storey building, part of the controversy and a source of legitimate concern in that such a building would be taller than other structures in the area. El-Gamal has been agnostic about height, stressing only that the local community is currently underserved in terms of both prayer space and recreational activities in which all may join. He now says, "If the community wants only four or five floors, it's going to be four or five floors." These issues should have been clarified early on, as should the issue of decision and rhetorical authority, that is, who gets to speak for the project.

A more subtle issue that has been unclear until (it seems) very recently is whether the proposed center would even include a mosque, or only a "prayer space." The difference seems to be (at least as clarified by Daisy Khan) that a mosque is duty-bound to admit any Muslim who wants to use it, whereas a prayer space may choose who enters and who does not. (Thus, if they are truly determined to keep out extremists, they need to opt for the more informal concept.) El-Gamal initially and for quite some time used the word "mosque" for what he was planning to include, but perhaps in ignorance of this technical distinction. He now calls the religious entity "Prayer-Space," but it is rather unclear whether he is maintaining that it is not technically a mosque. At any rate he continues to insist that extremists and hate purveyors will be excluded. This distinction is lost on journalists, who typically continue to use the term "mosque."

The issue of fundraising should also have been clarified well before any public statement of the plan, and again the two leaders appear to have deep differences here. Rauf wanted to raise money from all over the world, and to some extent had started doing that, apparently not ruling out donations from nondemocratic Arab nations such as Saudi Arabia. El-Gamal has insisted on limiting the fundraising to U.S. sources, focusing on New York. He also says that he will not accept money from groups that do not reflect "American values." He has now begun a massive fundraising campaign on this basis. And he has announced that the community center and the "prayer space" will be separate entities for legal and fundraising purposes, with both ultimately seeking separate nonprofit status. It's amazing that these issues were not thoroughly examined prior to any initiation of fundraising activity. The whole idea of accepting foreign funds for such a project is a very bad one, and Rauf's openness to it suggests a lack of judgment.

Even more important, the plan should not have moved forward without extensive consultation with New Yorkers of many faiths, with other Muslim leaders around the country, and with scholars and journalists. We have to be careful here: we don't want to suggest that all minority religions need to walk on eggshells as they attempt to exercise their constitutional rights. It does not seem to me that those planning to build a mosque in DuPage County outside Chicago, or in Murfreesboro, Tennessee, have an ethical obligation to engage in extensive community consultation, although political prudence suggests that they probably should. But the proximity to ground zero should have made this a special case, and it's clear that consultation was more or less totally absent, a source of complaint from local Muslim leaders as well as from other segments of the public. El-Gamal has now conceded this point: "Everything was backward," he said in August 2011. "We're going back to basics." He

envisages a long process of consultation: ground might not be broken for years, and consultation will determine the center's ultimate
shape and functions. The primary audiences to be consulted, he
added, will be Lower Manhattan residents of all faiths, and Muslims
who live in the greater New York area. The developers will also continue to evaluate the activities that are now taking place in the
building, "varying from art exhibits and yoga and Brazilian martial
arts classes to Muslim holiday observances and a discussion for
Muslim and non-Muslim children about bullying." This announcement is welcome, but too late, as El-Gamal acknowledges.

In hindsight, too, the whole alliance between the two leaders was
problematic. One can see what led the young El-Gamal to put the
dramatic, dynamic, well-connected, and intellectual Rauf in charge,
and the vision of the latter is to all appearances an admirable one.
But all along Rauf has had very little sense of the roots of the project in the community, and his grand vision probably would have
been better carried out somewhere else. As he acknowledged late in
the day, there was no particular reason for the center to be in Lower
Manhattan—apart, perhaps, from the symbolic significance of cele-
brating toleration on a site of hatred. Indeed, he recently said that
had he known of the pain his proposal would cause, he, as a man of
peace, would not have made it. But that was not going to solve the
problems of the need for space in Lower Manhattan. El-Gamal's
agenda was all about the needs of the community. Had he stuck to
that priority without Rauf's fanfare, perhaps this problem would
not have arisen.

All these criticisms seem fair, but let us return to one thing that is
not so fair. Unpopular minorities face demands on their behavior
that majorities do not typically face. They have to watch themselves
and hesitate, asking whether they are doing everything in their

power so as not to give offense. For majorities, by contrast, the world is made in their image, so to speak: the general shape of public culture expresses their sense of life, and they can relax, secure in the belief that their normal ways of behaving will not give offense: they define what "normal" is. This sense of internalized surveillance can cause great tension for well-intentioned minorities, and it may be that to hold Rauf and El-Gamal to such an exacting standard of reflection and consultation partakes in that burdensome demand.

Philosophy and Controversy: Constitutional Principles

We can say a lot about the case relying simply on good sense and decency. But now let's see how our three-pronged approach helps us think further.

One thing we can see right away, and it's very welcome, is that many if not most people are able to separate the issue of constitutional principle from the ethical issue, and virtually all (Newt Gingrich and Marty Peretz perhaps excepted) grant the fact that our Constitution gives Muslims the right to establish a mosque anywhere they want, so long as they hold the property rights and there are no other legal impediments. It is generally even conceded that zoning restrictions cannot be used to fence them out, given the way the area is currently zoned. Thus neither of the two hearings resulted in a divided vote. Moreover, virtually nobody is saying that our Constitution ought to be changed, that its provisions are deplorable, or that considerations of public security trump Muslims' right of religious free exercise.

In short, issues that would have gone a long way in Europe are going nowhere in the United States, and that's a relief. Nobody is calling for sweeping constitutional changes that would remove the free exercise rights in question, or grant an exception to them for this particular restriction. By contrast, the Swiss referendum removed the minaret from its antecedent constitutional protection; and the Italian *burqa* ban more recently removed a religious-freedom exception for Muslim religious dress that had previously been attached to a law forbidding clothing that covers the face. (I'm not clear how Italian law treats my other cases of facial covering: perhaps there is no need for the sort of wintry covering I describe, but there must be at least implicit exceptions for facial covering in certain professions and sports.)

Zoning law has often been a refuge for people who wish to deny a permit to construct a place of worship but don't want to advocate constitutional change. So it is in DuPage County, and this way of opposing mosque construction might survive constitutional scrutiny. Not all zoning restrictions are constitutional: the U.S. Supreme Court struck down a zoning restriction that the city of Cleburne, Texas, used to deny a permit for a home for people with mental retardation, saying that the reasoning behind the restriction didn't survive even the weak "rational basis" test because it was grounded in mere animus and fear.[28] So if the DuPage restriction ever made it to the courts, such questions would have to be asked. And any apparently neutral law of any sort that ruled the proposed center illegal would have to survive the withering scrutiny of Justice Scalia's *Lukumi* opinion, in which he determined that the general ban on animal slaughter was but an excuse to persecute Santeria worshippers.[29] At any rate, it's significant that such things are not happening in the Park51 case: there is no campaign to rezone Lower Manhattan. The struggle is being waged on the ground of the ethical issue alone.

It's highly significant, then, that the debate shows a strong U.S.

consensus in support of the constitutional principles I've been defending, principles that most of Europe has never accepted. The issue does not even require us to distinguish between the Lockean and the accommodationist position, since nobody is taking the position that the Muslims are asking for a special accommodation of their practices. And this fact corresponds to a deeper aspect of current American political culture. On many issues, our nation is deeply divided, but the free exercise of religion is not among those issues. Indeed, as my mention of Justice Scalia indicates, strong support for minority free exercise, understood at least in terms of Lockean equality, is a question on which a divided Supreme Court is not divided. Some U.S. conservatives (for example, former appellate judge and constitutional scholar Michael McConnell, and in at least some respects Chief Justice Roberts) favor accommodationism; others (Scalia) favor the Lockean approach. Both, however, agree that laws that appear neutral may fail to pass constitutional muster if they impose special burdens on minorities in ways suggestive of unfair treatment.

This is an idea that Europe has yet even to debate seriously, much less to embrace. The German decision that upheld a ban on the wearing of headscarves by public school teachers, while permitting nuns and priests to teach in full habit, is a perfect example of a Hialeah-style ordinance, and it would never pass muster in the United States. I have argued that the *burqa* bans fail in a similar fashion. This all suggests that Europe urgently needs to engage in a deep and searching debate about equality and what equal respect for citizens entails in the area of religion. In the United States, at least that much is common ground. Let's hope that this remains the case in the future. But the fact that Sarah Palin is not questioning these norms is somewhat reassuring.

When the protests over Park51 began, Cassandra, a stripper at New York Dolls, the strip club on Murray Street, around the corner from the proposed center, and one of two strip clubs very close to ground zero (the other being the Pussycat Lounge), worried at first that the call to prayer might wake up the neighbors, who like to sleep late. But when she was told that they didn't plan to use loud-speakers, she said she had no problem with the project. "I don't know what the big deal is," she said to a *Wall Street Journal* reporter. "It's freedom of religion, you know?"[30]

Philosophy and Controversy: Consistency

From now on, then, we are focusing on the ethical concern, and it's here that the issue of consistency becomes both urgent and thorny. So: are the objections to the proposed center instances of finding fault with an unpopular minority while not applying a similar scrutiny to the majority?

First, even had 9/11 been the result of a widespread conspiracy among all Muslim nations, it would not be consistent with general American practices to forbid new people, clearly innocent of that wrongdoing, from going about their business in that place. Justice Stevens recently made this point very forcefully, talking about his own feelings on seeing Japanese tourists visiting a memorial to the deaths at Pearl Harbor: "These people don't belong here. . . . We shouldn't allow them to celebrate the attack on Pearl Harbor even if it was one of their greatest victories."[31] But he concluded that he was mistaken in "drawing inferences" about the group of tourists, just because of ethnic similarity. Those tourists were not responsible for what their compatriots did; similarly, "the Muslims planning to build the mosque are not responsible for what an entirely different

224

group of Muslims did on 9/11." He concludes, "Ignorance—that is to say, fear of the unknown—is the source of the most invidious prejudice."

But as President Bush immediately emphasized, and as virtually all leaders have agreed, 9/11 was not the result of a worldwide Muslim conspiracy. It was the result of a criminal conspiracy by a specific terrorist organization, Al Qaeda. Our quarrel as a nation is with criminals, and with Al Qaeda, not with Islam and Muslims. So there would also be inconsistency if people were to treat the Park51 group as somehow standing for Al Qaeda, while not making similar associations between criminals who kill in the name of some other religion and that religion. Many criminals kill in the name of Christianity. We could argue that the Oklahoma City bombings had that aspect, although the militia movement contains many strands. Anders Behring Breivik was certainly proud of his Christian affiliation, and he clearly viewed his murders as part of a "holy war" between Christians and Muslims, so that is a far clearer case. We also should include the extremists who murder abortion doctors in the name of faith, since their actions are a type of terrorism, which has indeed been investigated as such by law-enforcement agencies, and yet Christian faith is not just the public justification but probably the true motive for those attacks. Many other terrorist groups have been Christian: the Ku Klux Klan and a range of white supremacist groups, among others. If those who express opposition to Park51 are associating all Muslims with Al Qaeda but would never think of associating all Christians with these crimes, then we should conclude that they are guilty of the type of inconsistency targeted in Chapter 4. The fact that some of these people have been hoodwinked by propaganda that tells them that all Muslims are part of a worldwide conspiracy with Al Qaeda to destroy America does not

change the case, since they are allowing themselves to be hoodwinked despite the fact that President Bush and a broad spectrum
of responsible political leaders have assured them that this is not
the case. Willed gullibility is no excuse.

A case that poses a very serious challenge to my charge of inconsistency, however, is that of the Carmelite convent on the site of
Auschwitz, which was brought up by Abraham Foxman of the Anti-
Defamation League in explaining his organization's opposition to
the proposed center. In 1984, Carmelite nuns erected a convent on
the part of the Auschwitz concentration camp called Auschwitz I, in
a building that once was a storehouse for the gas Zyklon B, used in
the gas chambers of the extermination camp.[32] They had the approval of church and government authorities but had conducted no
dialogue with the Polish public or the international Jewish community. A year later they added a large cross that had been erected for a
Mass celebrated on the Auschwitz II (Birkenau) death camp site by
Pope John Paul II in 1979. The cross was placed just next to Block 11,
a torture prison within Auschwitz I. The Church itself ordered the
Carmelites to move by 1989, but they remained until 1993 and left
the cross behind when they moved. Controversy continued about
the cross, dividing the government; meanwhile, hundreds of smaller
crosses were erected just outside Auschwitz, despite the opposition
of the country's Catholic bishops. By 1999, Parliament passed a law,
in consultation with Jewish organizations, giving the government
power to control what was present on the sites of all former camps.
But a leader of the procross opposition announced that he had
placed explosives under the site and would detonate them if the
government attempted to remove the crosses. He was arrested, the
smaller crosses were removed to a nearby monastery, and the large
cross remains.

This controversy is indeed parallel in many ways to the Park51 debate. Property issues are very different: the Polish government controls the property and no private group has any rights there. That does make a difference. In one case, the Carmelites were moving into a public site and changing it, without the permission of the government. In the other, El-Gamal owns the building and has legal title, as lessee from Con Ed, to the surrounding property. The ethical issues, however, do look rather similar. The anticonvent and anticross side insists that the convent and the subsequent crosses offend Jewish sensibilities, given especially the role played by the Catholic Church, both over the long haul, perpetuating the view that Jews killed Christ, and in the short term—since Pius XII was notorious for not doing anything to protest the Holocaust. The proconvent and procross side insists that the site was also used for Polish political prisoners and for famous Catholic resisters: both Father Maximilian Kolbe and Carmelite nun Edith Stein met their deaths there. So in both cases a group that shares a religion with the criminals is moving in where the criminals committed their crimes, and relatives of the victims of these crimes are offended. In both cases it is agreed that the occupants (or prospective occupants in the case of Park51) are not themselves guilty of any crimes and at least widely believed that their intentions are noble. In both cases, too, the group whose actions are protested can point to the fact that its own members suffered on the occasion of disaster: Catholics were killed at Auschwitz, Muslims died on 9/11.

Those are the analogies; where are disanalogies? First and most obvious, the convent and the subsequent crosses are actually on the site of Auschwitz, and that is precisely why they are there. They don't just happen to be in the vicinity of the site; they are on it, they refer to it, and they attempt to memorialize it. Nothing else is around, and there is no practical role for them to play in the region. Park51, by contrast, is in the middle of a bustling city, several city blocks from ground zero, with all sorts of other structures between it and the (future) 9/11 memorial, and structures of a totally nonsacred type, such as an off-track betting parlor and a strip club. And it has a practical role in the neighborhood, serving worshippers, families, and other local residents in a variety of ways. If it has a symbolic role (and this is part of the dispute between Rauf and El-Gamal, in which the symbolic vision of Rauf has by now been repudiated), it has always been secondary to the practical purpose.

The history of Catholic condemnation of Jews as Christ-killers is long and ugly, and there is absolutely no doubt that it played a significant role in the Holocaust, whether or not it played as large a role as some historians have believed. One has only to see the searing final moments of Part I of the Claude Lanzmann documentary film *Shoah* to see why Jews have good reason for offense. A Polish-Jewish man who survived the camps as a boy, in part because locals liked his singing, returns to the town where local Polish residents befriended him, hoping, years after the war, to reestablish some kind of mutuality and connection. It is a religious festival, and the local residents stream out of church. Having initially welcomed him, they then turn on him and exclaim, "The Jews killed Christ!" He weeps. In that sense, one can argue persuasively that the Roman Catholic Church (not the faith, but the organized church) is complicit in the Holocaust on a wide scale, even if many or (today) even most members of the religion abhor anti-Semitism. In the case of Islam, the record is far more murky and decentralized. There are extremist imams and mosques, but there are also far more imams and Muslims generally who abhor and denounce extremism. Particularly in the United States, this group is far more numerous than the extremist group, so that it hardly seems to make sense to impute blame to the religion as a whole. There are texts in both Christianity and Islam to which one can point if one wants to impute blame for violence, but everything depends on how those texts are interpreted, and the record of interpretation is simply far more uniform and centralized in the Catholic case. It is also relevant that the proposed center would serve American Muslims, who played no role at all in 9/11, since the culprits were foreigners. Polish Christians, by contrast, played a big role in the Holocaust.

Recently there has been some movement away from condemnation of the Jews for the killing of Christ. But on the site of Auschwitz, Pope Benedict, in 2006, conspicuously and controversially made no statement of apology. He blamed the Holocaust solely on "criminals" in the Nazi regime, and asked why God had allowed this to happen—clearly refusing to inquire why Catholics and the Church had allowed this to happen.

This brings us to the fact that the Roman Catholic Church is a hierarchically organized religion with a single authoritative leader whose teachings, even when not technically infallible, are normative for all members. And that teacher, Pius XII, remained culpably silent during the Holocaust, doing nothing that in his great power he might have done to stop mass murder. He also even collaborated with the Vichy regime, explicitly approving of some of its anti-Jewish laws. We cannot argue all the details of these matters here, but it is enough to establish that it is perfectly reasonable to impute partial blame for the Holocaust to the Church itself, and to judge that members of the Church who accepted its authority uncritically, without attempting to dissent or protest, bear at least some of the responsibility for that deadly policy of silence. Islam is not centralized—indeed less so even than Judaism—and thus it makes no sense at all to impute blame for the actions of Wahabist extremists to a Sufi who dissents from a large proportion of what that sect stands for. It's a little like blaming an American Reform Jew for the acts of the Israeli ultraorthodox, and of course one does sometimes get blamed in that way. But the appropriate reaction is to feel that the blamer ought to learn some history. Reform Judaism exists precisely because of a rejection of rabbinical authority and a search for autonomy.

The Catholic case seems genuinely difficult. It is reasonable for the Carmelites to seek to commemorate Christians who died at Auschwitz, and reasonable for Jews to feel offended. Park51 seems less difficult, and the offense is less plausibly attached to the actual proposal, once all facts are correctly stated—except through what Mill called a "purely constructive" injury. Although Foxman's invitation to examine the two cases together is a valuable one, it is not inconsistent to feel offended in the former case but not in the latter.

Searching for principled consistency helps us a lot here, revealing some genuinely hard cases and showing us that others are much less difficult. And it is commendable that people have sought consistency here, refusing the asymmetrical treatment of Muslims on account of their religion. On the whole, the U.S. debate is to be preferred to standard European debates about the *burqa*, because it does (at least centrally and typically) focus on the genuinely hard cases.

Philosophy and Controversy: Imagination

We have said, however, that consistency is not everything we need. We also need correct and informed moral perceptions, in order to

THE CASE OF PARK51

make sure that our arguments are not self-serving. And we've also suggested that these attitudes of curiosity, empathy, and friendship help to sustain commitments to good principles that might fray in times of stress. So what does the literary imagination show us about these cases? And who exercised the "inner eyes" well?

Empathy is just one ingredient in a moral argument. Putting yourself in the place of another does not tell you whether they are right or fair: only linking their view of the world to an overall ethical argument will do that. Empathy, however, does do something important, showing us the human reality of other people whom we might have seen as disgusting or subhuman, or as mere aliens and threats.

But to perform that function in a way that guides reflection well, empathy must direct itself to those whom we are inclined to see obtusely or inadequately, not just to those we already know and love. We saw that an unbalanced empathy can misdirect moral judgment, leading us to cozy up to the experience of someone appealingly like ourselves, and thus blocking us even more fully from a view of the full humanity of the people who are different. So more empathy is not always better. We need to figure out what our particular blind spots are likely to be, and how we can use empathy in a targeted rather than a narcissistic way, to address these. Our four authors in Chapter 5 responded to that challenge.

The Park51 case has some of the dangers of the criminal trial (discussed in Chapter 4): hearing the statements of victims who are part of "us," whom we assume to be good and loyal Americans, we may become not more perceptive but less perceptive about the situation and feelings of the many different types of Muslims involved in the debate, which is surely a large part of what a good ethical judge must try to understand. Thus, although Sarah Palin is on solid ground when she asks people to consider the feelings of the victims' families, she invites narcissism by not inviting the imagination to go further into more difficult and challenging terrain. People who think only of the victims are likely to be unbalanced in their sympathies, failing to see how the world looks through the eyes of stigmatized minorities.

One thing that we need, to prevent the imagination from going astray, is a lot of history and correct contextual facts. Insofar as victims' families are offended because they haven't done this mental work (seeing all Muslims as terrorists aimed at military conquest), their offense counts for far less. But how shall we ourselves get accurate information? Certainly there are many good accounts of Islam and the varieties of Islam that we can easily find; if we're in New York, we can talk to Muslims in our community. And if we're not, we can read reports of what they say to find out how they live. We can easily discover how many different countries they come from, what professions and jobs they have, how many died on 9/11. We might go out to talk to people in our community who have different religions. We might visit a mosque or Islamic school or community center. El-Gamal points out that he recently stopped to pray at a midtown mosque, and the service was led by a New York City police officer who was a Muslim. This is part of the complex reality that people need to come to grips with. At the very least, people could read the *Time* profile of Muslims in America, which would acquaint them with a wide range of different Muslim voices. We don't need to go to the scholarly lengths to which George Eliot went in her quest for understanding of the Jews in order to gain a far better understanding of contemporary Islam than most Americans currently have.

But we also need the counterparts of *Nathan der Weise, Daniel*

Deronda, and the children's books we discussed, and we need to have many conversations with Muslims about them. Other parts of the world have long had distinguished novelists for whom Muslim lives are central themes, from Naguib Mahfouz in Egypt to E. M. Forster writing about India to Vikram Seth and many other contemporary writers in India. Still, suggestions should particularly be sought from the Muslim-American community, and they should include both books in which problems of discrimination and suspicion are addressed and books in which being a Muslim is just a particular way of being American, not itself a center of drama or conflict. One article by a Muslim writer that makes a beginning of drawing up a book list for both children and adults is "Muslims in Children's Books," by Rukhsana Khan, in the *School Library Journal,* September 1, 2006. My colleague Aziz Huq has suggested the fiction of Nadeem Aslam, Daniyal Mueenuddin, Usma Aslan Khan, and Kamila Shamsie, all of whom deal with the experience of being Muslim in either Britain or the United States.

Bollywood movies are hardly American, and yet they are a fine way of understanding some of the religious complexities of India's inclusive democracy, where more than 160 million Muslims currently live, and which, despite tensions and conflicts, exemplifies admirable traditions of religious pluralism and respect. This tradition is particularly pronounced in Bollywood, which, like cricket, is a domain in which religious intermixing and amity are a huge and peaceful success. A particularly fine example of a film with that focus is *Lagaan,* a popular account of a group of villagers who beat a British team at cricket (in the late nineteenth century), but only through overcoming religious animosities and forming a genuinely united team. It's actually a good metaphor not only for India but for the United States as well.

At any rate, whatever concrete form it takes, some sort of self-education needs to precede any rush to judgment. This conspicuously did not happen in the case of Park51. Most Americans have an appalling level of ignorance about Islam. Few, for example, if asked to name the nations with the two largest Muslim populations in the world, would name Indonesia and India, both thriving democracies. Many assume that Muslims hail primarily or even only from Arab nations, and even more believe that Muslims have never been democratic citizens. They don't even think about Muslims from India, Indonesia, and Bangladesh. They certainly forget to include African-American converts to Islam (nearly a quarter of the Muslims in the United States are converts). They neglect the fact that a substantial number of Chinese Americans are Muslim. They do not even understand the distinction between Sunni and Shia. In short: they see a general outline of a shape, and they can't fill it in with human reality. What George Eliot asked for in the case of the Jews we should demand in the case of Muslims: curiosity, eager and mobile "inner eyes," and an openness to civic friendship.

Who passes the imagination test here? The developers certainly erred in not pondering the likely reactions of a wide range of Americans; had they done this imaginative work, or done more of it, they would surely have done much more explaining and consulting before the plans were announced, and it might be that the entire bitter controversy could have been avoided. They did, however, at least know their own community and its diversity, and they knew that it includes many who died on 9/11, who helped the victims during the attacks, and, of course, many more who mourn.

But who else imagined Muslim lives adequately? Well, in a down-to-earth, not culturally fancy way, many New Yorkers did, since living in New York means confronting the reality of difference on a daily basis, and usually (if one chooses to remain in New York) enjoying the energy it brings with it. "Cassandra" did all this: she asked the question that was pertinent (would those praying at the center wake up the neighbors) and gave a shrug to the rest, knowing that that's how life in New York is. She treated them, then, as human beings and fellow citizens who have a right to go about their business so long as they are not disturbing other people's business, rather than as conspirators and sworn enemies. Such an attitude, while it doesn't require high literature, does require a certain way of looking at those people, informed by an idea of humanity. As I said about the boys with the *tzizit*, so here: when the inner eyes function well, there's no need for prolonged or elaborate reflection. Similarly, President Bush said little in detail, and he probably did not conduct an exhaustive study of Islam or of Muslim lives, but he gave the right lead to people's imaginations after 9/11, and most of our nation's leaders have continued to do so, particularly when they celebrate Muslim holidays in a respectful and appropriate manner and welcome Muslim community leaders with respect. Mayor Bloomberg did so most convincingly, as someone who really did spend time with Muslims and, more generally, who deals on a daily basis with the population of an enormously diverse city.

The greatest failure of a wide range of opponents of the proposed center was simply not to acknowledge that Muslims are ubiquitous in New York, that they are policemen, computer techs, lawyers, doctors, teachers, in short, that they are in every walk of life in American cities; that their national origins are enormously diverse, including South Asia, the Middle East, but also Britain and other commonwealth countries, where many Muslims migrated before choosing life in the United States. It's a little difficult to believe that the people making strident general claims about Muslims aren't at some level aware of such facts, since it's virtually impossible for a non-Muslim American to go through life without associating with Muslims in a wide variety of capacities, and Muslims, unlike gays and lesbians in the old days, are rarely closeted. But often people just don't think about who their colleagues are, where their doctor comes from, and so forth. Probably the people who demonized the mosque project at that meeting in Sheboygan did not put it together with the doctor who treated them at the local hospital. That really does involve a failure of the inner eyes, and in an America with so many peaceful Muslims, it is a gross failure to cling to a conception of Muslims as all alike and all threatening to U.S. security.

In short, people thinking about American Muslims often fail, imaginatively, in a way very similar to a failure common in thinking about gays and lesbians: they accept a stock image that is framed in part by irrational fear (gays are sources of contagion, gays will undermine heterosexual marriage), and they use that image to think about public choices rather than actually looking at the people who are in front of them, people who are tremendously varied and individual, pursuing a wide range of human purposes. It was something like this failing, too, that Ralph Ellison was targeting in *Invisible Man:* the reason his hero declared himself "invisible" was that a stock scare image of "the black man" dominated thinking, and this scary figure was not a real individual person with a profession, with a specific set of family relations, with a specific set of friends and hopes and fears, and so forth. It's that generalized image, superimposed on varied human reality, that produces the incidents by now both numerous and notorious, in which a taxi driver refuses to stop on Park Avenue for an African-American professor dressed in a suit; in which women clutch their handbags on seeing an African-American professional man in a tweed jacket in the supermarket;

and so on. So too here: the fantasy image of a Muslim conspirator, bent on world domination, takes over from any empirical reality; and of course this is all the more likely to happen because part of the stereotype (as in the case of Jews in the *Protocols*) is that the enemy is a master of disguises. Thus the reassuring neighborly appearance of a Muslim New Yorker is no reassurance that this person is not a radical bent on world domination—as the expensive suit of the professor on Park Avenue ought to have provided reassurance that he was not about to hold a gun to the taxi driver's head. The fiction tells us that all cues coming from the world of reality are part of the plot.

It's not rational to dismiss the fear of Muslim terrorism. That fear is rational in the light of history and current events, and that rational fear ought to guide sensible public policy. That's why I've said that airport profiling, if intelligently done (without some of the crude errors that have actually been made, such as thinking that if the name Ali is on a no-fly list, every person with that name ought to be given a hard time), is a legitimate response to a reasonable fear. But it's simply not reasonable to believe that all one's neighbors are fiends in disguise.

In sum, Park51 was a set of good ideas too hastily put forward, with too little clarification of goals and concepts and much too little consultation with the local community. Once that rush to publicity happened and controversy was generated (often highly irresponsibly), two positions seemed plausible. Both positions grant the wisdom of our basic constitutional principles, but they differ about what ethics and respect for others dictate. The anticenter position is that in this case, sensitivity to public sentiment should lead to relocation—even if the fears of the public are based on stigma and misinformation. The Bloomberg position is that one of America's best achievements is its acceptance of diversity, and that welcoming the center is an ethically admirable act, as well as an expression of a type of civic friendship that solidifies and sustains constitutional principles. Notice that both positions presuppose the nonviolence and basic decency of the developers' intentions, and thus do not even consider what ethics would demand if they were themselves hate-mongers. As I've already said apropos of the Ku Klux Klan, hate-mongering by a group may still be constitutionally protected, but it can and should be publicly protested, and that would be my position, too (and, presumably, that of both Cohen and Bloomberg) were the facts about the developers and their intentions completely different.

In my view, Bloomberg has the better understanding of what has produced and sustained a robust regime of religious freedom and respect in the United States, and of what is required to develop and sustain it for the future. One cannot simply cave in to the fear of hatred, or allow the bounds of policy to be determined by the vehement opposition of people who (however admirable in other respects) are bigoted and misinformed on the issue. Nor does Cohen seem right that the creation of the center would lead to a spiraling climate of hatred. Even if reactive violence were in the offing (as with the integration of the South in the 1950s and 1960s), it certainly doesn't follow that reasonable and decent people should back down before that threat—rather than making sure that crime is both prevented and punished. But Bloomberg's New York is not Governor Wallace's Alabama, and in this case the reaction of Cassandra probably points the way: America in general, and New York in particular, are capacious enough and imaginative enough to contain differences, as so often they have before. If we don't all insist on decency and inclusion, the nation will subtly have become a different nation, one more suspicious of foreigners, more insistent on homogeneity. This would be a tremendous loss.

On Wednesday, September 21, 2011, Park51 opened its doors to the public with a photo exhibit titled "NYChildren: A Child from Every Country, All Living in New York City." The website, park51.org, offers the slogan, "Building Hope, Building Community, Building Beauty." It contains stories of immigrants, including "What Is Possible: A Woman's Journey from Iran to America," an interview with El-Gamal, a discussion with a prominent rabbi, a section entitled "Park51 and Patriotism," with images of America's founders connected to a discussion of religious freedom that quotes from a woman who lost a sister on 9/11, a discussion of Islamic environmentalism with a prominent African-American Muslim leader, and a variety of other community-oriented materials. Surprisingly little publicity attended the opening.

The future of Park51 has yet to be written. But at least it seems likely at this point that it will be written by ordinary New Yorkers, not by national media or bloggers. Ordinary New Yorkers are tough and skeptical and yet not incapable of friendship. So it may even be written well.

7

OVERCOMING THE POLITICS OF FEAR

Our search for an ethical response to the politics of fear began with Socrates in ancient Athens. Athens was in many ways a great democracy, but its people—therefore its politics—were prone to the appeals of irresponsible demagogues and to the usual human failings of sloppiness, deference to tradition, and selfish partiality. Socrates challenged his culture to lead the "examined life," creating a democracy that would be thoughtful rather than impetuous, deliberative rather than unthinkingly adversarial. At the same time, he challenged each individual citizen to take charge of his political life, searching for reasons rather than just making confident assertions, demanding consistency in judgments rather than allowing each person to make a special case for himself. (Only men were citizens in ancient Athens.)

Socrates' response to the defects of his democracy was promising but incomplete. It lacked three elements that any Socratic response today must have. First, it lacked an awareness of the diversity of people and ways of life, and a determination to include all people and groups in democracy's conversation. Socrates tried: he famously said that in the underworld, after death, he would converse with women—whom Athenian custom kept secluded, and whom he therefore could not address during his lifetime (a reminder that the issue of female seclusion has deep roots in a culture that is regarded as the cradle of Western civilization). He also questioned a slave boy, showing that this boy had as agile a mind as any other person and could quickly understand basic principles of mathematics (a reminder that this same cradle of civilization defended that cruel institution). In some respects he did confront people from afar, since Athens did contain resident aliens—although it allowed them few legal rights and sometimes threatened their lives. (Aristotle, an alien, was forced to flee Athens twice.) But even had Socrates been able to address the entire range of human beings who were present in Athens during his time, the city was very small, and it simply did not contain anything like the huge human variety of modern democracies, with their enormous range of religious views, of ethnic origins, of tastes and preferences. So a modern Socratism must establish respectful conversations across a far wider terrain, and this requires historical and social understanding of a type that Socrates did not possess and did not even seek.

Second, Socrates had no idea that respect for human beings required an acknowledgment that there are many different religious and secular ways of life, and that people have a right to seek life's meaning in their own way, in accordance with their own consciences. It's not so much that Socrates believed in a single idea of good and was not a moral relativist. Many if not most people who believe in liberty of conscience today also believe that their own view is correct and that other views are, at least in some respects, incorrect. The insight that Socrates lacked was that politics and government have no business telling people what God is or how to find the meaning of life. Even if governments don't coerce people, the very announcement that a given religion (or antireligion) is the preferred view is a kind of insult to people who in all conscience cannot share this view and wish to continue to go their own way. And that is a point that Socrates, and many philosophers after him, have utterly failed to understand.

Indeed, the idea of equal liberty of conscience took a surprisingly long time to take hold in the Western tradition. The European wars of religion ended in a grudging compromise, as some nations established Roman Catholicism and others Protestantism—but none sought principles that showed equal respect to the consciences of all. Even when minorities (Jews, for example) began to be officially tolerated, it was usually the sort of grudging toleration criticized by George Washington as hierarchical, not an acknowledgment that all human beings have equal rights to liberty. Even in the nineteenth century, when many internationally minded thinkers began to talk of a universalistic "religion of humanity" that would link all human beings in a culture of human rights and compassion, they imagined it as a replacement for traditional religion, which would, they thought, quickly be seen as old-fashioned and retrograde, and would be strongly discouraged. In trying to build political institutions around this possibility, they really didn't show much respect for people for whom those religions were defining features of life.

Interestingly, the missing idea existed far earlier in India: from at least the time in the second century B.C.E. when Ashoka, an emperor who converted from Hinduism to Buddhism, set up pillars announcing edicts of mutual respect and toleration between the religions. The same idea was developed much further, and over a wider and more diverse territory, in the Muslim Moghul empire, when Akbar, an observant Muslim, established policies of toleration in his entire domain. Akbar had some influence in Europe, and his ideas were well known, but European sectarianism and arrogance proved stronger—all the way through the subsequent history of the Raj, to such a degree that Winston Churchill could say that Hindus are a "beastly people with a beastly religion" without getting into any political difficulty as a result.

The idea that political principles should not plump for one religion over others and should show equal respect to the liberty of all did a lot better in the American colonies and, ultimately, in the new nation, which forged basically adequate principles for dealing with today's problems of religious diversity and suspicion. The reality, however, has always been less glorious than the principles, as Roman Catholics, Mormons, Jehovah's Witnesses—and of course Native Americans—all fared ill in concrete searches for equality. Hindus, Muslims, and Buddhists, largely kept at bay by immigration policy, were not even seriously considered until very recently.

The failure of good principles to guide reality consistently reminds us of the third thing Socrates lacked: a curious imagination. To some extent he did have one, as he sought out the slave boy and as he announced his plan to question women in the afterlife. And other Greeks did much more in this direction. Historian Herodotus traveled all over the known world and reported the ways of life of many different peoples with a genuine curiosity and a surprising absence of cultural chauvinism. Athenian tragedy repeatedly turned to the experiences of women, of foreigners, even on occasion of slaves, inviting the audience to inhabit these unfamiliar perspectives, and suggesting that this imaginative activity was relevant to political choice. India, meanwhile, did a lot along these same lines. The great poet Kalidasa, in the fifth century C.E., wrote a poem, *Megadhuta*, that imagines a cloud traveling all around India—to bring a message from one lover to another, but in the process observing with loving curiosity the ways of life of people in different regions. Cross-religious imagination was a major theme in Sufi Muslim poetry during the Moghul empire. No doubt each national tradition has its own ways of developing these themes. In Europe, the literary tradition of curiosity and friendship has had many descendants, as Chapter 5 recorded, each addressing the specific problems of the "inner eyes" in their own time.

Today, we at least know what good political principles look like in the area of religious respect and human equality. In the United States, and in a much more uneven way in Europe, such principles are even recognized in law and guide public life. They remain fragile, however, in times of fear. Like railroad tracks, they guide the train well until some disaster, whether a system failure or an earthquake, causes it to go off the tracks. And today we see all too many cases in which panic is causing derailment.

The poet Walt Whitman said: "To hold men together by paper and seal or by compulsion is no account,/ That only holds men together that aggregates all in a living principle." Laws are made by people, and they can be altered and repealed should those same people change their ways of seeing one another. So a political culture that is to remain stable needs to think about people and how they see the world. And people are not terribly reliable: they tend to be wrapped up in their own concerns, and are often obtuse toward their neighbors. Our current climate of fear shows that people are all too easily turned away from good values and laws, in a time of genuine insecurity and threat.

Our time is genuinely dangerous. As we have seen, many fears are rational, and appeals to fear have a role to play in a society that takes human life seriously. Still, at this point, the balance has all too often shifted in the other direction, as irresponsibly manufactured fears threaten principles we should cling to and be proud of. To counteract the baneful tendency to narrow our sights in a focus on the all-important self, we need, first of all, each of us, the Socratic (and Christian-Kantian) commitment to examine our choices to see whether they are selfish, whether they make a privileged case of ourselves, ignoring the equal claims of others. And we need, equally, the inner spirit that must animate the search for consistency, if it is not to remain a hollow shell: we need, that is, the spirit of curiosity and friendship.

Notes

1.   A TIME OF ANXIETY AND SUSPICION

1. In what follows, I use the word *burqa* to refer to both *burqa* and *niqab*. The commonly accepted distinction is that a *burqa* is a full-body covering with a mesh screen for the eyes; a *niqab* is a face veil, typically attached to a full-body covering, which has a slit for the eyes.

2. "Italian Law to Ban Veil Wins Early Approval," *Sydney Morning Herald*, August 4, 2011.

3. Ian Fisher, "Italian Woman's Veil Stirs More Than Fashion Feud," *New York Times*, October 15, 2004.

4. See Legifrance (public service for diffusion of the law), Loi no. 2004-228 du 15 mars 2004, version in force November 7, 2011. Available at http://www.legifrance.gouv.fr/affichTexte.do?cidTexte=JORFTEXT000000417977&dateTexte=.

5. Stephen Schwartz, "Kosovo Says No to the Headscarf in Public Schools," *Weekly Standard*, April 14, 2010.

6. "Dutch Government Pact Bans Burqa," *Reuters*, September 30, 2010, available at http://www.reuters.com/article/2010/09/30/us-dutch-politics-idUSTRE68151420100930; "Another Spanish Town Bans Burqa in Public," *Fox News*, September 6, 2011, available at http://www.foxnews.com/world/2011/09/06/another-spanish-town-bans-burqa-in-public/; "Belgian Lawmakers Pass Burka Ban," *BBC*

News, April 30, 2010, available at http://news.bbc.co.uk/2/hi/europe/8652861.stm.

7. "Swiss Court Upholds Basketball Hijab Ban," *Muslim News* (UK), February 26, 2010, available at http://www.muslimnews.co.uk/paper/index.php?article=4517.

8. "Russian Muslims Hail Headscarf Ruling," *BBC News,* May 15, 2003, http://news.bbc.co.uk/2/hi/europe/3031379.stm; "Russian Pupil Fired from School for Wearing Hijab," *Union of Islamic World Students,* September 28, 2010, http://www.rohama.org/en/pages/?cid=2921; "University in Russia's North Caucasus Bans Muslim Headscarves," *Ria Novosti,* December 23, 2010, http://en.rian.ru/russia/20101223/161905836.html.

9. Nick Cumming-Bruce and Steven Erlanger, "Swiss Ban Building of Minarets on Mosques," *New York Times,* November 29, 2009.

10. "Giunta leghista: niente kebab in centro," *Corriere Della Sera* (Italy), August 19, 2009, available at http://www.corriere.it/politica/09_agosto_19/kebab_vietato_giunta_leghista_capriate_san_gervasio_7a6a8484-8ceb-11de-90bb-00144f02aabc.shtml.

11. "Anti-Immigrant Italians Find New Foe: Food From Abroad," *The Observer* (UK), November 14, 2009, available at http://www.guardian.co.uk/world/2009/nov/15/italys-kebab-war-hots-up.

12. "Muslim Headscarves Unveil Attitudes and Opinions," *YLE* (Finland), October 8, 2008, available at http://www.yle.fi/uutiset/news/2008/10/muslim_headscarves_unveil_attitudes_and_opinions_354627.html.

13. KGS, "Muslim Women's Head Scarf Use at Work Causes Controversy," *Tundra Tabloids,* February 2, 2009, available at http://tundratabloids.com/2009/02/finland-muslim-head-scarf-controversy.html. The Helsinki Osuus store in Elanno has this policy, and some K-food stores have adopted it.

14. "Raasepori Schools Frown On, But Will Allow, Islamic Scarves," *YLE* (Finland), May 19, 2010, available at http://www.yle.fi/uutiset/news/2010/05/raasepori_schools_frown_on_but_will_allow_islamic_scarves_1695371.html.

15. Anu Ilomäki, "No Special Meals for Muslim Children at Helsinki and Espoo Municipal Playgrounds," *Helsingin Sanomat* (Finland), June 16, 2007, available at http://www.hs.fi/english/article/No+spe cial+meals+for+Muslim+children+at+Helsinki+and+Espoo+ municipal+playgrounds/1135228145208. The only special meal currently offered is one for the lactose-intolerant. Since the primary Muslim concern was having an alternative to pork, one can assume that the concerns of Jewish children are also unaddressed.

16. "All Nationalities Welcome during 'Muslims-only' Hours at Helsinki Public Swimming Pools," *Helsingin Sanomat* (Finland), June 22, 2009, available at http://www.hs.fi/english/print/1135247093619. The issue is that Muslim women believe it immodest to be seen naked by another woman, which means that they want to use the showers one by one, and non-Muslim Finnish women object to this. This article uses the term "Finns" in a way that implies that the Muslim women are not Finnish.

17. Steven Erlanger, "Norway Suspect Denies Guilt and Suggests He Did Not Act Alone," *New York Times*, July 25, 2011.

18. Neil Sears, "'Vlad the Impaler Was a Genius': The Crazed and Hate-Filled 'Manifesto' of the Mass Murderer," *Daily Mail* (UK), July 25, 2011.

19. Mark Hughes and Gordon Rayner, "Norway Killer Anders Behring Breivik Had Extensive Links to English Defence League," *The Telegraph* (UK), July 25, 2011; "Norwegian Murderer Had Links with Anti-Muslim Groups in Israel, UK and USA," *English Islam Times*, July 26, 2011, avialable at http://www.islamtimes.org/vdce7n8v. jh8fxik1bj.html.

20. "Norway Attacks: National Front Member Suspended For Defending Anders Behring Breivik," *The Telegraph* (UK), July 26, 2011.

21. "Italy MEP Backs Ideas of Norway Killer Breivik," *BBC News*, July 27, 2011, http://www.bbc.co.uk/news/world-europe-14315108.

22. Edwin S. Gaustad and Leigh E. Schmidt, *The Religious History of America*, rev. ed. (New York: HarperCollins, 2002), 67, 170.

23. Ibid., 43.

24. Ibid., 170.
25. Ibid., 352; Gary L. Ward, *Mormonism I: Evangelical Christian Anti-Mormonism in the Twentieth Century* (New York: Garland, 1990).
26. Leonard Dinnerstein, *Antisemitism in America* (New York: Oxford University Press, 1994).
27. "Jewish Prayer Ritual Causes LA Flight Lockdown," *CBS News,* March 14, 2011, available at http://www.cbsnews.com/stories/2011/03/14/national/main20042769.shtml.
28. Laurie Goodstein and Tamar Lewin, "Victims of Mistaken Identity, Sikhs Pay a Price for Turbans," *New York Times,* September 19, 2001; Laurie Goodstein, "A Nation Challenged: Civil Rights; American Sikhs Contend They Have Become a Focus of Profiling at Airports," *New York Times,* November 10, 2001.
29. Ken Maguire, "American Sikhs Decry Screenings," *New York Times,* November 6, 2010.
30. "U.S. Military Quietly Opens Up to Sikhs," *Today in the Military,* September 10, 2010, available at http://www.military.com/news/article/us-military-quietly-opens-up-to-sikhs.html.
31. "Protesters Arrested for Disrupting First Hindu Senate Prayer," *CNN,* July 12, 2007, available at http://politicalticker.blogs.cnn.com/2007/07/12/protesters-arrested-for-disrupting-first-hindu-senate-prayer/.
32. "Airline Apologises after Muslim Woman Wearing a Headscarf is Thrown Off Flight for 'Suspicious Behaviour,'" *Daily Mail* (UK), March 17, 2011.
33. "Muslim Woman Sues Disneyland Over Headscarf," *The Telegraph* (UK), August 19, 2010.
34. "Muslim Disney Employee Agrees to Wear a Beret over Her Hijab after Theme Park Objected to Her Head Scarf," *Daily Mail* (UK), September 29, 2010.
35. "Controversy Shrouds Muslim Women's Head Coverings," *USA Today,* April 15, 2010.

36. Laurie Goodstein, "Georgia: Lawsuit Over Muslim Woman's Head Scarf," *The New York Times*, December 15, 2010.

37. Joseph Ruzich, "DuPage Zoning Panel Opposes Plan for Mosque Near Willowbrook," *Chicago Tribune*, January 14, 2011.

38. "Naperville Not Putting Out Welcome Mat for Islamic Religious Center," *Chicago Tribune*, October 7, 2011.

39. Robbie Brown, "Incidents at Mosque in Tennessee Spread Fear," *New York Times*, August 30, 2011; "Justice Department Wades into Tennessee Mosque Controversy on Side of Islam," *Fox News*, October 18, 2010, http://www.foxnews.com/politics/2010/10/18/justice-department-wades-tennessee-mosque-controversy-islam/.

40. "Man Charged with Mosque Threat Ruled Incompetent," *CBS Detroit*, August 22, 2011, http://detroit.cbslocal.com/2011/08/22/man-charged-with-mosque-threat-ruled-incompetent/.

41. Nationwide Anti-Mosque Activity (map), American Civil Liberties Union, n.d., available at http://www/aclu.org/map-nationwide-anti-mosque-activity.

42. Garrett Epps, "In Sharia Law Ban, Oklahoma Juggles Dynamite," *Atlantic*, November 16, 2010.

43. James McKinley, "Oklahoma Surprise: Islam as an Election Issue," *New York Times*, November 14, 2010.

44. James C. McKinley, Jr., "Judge Blocks Oklahoma's Ban on Using Shariah Law in Court," *New York Times*, November 29, 2010.

45. Aziz Huq, "Defend Muslims, Defend America," *New York Times*, June 19, 2011.

46. Zaid Jilani, "Report: At Least 13 States Have Introduced Bills Guarding Against Non-Existent Threat of Sharia Law," *Think Progress*, February 8, 2011, http://thinkprogress.org/politics/2011/02/08/142590/sharia-states/.

47. Bob Smietana, "Tennessee Bill Would Jail Shariah Followers," *USA Today*, February 23, 2011.

48. See Huq, "Defend Muslims, Defend America"; and Steven Green

house, "Muslims Report Rising Discrimination at Work," *New York Times,* September 23, 2010.

49. J .H. H. Weiller, "To Be a European Citizen: Eros and Civilization," Center for European Studies, University of Wisconsin-Madison, working paper, Spring 1998, available at http://uw-madison-ces. org/sites/ces.wisc.edu/files/weiler.pdf.

50. Jacob Katz, *Out of the Ghetto* (Cambridge, MA: Harvard University Press, 1973).

51. Eric Hobsbawm, *Nations and Nationalism since 1780: Programme, Myth, Reality* (London: Cambridge University Press, 1990); Graham Robb, *The Discovery of France* (New York: Norton, 2007); Linda Colley, *Britons: Forging the Nation 1707–1837* (New Haven: Yale University Press, 1992).

52. George Mosse, *Nationalism and Sexuality: Middle-Class Morality and Sexual Norms in Modern Europe* (Madison: University of Wisconsin Press, 1985).

53. Anssi Paasi, *Territories, Boundaries and Consciousness: The Changing Geographies of the Finnish-Russian Border* (Chichester: John Wiley and Sons, 1996), 79–97.

54. Maureen O'Donnell, "S. Side St. Pat's Parade Yanks Mat from Buchanan," *Chicago Sun-Times,* March 9, 1996.

55. See Martha C. Nussbaum, *The Clash Within: Democracy, Religious Violence, and India's Future* (Cambridge, MA: Harvard University Press, 2007).

2.   FEAR: A NARCISSISTIC EMOTION

1. Diogenes Laertius, *Lives of the Philosophers,* Life of Pyrrho, IX.1.

2. Ibid., IX.63.

3. For both, see the excellent collection of texts in Paul Mendes-Flohr, ed., *The Jew in the Modern World* (New York: Oxford University Press, 2011), 336–342.

4. Joseph LeDoux, *The Emotional Brain: The Mysterious Underpinnings of Emotional Life* (New York: Simon and Schuster, 1996); Joseph

LeDoux, "Emotional Memory Systems in the Brain," *Behavioural Brain Research* 58 (1993), 69–79; Joseph LeDoux, "Emotion, Memory, and the Brain," *Scientific American* 270 (1994), 50–57.

5. LeDoux, "Emotion, Memory, and the Brain," 56

6. Ibid., 57.

7. See Jenefer Robinson, "Startle," *Journal of Philosophy* 92 (1995), 53–74. Both fright and "startle" still involve cognition in the sense that they involve transmission and processing of information, as well as some rudimentary appraisal of the situation; they just do not involve reflection or self-conscious awareness.

8. John Stuart Mill, *Utilitarianism*, chapter 5.

9. Erich Maria Remarque, *All Quiet on the Western Front*, trans. Brian Murdoch (London: Random House, 1994; original German publication 1929), 37.

10. Ibid., 150.

11. A good treatment of this issue is Corey Robin, *Fear: The History of a Political Idea* (New York: Oxford University Press, 2004).

12. Aristotle, *Rhetoric*, 1382a21 2, my translation.

13. Ibid., 1382b31 2.

14. In his biological works, Aristotle insists that fear is present in all animals, in a way that other emotions such as grief, anger, and compassion are not. See Juha Sihvola, "Emotional Animals: Do Aristotelian Emotions Require Beliefs?" *Apeiron* 29 (1996), 105–144.

15. See Cass R. Sunstein, *Risk and Reason: Safety, Law, and the Environment* (Cambridge: Cambridge University Press, 2002), 33–35, with references to the psychological literature.

16. See Timur Kuran, "Ethnic Norms and Their Transformation through Reputational Cascades," *Journal of Legal Studies* 27 (1998), 623–659; and Sunstein, *Risk*, 37–39.

17. Sudhir Kakar, *The Colors of Violence: Cultural Identities, Religion, and Conflict* (Chicago: University of Chicago Press, 1996).

18. Solomon Asch, "Opinions and Social Pressure" (1955), http://www.panarchy.org/asch/social.pressure.1955.html.

19. Anne Hollander, *Sex and Suits* (New York: Kodansha Globe, 1995).

20. For all these, with examples from the pamphlet literature, see Martha C. Nussbaum, *From Disgust to Humanity: Sexual Orientation and Constitutional Law* (New York: Oxford University Press, 2010).

21. See, for example, Otto Weininger, *Sex and Character* (1906; New York: Howard Fertig, 2003), in which Jews are compared to women in this respect.

22. See Sander Gilman, *The Jew's Body* (New York: Routledge, 1991); Sander Gilman, *Creating Beauty to Cure the Soul: Race and Psychology in the Shaping of Aesthetic Surgery* (Durham, NC: Duke University Press, 1998).

23. The Greeks, by contrast, thought the circumcised penis cleaner, though less beautiful.

24. The 2010 Human Development Report, United Nations Development Programme, available at http://hdr.undp.org/en/, cites 62.0 percent of Swiss women and 74.5 percent of Swiss men as having at least secondary education; labor force participation rates are 76.6 percent and 87.8 percent, respectively.

25. Ashley Hall, "Media Rushed to Judgment in Norway Attacks," ABC News (Australia), July 26, 2011, available at http://www.abc.net.au/news/2011-07-25/media-rushed-judgment-in-norway-under-fire/2809786/?site=sydney.

26. Magnus Nome, "Why Let Facts Ruin the Story?" Open Democracy, August 8, 2011, available at http://www.opendemocracy.net/magnus-nome/why-let-facts-ruin-story-norwegian-comments-on-us-coverage-of-norway-terror.

27. Genevieve Long Belmaker and Jack Phillips, "Media Slammed for Linking Islam to Norway Attacks," *Epoch Times*, July 27, 2011.

28. "Norway Attacks 'A Sign,' Say Far Right," *Herald Sun* (Australia), July 27, 2011.

29. http://uk.reuters.com/article/2011/07/23/uk-norway-killer-idUKTRE76M1OJ20110723.

30. Eugene Robinson, "Stoking Irrational Fears about Islam," *Washington Post*, April 7, 2011.

31. Ibid.
32. Aziz Huq, "Defend Muslims, Defend America," *New York Times*, June 19, 2011.
33. For the chart and the account of the group, see Spencer Ackerman, "After Oslo, Group Accuses Thousands of Being Homegrown Terrorists," *Wired*, July 25, 2011, available at http://www.wired.com/dangerroom/2011/07/thousands-accused/.
34. Spencer Ackerman, "FBI 'Islam 101' Guide Depicted Muslims as 7th-Century Simpletons," *Wired*, July 27, 2011, available at http://www.wired.com/dangerroom/2011/07/fbi-islam-101-guide/.
35. Ibid.
36. Danios, "Pamela Geller Hiding Identity of Norwegian Terrorist (Or Possible Future Terrorist)," *Loonwatch*, July 31, 2011, available at http://www.loonwatch.com/2011/07/pamela-geller-hiding-the-identity-of-norwegian-terrorist-or-possible-future-terrorist/.
37. Murdoch borrows this term from Buddhist ethics, in which she had a lifelong interest.
38. Iris Murdoch, *The Black Prince* (New York: Penguin, 2003), p. 183.

3. EQUAL RESPECT FOR CONSCIENCE

1. See Amartya Sen, *The Argumentative Indian* (London: Allen Lane, 2005).
2. Christine Korsgaard, *Fellow Creatures: Kantian Ethics and Our Duties to Animals*, The Tanner Lectures on Human Values, vol. 25/6 (2004), 79–110.
3. See Richard Sorabji, *Animal Minds and Human Morals: The Origins of the Western Debate* (Ithaca, NY: Cornell University Press, 1993).
4. One because of the possibility of human cloning.
5. Martha C. Nussbaum, *Frontiers of Justice: Disability, Nationality, Species Membership* (Cambridge, MA: Harvard University Press, 2006); Martha C. Nussbaum, "The Capabilities of People with Cognitive Disabilities," in *Cognitive Disability and Its Challenge to Moral Philosophy*, ed. Eva Kittay and Licia Carlson (Malden, MA: Wiley-Blackwell, 2010), 75–96.

6. The famous words "to bigotry . . . no assistance" and also the words
   "liberty of conscience and immunities of citizenship" are directly
   quoted by Washington from the letter addressed to him by the He
   brew Congregation at Newport, and signed by its warden Moses
   Seixas. Washington's letter is quoted in many places, often with minor variations in punctuation or even wording. I have checked this
   version against the photograph of the original in Washington's
   (very clear) hand. See http://gwpapers.virginia.edu/documents/he-
   brew/reply.html.

7. John Locke, *A Letter Concerning Toleration* (1689; Amherst, NY: Pro-
   metheus Books, 1990).

8. Ibid., 69.

9. Ibid.

10. Ibid.

11. Ibid., 59.

12. *Church of the Lukumi Babalu Aye v. City of Hialeah*, 508 U.S. 520 (1993).

13. *A Letter Concerning Toleration*, 47–48.

14. *Fraternal Order of Police v. City of Newark*, 170 F. 3d 359 (3d Cir. 1999).

15. Ibid., 365.

16. See Michael McConnell, "The Origins and Historical Understand-
    ing of Free Exercise of Religion," *Harvard Law Review* 103 (1990),
    1409 ff.

17. The Quakers wrote to Washington first, expressing gratitude for re-
    ligious freedom and pointing out that they are good citizens, con-
    tributing to the support of the poor and to civil government.

18. *Stansbury v. Marks*, 2 Dall. 213 (Pa. 1793); *People v. Philips*, New York
    Court of General Sessions, 1813.

19. The decisive case was *Cantwell v. Connecticut*, 310 U.S. 296 (1940).

20. *Sherbert v. Verner*, 374 U.S. 398 (1963).

21. See *U.S. v. Seeger*, 380 U.S. 163 (1965), and *Welsh v. U.S.*, 398 U.S. 333
    (1970).

22. 406 U.S. 205 (1972).

23. See my discussion in Martha C. Nussbaum, *Liberty of Conscience: In*

Defense of America's Tradition of Religious Equality (New York: Basic Books, 2008), ch. 4.

24. 494 U.S. 872 (1990).

25. Ibid., 909.

26. This controversy is more fully described in Nussbaum, *Liberty of Conscience*, ch. 5.

27. 521 U.S. 507 (1997).

28. See detailed enumeration in Nussbaum, *Liberty of Conscience*, ch. 4.

29. 544 U.S. 709 (2005).

30. See Christopher L. Eisgruber and Lawrence G. Sager, discussed in Nussbaum, *Liberty of Conscience*, ch. 4.

31. This is, basically, the course I take in *Liberty of Conscience*.

32. *U.S. v. Seeger*, 380 U.S. 163 (1965), *Welsh v. U.S.*, 398 U.S. 333 (1970). The cases, however, involved statutory interpretation, and thus cannot be understood as a general mandate for such policies.

33. Kent Greenawalt, *Religion and the Constitution*, vol. 1: *Free Exercise of Fairness* (Princeton: Princeton University Press, 2006), chaps. 4 and 5.

34. *Rosenberger v. Rector and Visitors of the University of Virginia*, 515 U.S. 819 (1995).

35. The Central Human Capabilities

   1. Life. Being able to live to the end of a human life of normal length; not dying prematurely, or before one's life is so reduced as to be not worth living.

   2. Bodily Health. Being able to have good health, including reproductive health; to be adequately nourished; to have adequate shelter.

   3. Bodily Integrity. Being able to move freely from place to place; to be secure against violent assault, including sexual assault and domestic violence; having opportunities for sexual satisfaction and for choice in matters of reproduction.

   4. Senses, Imagination, and Thought. Being able to use the senses, to imagine, think, and reason—and to do these things in a "truly

257

human" way, a way informed and cultivated by an adequate education, including, but by no means limited to, literacy and basic mathematical and scientific training. Being able to use imagination and thought in connection with experiencing and producing works and events of one's own choice, religious, literary, musical, and so forth. Being able to use one's mind in ways protected by guarantees of freedom of expression with respect to both political and artistic speech, and freedom of religious exercise. Being able to have pleasurable experiences and to avoid non-beneficial pain.

5. *Emotions.* Being able to have attachments to things and people outside ourselves; to love those who love and care for us, to grieve at their absence; in general, to love, to grieve, to experience longing, gratitude, and justified anger. Not having one's emotional development blighted by fear and anxiety. (Supporting this capability means supporting forms of human association that can be shown to be crucial in their development.)

6. *Practical Reason.* Being able to form a conception of the good and to engage in critical reflection about the planning of one's life. (This entails protection for the liberty of conscience and religious observance.)

7. *Affiliation.*

   A. Being able to live with and toward others, to recognize and show concern for other human beings, to engage in various forms of social interaction; to be able to imagine the situation of another. (Protecting this capability means protecting institutions that constitute and nourish such forms of affiliation, and also protecting the freedom of assembly and political speech.)

   B. Having the social bases of self-respect and non-humiliation; being able to be treated as a dignified being whose worth is equal to that of others. This entails provisions of non-discrimination on the basis of race, sex, sexual orientation, ethnicity, caste, religion, national origin.

8. *Other Species.* Being able to live with concern for and in relation to animals, plants, and the world of nature.

9. *Play.* Being able to laugh, to play, to enjoy recreational activities.

10. *Control over One's Environment.*

   A. *Political.* Being able to participate effectively in political choices that govern one's life; having the right of political participation, protections of free speech and association.

   B. *Material.* Being able to hold property (both land and movable goods), and having property rights on an equal basis with others; having the right to seek employment on an equal basis with others; having the freedom from unwarranted search and seizure. In work, being able to work as a human being, exercising practical reason and entering into meaningful relationships of mutual recognition with other workers.

4. IMPARTIALITY AND THE EXAMINED LIFE

1. My own translations. I retain the old-fashioned word "mote" because the image is so famous; "speck of sawdust" is used by some good modern translations.

2. http://news.bbc.co/uk/2/hi/6159046.stm.

3. http://news.bbc.co.uk/2/hi/uk_news/politics/5413470.stm.

4. http://www.dailymail.co.uk/news/article-1249812/Justice-Secretary-Jack-Straw-rejects-burka-ban-Muslim-women.html.

5. Judge Janet Thorpe, quoted in http://news.bbc.co.uk/2/hi/americas/2970514.stm.

6. "The Case of Mrs. Sultaana Freeman," American Civil Liberties Union of Florida, n.d., available at http://www.aclufl.org/issues/religious_liberty/freemanstatement.cfm.

7. Ibid.
8. See, for example, http://www.nbcwashington.com/news/local/ Hairline-Headline—A-New-Rule-for-Dcs-DMV-90857884.html. Alex Cameron, "Muslim Woman Wins Driver's License Fight," News9 (Oklahoma City), February 19, 2009.
9. *City of Chicago v. Morales,* 527 U.S. 1 (1999). The plurality of opinions in this 6–3 vote makes it a very complicated case to sort out; both the vagueness and the liberty arguments clearly command a majority, but they are expressed somewhat differently in the four different opinions on the majority side. Given the narrowness of the holding, the city was able to pass a rather similar law under which it's plausible to think that wearing gang colors plus ethnicity still matters to enforcement.
10. See Aziz Huq, "Defend Muslims, Defend America," *New York Times* June 19, 2011. Huq, a law professor at the University of Chicago, is talking about the preemptive bans on "Sharia law," but his point applies to a range of other cases.
11. Municipal Code sec. 36034.
12. See volokh.com/2011/05/18/substantive-dignity-dwarf-throwing-burqa-bans-and-welfare-rights/.
13. Peter Allen, "Nicolas Sarkozy Says the Burqa Is 'Not Welcome' in France," *Telegraph* (UK), June 22, 2009.
14. See my "Objectification," in Martha C. Nussbaum, *Sex and Social Justice* (New York: Oxford University Press, 1999), 213–239, discussing and engaging critically with a large feminist literature.
15. See Martha C. Nussbaum, *Liberty of Conscience: In Defense of America's Tradition of Religious Equality* (New York: Basic Books, 2008), ch. 5, for much more detail on these cases.
16. Paul Blanshard, *American Freedom and Catholic Power,* 2nd ed., rev. and enl. (Boston: Beacon Press, 1958), 88.
17. *Swann v. Pack,* 527 S.W. 2d 99 (Tenn. 1975).
18. *Bob Jones v. U.S.,* 461 U.S. 574 (983).
19. See Edward O. Laumann and Robert T. Michael, eds., *Sex, Love, and*

Health in America: Private Choices and Public Policies (Chicago: University of Chicago Press, 2000), and Edward O. Laumann, John H. Gagnon, Robert T. Michael, and Stuart Michaels, *The Social Organization of Sexuality: Sexual Practices in the United States* (Chicago: University of Chicago Press, 1994).

20. There is no explicit restriction to "public accommodations," but the ban is enforced only there. Upper-caste parents still overwhelmingly resist lower-caste marriages for their children, no doubt applying familiar types of coercive pressure, and in some cases continuing to practice untouchability in their homes.

21. *Barnes v. Glen Theater,* 501 U.S. 560 (1991), concurring opinion by Justice Souter. I criticize Souter's analysis in Martha C. Nussbaum, *From Disgust to Humanity: Sexual Orientation and Constitutional Law* (New York: Oxford University Press, 2010), ch. 6. Souter is alone in his analysis, in this case decided by a 5–4 vote, but because his rationale for upholding the ban is narrower than that of the other members of the majority, his is the controlling opinion.

22. James Joyce, *Ulysses* (New York: Modern Library, 1961), 731.

23. Ear surgery was the only form of surgery I have ever had to date. It was utterly unnecessary and dictated by parental vanity.

24. Amy Chua, *Battle Hymn of the Tiger Mother* (New York: Penguin, 2011); also Amy Chua, "Why Chinese Mothers Are Superior," *Wall Street Journal,* January 8, 2011.

25. 406 U.S. 205 (1972).

26. The *burqa* has no direct Quranic authority: it is a matter of interpretive tradition. In some communities (e.g., Bengal) face-covering is unknown.

27. Joan Wallach Scott, *The Politics of the Veil* (Princeton: Princeton University Press, 2007), 127.

28. *Pierce v. Society of Sisters,* 268 U.S. 510 (1925).

29. There are, of course, difficult questions here, such as the question of accommodations for doctors who are unwilling to perform abortions on religious grounds. My view is that such accommodations

for individuals should be granted, but only in combination with a strong guarantee that a woman has other options for the exercise of her legal rights; and similarly for other cases.

30. See my "Teaching Patriotism," *University of Chicago Law Review*, forthcoming 2012.

5. RESPECT AND THE SYMPATHETIC IMAGINATION

1. See Barbara Herman, *The Practice of Moral Judgment* (Cambridge, MA: Harvard University Press, 1996), arguing that a Kantian ethic relies on cultivated perception.

2. This work is summarized in his *magnum opus, Altruism in Humans* (New York: Oxford University Press, 2011), with complete bibliography of earlier publications. His earlier work is discussed in C. Daniel Batson, *The Altruism Question: Toward a Social Psychological Answer* (Hillsdale, NJ: Lawrence Erlbaum, 1991).

3. See Susan Bandes, "Empathy, Narrative, and Victim Impact Statements," *University of Chicago Law Review* 63 (1997), 361–412.

4. See *Woodson v. North Carolina*, 428 U.S. 280 (1976).

5. As he notes, Barbados permitted religious liberty *de facto* and with the approval of Charles II, but no official charter guaranteed religious liberty to all prior to the Rhode Island charter of 1658. For an extensive account of the Charter, and of Williams's thought and life in general, see Martha C. Nussbaum, *Liberty of Conscience: In Defense of America's Tradition of Religious Equality* (New York: Basic Books, 2008), ch. 2.

6. The major sources for Williams's thought are Roger Williams, *The Correspondence of Roger Williams,* ed. Glenn La Fantasie (Providence, RI: Brown University Press, 1988), hereafter C I and C II, followed by the page number in each case; and *The Complete Writings of Roger Williams* (New York: Russell and Russell, 1963), in seven volumes, of which the first is *A Key into the Language of America*, the 1643 book with which we shall be most concerned.

7. C I, 379.
8. See the detailed account in C I, 12–23, "Editorial Note."
9. As I discuss in Nussbaum, *Liberty of Conscience*, this novel legal argument anticipates by more than three hundred years the argument of the Australian Supreme Court in the famous case *Mabo v. Queensland* (1992).
10. C II, 610.
11. *Key into the Language of America*, 85.
12. *Mabo v. Queensland* (1992), 175 CLR 1.
13. C II, 750.
14. C II, 751.
15. C II, 535, 541, citing the Charter.
16. C II, 611.
17. For example, C II, 534, complaining about the refusal of the English to pay his emissary: "These very Barbarians when they send forth a publike messenger they furnish him out, they defray all paymts, they gratifie him with Rewards, and if he prove lame and sick and not able to returne, they visit him and bring him home upon their shoulders (and that many Scores of miles) with all Care and Tendernes."
18. *Key into the Language of America*, 47.
19. C II, 754.
20. C I, 387.
21. *Key into the Language of America*.
22. Ibid., 164–165.
23. Ibid., 167.
24. *Pew Global Attitudes Project,* Pew Research Center, released July 21, 2011, at http://pewglobal.org/2011/07/21/muslim-western-tensions-persist/1/.
25. A fine treatment of all these prejudices in England, with a particularly detailed history of the "blood libel" and a host of compelling examples, is the brilliant book by Anthony Julius, *Trials of the*

Diaspora: A History of Anti-Semitism in England (New York: Oxford University Press, 2010).

26. William Shakespeare, *Merchant of Venice*, I.iii.

27. I use the version in Mendes-Flohr, ed., *The Jew in the Modern World* (New York: Oxford University Press, 2011), 27–34.

28. See an extract in ibid., 66–68.

29. A good English version is in ibid., 67–72. The complete German text can be found online from Project Gutenberg. The story of the rings derives ultimately from Boccaccio.

30. Julius, *Trials of the Diaspora*, emphasizes the continuity of anti-Jewish stereotypes, some of them refurbished today as anti-Israel stereotypes.

31. Thomas Babington Macaulay, *Civil Disabilities of the Jews*, 1831, extracted in Mendes-Flohr, *The Jew in the Modern World*, 168–171.

32. Quoted in Julius, *Trials of the Diaspora*, 212–213.

33. See Julius, *Trials of the Diaspora*, and the fascinating account in Gertrude Himmelfarb, *The Jewish Odyssey of George Eliot* (New York: Encounter Books, 2009).

34. George Eliot, *Daniel Deronda* (London: Penguin, 1967), 411.

35. Ibid., 412.

36. Eliot does not ignore anti-Semitism, as we have already seen, and she addresses it head on in the title of the final and longest essay in her last book, *The Impressions of Theophrastus Such*, which is entitled "The Modern Hep! Hep! Hep!" alluding to the cries of the Crusaders bent on destroying Jews.

37. Julius, *Trials of the Diaspora*, 207–208.

38. Marguerite de Angeli, *Thee, Hannah!* (1940; Scottsdale, PA: Herald Press, 2000).

39. Marguerite de Angeli, *Bright April* (New York: Doubleday, 1947).

40. One might also complain that April and Miss Cole, her Brownie leader, are very "white" in feature, but that is not the case with her mother, or with the men of the Bright family.

6. THE CASE OF PARK51

1. Andrew Grossman, "For Strippers Near Ground Zero, It's Business as Usual Amid Mosque Uproar," *Wall Street Journal*, August 19, 2010.

2. "Sharif El-Gamal: 'I Am Going to Do Everything Humanly Possible to Make This Project Happen,'" *PBS Frontline*, September 27, 2011, http://www.pbs.org/wgbh/pages/frontline/religion/man-behind-mosque/sharif-el-gamal-i-am-going-to-do-everything-humanly-possible-to-make-this-project-happen/.

3. See Aziz Poonawalla and Shahed Amanullah, "We Want to Build Park51 So It Has Something for Everyone," *Altmuslim*, July 24, 2010, available at http://www.altmuslim.com/a/a/n/3866.

4. Ibid.

5. See James Fanelli, "Park51 developer Sharif El-Gamal Has a History of Run-ins with the Law," *New York Daily News*, August 28, 2010.

6. Zeyno Baran, ed., *Understanding Sufism and Its Potential Role in U.S. Policy*, Nixon Center Conference Report, Hudson Institute, March 2004, available at http://www.hudson.org/files/publications/Understanding_Suffism.pdf.

7. Edward C. Dimock, Jr., "Rabindranath Tagore—'The Greatest of the Bauls of Bengal,'" *Journal of Asian Studies*, 19, no. 1 (November 1959): 33–51.

8. See "Imam Feisal Abdul Rauf," American Society for Muslim Advancement, available at http://asmasociety.org/about/b_rauf.html.

9. Feisal Abdul Rauf, "Building on Faith," *New York Times*, September 7, 2010.

10. Anne Barnard, "Parsing the Record of Feisal Abdul Rauf," *New York Times*, August 21, 2010.

11. See Michael Rubin, "Who Is Responsible for the Taliban?" March 2002, available at http://www.michaelrubin.org/1220/who-is-responsible-for-the-taliban.

12. Ralph Blumenthal and Sharaf Mowjood, "Muslim Prayers and Renewal Near Ground Zero," *New York Times,* December 8, 2009.
13. Justin Elliott, "How the 'Ground Zero Mosque' Fear Mongering Began," *Salon,* August 16, 2010, available at http://www.salon.com/2010/08/16/ground_zero_mosque_origins/.
14. Anne Barnard and Alan Feuer, "Outraged, and Outrageous," *New York Times,* October 8, 2010.
15. Javier C. Hernandez, "Vote Endorses Muslim Center Near Ground Zero," *New York Times,* May 26, 2010.
16. Bloomberg quote in Michael Barbaro and Javier C. Hernandez, "Mosque Plan Clears Hurdle in New York," *New York Times,* August 3, 2010.
17. Kirk Semple, "Opponent Seeks to Block Construction of Downtown Mosque," *New York Times,* January 11, 2011.
18. John Bayles, "Park51 Rift Grows: Remarks by New Imam Spark Debate," *Downtown Express* 20, no. 38 (February 2–8, 2011).
19. *New York Times,* December 9, 2009.
20. CNSNews, July 25, 2010.
21. Justin Elliott, "Nadler: Attacks on Mosque 'Shameful and Divisive,'" *Salon,* August 5, 2010.
22. *New York Times,* Wednesday August 4, 2010.
23. Roger Cohen, "Harvest of Anger," *New York Times,* September 9, 2010.
24. *New York Times,* August 13, 2010.
25. *New York Times,* August 14, 2010.
26. See Robert A. Pape, *Dying to Win: The Strategic Logic of Suicide Terrorism* (New York: Random House, 2005).
27. Rauf, "Building on Faith."
28. *City of Cleburne v. Cleburne Living Center, Inc.,* 473 U.S. 432 (1985).
29. *Church of the Lukumi Babalu Aye v. City of Hialeah* (91–948), 508 U.S. 520 (1993).
30. Grossman, "For Strippers Near Ground Zero."

31. "Justice Stevens on 'Invidious Prejudice,'" *New York Times*, November 9, 2010.

32. For exhaustive coverage of these events, see Carol Rittner and John K. Roth, eds., *Memory Offended: The Auschwitz Convent Controversy* (New York: Praeger, 1991), an edited collection of essays.

INDEX

INDEX

Helsinki, 5
Heretics, 136, 137
Herodotus, 243
Heterogeneity, 7, 13, 17, 135
Hialeah, Florida. *See Church of the Lukumi Babalu Aye v. City of Hialeah*
Hiddenness, 23–24, 25, 37, 38–39, 46
High heels, 130, 131
Hijab, 9
Himmelfarb, Gertrude, 173
Hindus, 8, 17, 36, 121, 191, 242, 243
HIV/AIDS, 125
Hoasca, 84
Hobsbawm, Eric, 14
Hollander, Anne, 36
Holocaust, 227, 228, 229
Holocaust Museum, 211
Holyland Foundation, 52
Home schooling, 137–138
Homogeneity, 14–16, 96, 136, 137, 144
Homosexuality, 36–37, 175, 202, 203, 204, 236
Hughes, Karen, 192
Human rights, 65, 119, 242
Human rights movement, 62
Humans, as end not means, 62–63, 101–102, 103, 131, 140
Huq, Aziz, 12, 51, 233, 260n10
Hurricane Irene, 40–41
Hypocrisy, 3, 102–104. *See also* Consistency/inconsistency

Imagination, 257n35; and approval, 143; and close vs. distant groups, 146–148; curious and sympathetic, 21; and de Angeli, 179, 183; and Eliot, 168, 169, 170, 172, 174; and Ellison, 140, 166; and empathy vs. fear, 146; and factual truth and curiosity, 186; and good principles, 139, 140, 205; and helping behavior, 145–146; and India, 243–244; and Less-

ing, 163; and lives of American Muslims, 214; and minority perspective, 59; and moral life, 186–187; as mundane and nonconscious, 144; and other's point of view, 3; and Park51, 230–237; participatory, 143, 144, 145, 146; and respect, 141–144; and Socrates, 243. *See also* Empathy
Immigration: and Australia, 17–18; and core values and political culture, 137; and Europe, 61, 94, 95, 137, 142; and Finland, 14; illegal, 16; and Lockean tradition and accommodationism, 94; in Switzerland, 43–44, 46–47, 48, 56; in United States, 16–17, 18
Impartiality, 57, 90
Inconsistency. *See* Consistency/inconsistency
India: airport security in, 42; and Churchill, 243; and democracy, 53, 212, 233, 234; economic equality in, 16; imagination in, 243–244; law and religious freedom in, 69; national identity in, 16, 17, 18; religious toleration in, 60, 242; Sufism in, 191; untouchability in, 121, 261n20
Indian Constitution, 121
Indonesia, 53, 212, 234
Ingraham, Laura, 194–195
Injury, purely constructive, 202, 203, 230
Inner eyes. *See* Imagination
Invasion of the Body Snatchers, 23–24
Iraq, 193
Islam: and accommodationism, 79; Al Qaeda as distortion of, 213; American ignorance about, 234; and Borghezio, 6; and *burqa*, 104, 115, 119; different sects of, 229–230; as equated with violence, 200; and extremism, 41, 192, 228–229; face covering in, 24; and France, 136; and Gingrich, 210–211; and 9/11 attacks, 225; and Norway, 49–50; Obama

Self-examination, 99–100, 102
Selfishness, 57, 101, 104
Seneca, 66
Senses, 257n35
Separation, of church and state, 132
Seth, Vikram, 233
Sexuality, 14, 136
Shakespeare, William, *The Merchant of Venice*, 159, 166, 171
Shamsie, Kamila, 233
Sharia law, 11–12, 45, 104. *See also* Islam
Sherbert, Adell, 79, 86
Sherbert v. Verner, 79–80, 81, 83, 86, 87, 88
Shoah, 228
Sibelius, Jean, 15
Sikhs, 8
Skokie, Illinois, 118, 201
Smith, Al, 80–81, 86
Snake handling, 119, 120
Socrates, 2, 33, 98–100, 102, 130, 240–242, 243, 245
Socratic-Kantian argument, 167
SoHo Properties, 189
South Africa, 16
South Asia, 235
Southern Europe, 7
Southern Poverty Law Center, 53
Southwest Airlines, 8–9
Spain, 4, 104, 129, 130, 158, 193
Spencer, Robert, 48–49, 52–53, 55, 195; *The Truth about Mohammed*, 52, 53, 54
Sri Lanka, 216
Stansbury v. Marks, 256n18
Startle, 26–27, 36, 40, 253n7
States, 83–84, 89–90
Statue of Liberty, 16
Stein, Edith, 227
Stevens, John Paul, 224–225
Stigmatization, 43, 51, 113, 121, 126, 186
Stockham, Roger, 10–11
Stoics, 62, 63, 65, 66, 67
Stop Islamisation of Europe (SIOE), 50, 51

Stop the Islamicization of America, 52–53, 195
Stowe, Harriet Beecher, 168
Straw, Jack, 105–106
Substantial burden, 78, 120, 129, 143
Sufism, 200, 212, 230, 244
Survival, 25, 27, 30, 31, 32, 56
Swiss People's Party, 44
Switzerland, 13, 56, 254n24; minarets in, 4, 9, 13, 43–48, 56, 222; Muslim headscarf in, 4
Sympathy, 28, 29, 56, 96; for close vs. distant groups, 147–148; and criminal trials, 147; and de Angeli, 183; and Eliot, 171; and imagination, 144–145; and moral life, 186. *See also* Empathy

Tagore, Rabindranath, 192
Taliban, 192–193
Tamil Tigers, 216
Tea Party, 196
Tennessee, 12
Terrorism, 54; and bans on *burqa*, 107–108; fear of, 237; and Gingrich, 211; and Hamas, 193; and Islam, 211, 212; murder of abortion doctors as, 225; and Muslims, 216, 232, 236–237; and Norway, 49–50; and Peretz, 212; precautions against, 41–42; and Tamil Tigers, 216
Thucydides, *History of the Peloponnesian War*, 32
Time magazine, 214–216, 232
Toleration, 70, 181, 206, 217, 242
Tourette's Syndrome, 113
Transparency, 105–106, 111–114, 132
Transportation Security Administration (TSA), 8
Truth, 31, 185, 186. *See also* Facts
Turkey, 121, 129
Turner, Bob, 198
Tyler, Tom, 51
Tzizit, 141, 142, 235